THE CELTIC SOUL FRIEND

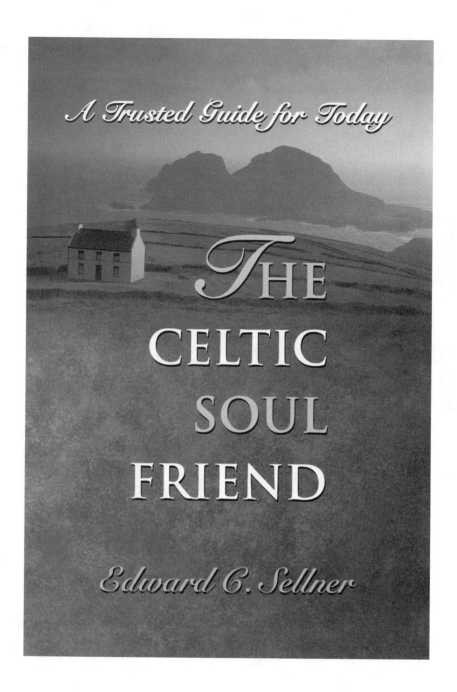

A Trusted Guide for Today

THE CELTIC SOUL FRIEND

Edward C. Sellner

ave maria press   Notre Dame, Indiana

---

www.avemariapress.com

International Standard Book Number: 0-87793-967-5

Cover and text design by Katherine Robinson Coleman

Illustration p.107 by Susan McLain

Maps by Brian C. Conley

Printed and bound in the United States of America.

Library of Congress Cataloging-in-Publication Data
Sellner, Edward Cletus.
The Celtic soul friend : a trusted guide for today / Edward C. Sellner.
    p. cm.
Includes bibliographical references.
ISBN 0-87793-967-5 (pbk.)
1. Spirituality--Celtic Church. 2. Spiritual direction. I. Title.
BR748 .S45 2002
248'.089'9162--dc21

                  2001005299
                  CIP

For Donald Allchin and Benedicta Ward, S.L.G.

Anyone without a soul friend is like a
body without a head.

—St. Brigit of Kildare

In every generation wisdom lives in holy
souls and makes them friends of God.

—Wisdom 7:27

Ireland

Derry

Bangor

Glencolumbkile

Nendrum
Downpatrick

Irishmurray
Armagh
Devenish

Louth

Mayo
Kells
Monasterboice

Clonbroney

Clonard
Finglas

Inisbofin
Anaghdown
Clonmacnoise
Durrow
Tallaght

Clonfert
Kildare

Aran Islands
Birr

Kilfenora
Saighir
Glendalough

Dysert O'Dea

Scattery
Island
Kilkenny

Cashel
Ferns

Emly

Ardfert
Killeedy
Lismore

Gallerus

Cork
Ardmore

Gougane Barra

Skellig Michael

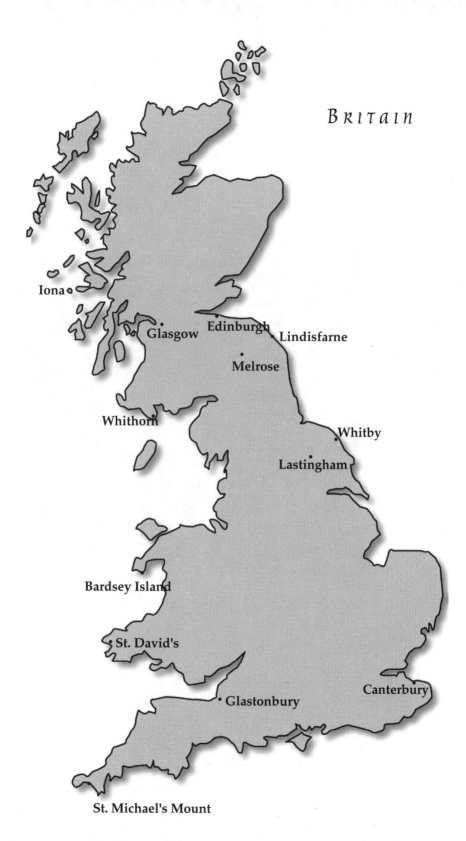

Britain

Iona

Glasgow   Edinburgh   Lindisfarne

Melrose

Whithorn

Whitby

Lastingham

Bardsey Island

St. David's

Canterbury

Glastonbury

St. Michael's Mount

Brittany

Canildut
St. Renan
Brest
Loperhet · Daoulas
· Landévennec
St. Nic
· Locronan

St. Pol-de-Léon
· St. Vougay
Dirinon
· Sizun
· St. Thégonnec

Batz

St. Efflain
Plestin-les-Grèves
Guingamp
· Gurunhuel
Bourbriac

Tréguier
· Plouha

Chatelaudren
· Hellion
St. Brieuc

Lavret
▷ Bréhat

St. Cast

St. Malo
· St. Servan (Aleth)

· St. Suliac

Dinan

· Quimper

· Le Faouët
· St. Fiacre
· Kernaskléden
· Quimperlé
· Locminé

· Rennes
· St. Léry
· Paimpont

Carnac
· Vannes

Pointe
de Colomban
Quiberon

· Kernévelan

· Nantes

contents

Introduction

Tyf yr hyn sydd or hyn a fu.
That which is comes from that which was.

Old Welsh Proverb

All my life I have been "haunted by waters," a haunting mysteriously linked with my love of Ireland and of my ancestors who came from there.[1] On my first visit to Ireland in 1982 with my wife, JoAnne, I had a powerful "déjà vu" experience when we walked the grounds of Glendalough, the home of St. Kevin. Near the magnificent round tower, located not far from the clear lakes, and surrounded by the Wicklow Mountains, I experienced a strong intuitive sense that I had been there before. Some years later, when I went back to that holy site with JoAnne, her parents, and my mother, another curious thing happened on a walk with my father-in-law after dinner at the hotel. Passing by the river that flows through the valley, I distinctly heard the rushing waters singing. I mean, melodious voices in the water, under the stones and rocks, singing and talking with each other! It was only when I read *Angela's Ashes* by Frank McCourt and his telling of how his mother believed the River Shannon sang that I discovered I was not crazy.[2]

One of the earliest dreams that I can remember took place in young adulthood when I was trying to decide what to do with my life. In the dream, filled with vivid colors and loud sounds, I find myself on a seashore looking out across yellow sands to the deep blue horizon where ocean and sky meet. I stand there waiting expectantly. Suddenly dark clouds come racing across the skies, and peals of thunder, preceded by bright flashes of lightning, fill my ears. I am frightened by this awesome manifestation of nature's power, and turn and run from it, down the beach.

At the time of this dream, I did not know that the ancient Celts believed in a god of thunder, Taranis, and that the divine manifested itself in nature, weather, and storms; nor that lightning, in particular, was symbolic of life-giving forces and illumination, enlightenment. In retrospect, this dream was saying, loudly, "Pay attention!" and perhaps also, "Don't run away." But I didn't understand all this at the time. Now I have come to see that at least the opening scene of my dream typifies a basic stance of mine that has developed over the years as a teacher, scholar, and spiritual writer: my looking across the vast expanse of water, back to Europe, back to the land of my ancestors; my yearning to be connected with them, with my spiritual inheritance, with the living past. Yearning, most of all, for wholeness, for wisdom, for God. The words of the Irish poet, Stephen Gwynn, express well my own feelings and passions about the overwhelming beauty of the land, its people, and its rich heritage:

> Ireland, O Ireland!
> Center of my longings,
> Country of my fathers, home of my heart.
> Overseas you call me: Why an exile from me?
> Wherefore sea-severed, long leagues apart?
> Pearly are the skies in the country of my fathers,
> Purple are the mountains, home of my heart;
> Mother of my yearning, love of all my longings,
> Keep me in remembrance, long leagues apart.[3]

Almost a decade after my first visit to Glendalough, I stood on the cliffs of Skellig Michael, a small island off the western coast of Ireland, gazing across at the long leagues of water I had just traversed and down at one of the most ancient sites of the early Celtic Church. I felt exhilarated, filled with a profound sense of gratitude and joy, what C. S. Lewis associates with an experience "as if from a depth not of years but of centuries."[4] In some ways, my boat trip there in the bright rays of the afternoon sun, so soon after my father's sudden death, and my climb to the rugged heights of the island seemed like the culmination of a lifelong quest. Not only was I feeling closely linked with my ancestral past, but, after years of research and writing about the Celtic saints and travel to many of the early sites connected with them, I was finally seeing, in person, the beehive-shaped cells, stone oratory, and carved crosses of one of the earliest settlements of the Irish church, still in almost perfect shape, as if untouched by time.

What I realized, as I stared at the ruins on Skellig Michael, and what contributed to my exhilaration was how much the beehive huts below me were symbols of one aspect of my Irish heritage that I had been studying since graduate school at the University of Notre Dame. When I had first heard the word *anamchara,* Gaelic for "friend of the soul" or "soul friend," in a theology course on reconciliation, the concept had caught my attention and my imagination. For me, the word had named immediately significant relationships with certain loving relatives, friends, and mentors that endured the passages of time, geographical distance, and even the physical separation that death brings. The beehive cells now below me symbolized these relationships of depth and enduring love.

Like the desert fathers and mothers whose ascetic spirituality they had incorporated into their own, the Christians of the early Celtic Church opened their cells—and hearts—to fellow-monks and protégés who came to visit them. As in the story of Abba Moses who admonishes his followers to "sit in your cell and it will teach you everything,"[5] Celtic Christians too valued that space as a place of revelation. They believed, as one of their own desert heroes, John Cassian, had written, that an eternal quality characterizes all relationships of genuine intimacy: "There is one kind of love which is indissoluble," he says, "what no interval of time or space can sever or destroy, and what even death itself cannot part." "With God" and "the union of character," Cassian adds, friends are joined together "in a common dwelling."[6] Knowing this, it came to me then, as I stood out on that island surrounded by ocean waters, that to be a soul

———— ❧ ————

friend is to provide a cell, a place of sanctuary to another where, through our acceptance, love, and hospitality, he or she can grow in wisdom, and both of us in depth.

The belief that there are relationships that can be especially helpful for personal growth and the acquisition of wisdom is not unique to the Celts or Celtic lands. Teachers, mentors, and benevolent helpers have been identified by many spiritual traditions in the history of humankind. The philosopher of the Greeks, the shaman of native tribes, the rabbi of the Jews, the guru of the Hindus, the Zen Master of the Buddhists, the *staretz* of Eastern Orthodox Christians—all are considered by their followers as important resources for their spirituality. Still, the *anamchara* of the early Celtic Church has a unique value of its own, for it came to be closely associated in Christianity with ongoing transformation, a process of conversion-reconciliation that included frequent self-disclosure to a soul friend. This practice of confession and spiritual guidance was eventually recognized as one of the seven great sacraments in the Roman Catholic church at the Council of Trent in the sixteenth century. In the twentieth century, the practice became a part of the steps to recovery recommended by such self-help groups as Alcoholics Anonymous. With its one-to-one focus, Celtic soul-friendship contributed greatly to Western culture's emphasis on the integrity and worth of the individual person and upon his or her spiritual and psychological development. Our modern therapeutic and counseling professions find their roots in this ministry. Soul friendship also affected the entire history of Christian spirituality, affirming as it did the conviction that a person's relationship with God can take the form of effective dialogue, and that whenever sins or faults, grief or human vulnerability are openly and honestly acknowledged, healing begins and God's presence is experienced, sometimes unforgettably.

The value of this relationship, especially for and by lay Christians, is being rediscovered today. Despite differing ecclesial backgrounds and loyalties, many people are finding a great deal of meaning in relationships of friendship and mentoring. Many too have been professionally involved in a ministry of spiritual direction or companionship for years, while more are wondering whether they should be. Increasing numbers are presently participating in theological and spiritual formation programs which will better prepare them to do the great varieties of pastoral care which that type of ministry encompasses. Aside from church settings or specifically Christian forms of ministry, all sorts of support groups, many of them following the Twelve Steps of Alcoholics Anonymous, have come to acknowledge, as Steps Four and Five advocate, the importance of sharing their stories with a trusted guide in order to be set free of their addictions and the guilt and shame associated with them. Others have experienced the tremendous contribution of those who act as sponsors in ways that not only help them maintain some degree of sanity and sobriety, but also enrich them spiritually, frequently in unexpected ways.

This book is about the origins, history, and meaning of soul friendship as expressed in various pre-Christian and Christian writings. Primary sources for an understanding of soul friendship are the stories that were written down in the early medieval and medieval periods, especially the Lives or hagiographies of the Celtic saints. In the history of Christian spirituality, hagiography is the genre of writing that developed which is specifically concerned with the lives and holiness of these spiritual leaders. The term comes from two Greek words: *graphe*, which means "writing," and *hagoi*, "about saints." The wealth of information found in the Celtic hagiographies sheds light not only upon specific saintly soul friends, but upon the environment in which they lived, the political and ecclesiastical landscape which they inhabited, and the spirituality that united them. Although there was great diversity among the Celtic Churches, especially if one considers their geographical locations as well as the differences that naturally arose over the centuries, these Lives of the saints paint a fairly coherent picture of that Celtic Church, revealing common themes and purposes, as well as the meaning of soul friend relationships.

Celtic spirituality out of which the *anamchara* emerged as a distinctive form of friendship and mentoring is also examined here. If, as is true, some of the greatest and most influential storytellers of Western history, from Virgil[7] to Abraham Lincoln,[8] were of Celtic stock, we can posit how much Celtic spirituality has richly influenced directly or indirectly numerous wisdom figures down through the centuries, including the Venerable Bede, Alcuin, Bernard of Clairvaux, Aelred of Rievaulx, Hildegard of Bingen, Francis of Assisi, Meister

Eckhart, Joan of Arc, Dante Alighieri, George Herbert, John Henry Newman, Gerard Manley Hopkins, C. S. Lewis, Evelyn Underhill, Teilhard de Chardin, and Thomas Merton. In many ways, this spirituality is the foundation of Anglican, Episcopalian, and Methodist spiritualities. Because of the Christian Celts' love for the desert fathers and mothers, it has a great affinity too with that of the Eastern Orthodox and its tradition of the spiritual guide or *staretz*. With its focus upon nature and women's gifts, its love of storytelling, drumming, and dance, its respect for ancestors, visions, and dreams, it finds resonance with Native American and African spiritualities. With its non-dualistic perspective on nature, spirit, and genders, it is similar to the great spiritual traditions of the East which see no conflict between our "spiritual" side and our "natural" side, nor between our masculine and feminine energies which as *yin* and *yang* are part of a larger, unifying whole.

Increasing numbers of people today, whether closely linked with church communities or not, are attracted to Celtic spirituality's inherent beauty and wisdom, acknowledging that it has much to teach them about the quality of their own spiritual life, the ecological survival of our planet, the importance of women's leadership, and the need to reach out to and include the marginalized of our society and churches. This Celtic spirituality is not, Donald Allchin reminds us, "a romantic ideal divorced from the complexities of our life in space and time. . . ." Because it affirms ecumenism, ecology, and a wholistic awareness of life, it provides, he says, "a very particular Christian vision"—a vision, I would add, that especially fits the twenty-first century.[9] As John Macquarrie prophetically stated over thirty years ago: "Although it [Celtic spirituality] belongs to a culture that has almost vanished it fulfils in many respects the conditions to which a contemporary spirituality would have to conform."[10]

Chapter one of this book begins with an examination of the historical origins of the soul friend as found in the ancient Celts and their spiritual leaders, the druids and druidesses. In chapter two the desert fathers and mothers are discussed who, with their own spiritual mentoring, influenced the rise of soul friendship in Celtic lands. Chapter three relates the coming of Christianity to Celtic lands and the leadership the Celtic soul friends gave in its establishment, while chapter four discusses the "lasting beauty" of the early Celtic Church in its landscape and spirituality. In chapter five the hagiographies themselves are examined, and how the eighth-century reform movement called the Celi De Movement, in particular, contributed to the emerging soul friend ministry. Chapter six investigates the documents from the Celtic Church that specifically describe the professional and personal dimensions of *anamchara* relationships. In the conclusion, history and the contemporary dimensions of soul friendship are brought together.

If memory is both our greatest teacher, as St. Augustine believed,[11] and the mother of creativity, as the American psychiatrist Rollo May posits,[12] then our collective memory as expressed in our spiritual traditions can be a rich source of ongoing guidance for us all. This knowledge of the living presence of the past, the continuity of life and prayer through the centuries, is essential to spirituality and effective ministry today. Whether we are lay or ordained, our personal and professional lives are dependent upon both the ability of accurately "reading" the signs of the times, *our* times, as well as upon developing a familiarity with and critical appreciation of our spiritual traditions. From those traditions, we might discover a common heritage and common bonds that transcend theological and ecclesial differences that continue to divide us. As Thomas Merton suggests, "If I can unite in myself, the thought and devotion of Eastern and Western Christendom, the Greek and Latin Fathers, the Russian with the Spanish mystics, I can prepare in myself the reunion of divided Christians. From that secret and unspoken unity in myself can eventually come a visible and manifest unity of all Christians."[13] By knowing our spiritual traditions, we might also find personal resources for ourselves that we didn't know we had: insights into contemporary conflicts, hope in the midst of institutional malaise, creative possibilities never before imagined. To be a good friend, to be an effective spiritual mentor or, really, any kind of reconciler in our families, churches, and communities, we need to know our spiritual traditions and open ourselves to what they have to teach us. I hope this book will contribute to a deeper awareness and understanding of what one significant resource, the Celtic soul friend tradition, has to offer the reader's own life, leadership, and spirituality.

———— ✺ ————

This book on soul friendship could not have been written without the love of my family and the support of a community of friends. I am grateful to JoAnne, and our sons, John and Daniel, for their patience and love while I pursued the daemons of my heart either in foreign lands or while sitting in my study at my word-processor. I also want to thank those scholars and good friends who have met with me on my numerous journeys, answered my questions, and guided me to people, books, and places of which I was unaware. In Ireland, I am indebted to Diarmuid O'Laoghaire, Ronan Drury, Enda McDonagh, Tess Harper, Dara Molloy, Padraig O'Fiannanchta, Kim McCone, Peter O'Dwyer, Maureen Groarke, Joseph Maguire, Ben Kimmerling, Marcus and Noleen Losack, Michael Rodgers, Mary Minehan, John O'Donohue, Marge Fallon, Annya O'Connor, Cathal O'Sullivan, and the late Cardinal Tomas O'Fiaich; in England, to Benedicta Ward, Helen Columba, Savas Zembillas, Margaret and the late Peter Hebblethwaite, Shirley Toulson, Shirley duBoulay, and Richard Sharpe; in Scotland, to Noel Dermot O'Donoghue; in Wales, to Donald Allchin, Esther deWaal, Mary and Antony Lewis, Val and Wyn Buick, and Brian Brendan O'Malley; in France, to Jerome, Maud, and Yvon Orial, Philippe Story, Pere Mikael and the Celtic-Orthodox community Sainte-Presence at Saint-Dolay; and in Switzerland, Ian Baker, Kathrin Asper, and John Hill.

I am appreciative too of my friends at home who offered me encouragement and attentive ears: Ken Schmitz and Judy Jackson, Mark Scannell and Elaine Gaston, Susan and Phil McLean-Keeney, Kay VanderVort, Mary Kaye Medinger, Patrick Schaeffer, Jim Walsh, Bill McCollam, Eric Nelson, Tom Delaney, Erwin Templin, Peter Zambrano, Andrew Mohring, Greg Madsen, Craig Wood, Mary Pauluk, Skip Patnode and Anita Neumann, Colleen and Steve Hegranes, Brian Bruess, Kate Dayton, Joseph Speranzella, Jim Olsen, Matt Lucas, Chris Narins, Randy Capelle, Gayle Foster Lewis, Kathleen Moriarty, Jim Rogers, Todd Deutsch, Kevin Underkofler, Gretchen Berg, Andrew Birmingham, Steve Rinker, David Schmit, Rosemary Haughton, James Charles Roy, Michael Downey, Bob Ludwig, David Hunter, and Arthur Holder. Last, but definitely not least, I want to thank my colleagues and students at the College of St. Catherine, especially Andrea J. Lee, IHM, our president. It is the college's intellectual environment and special encouragement of

———— 🙠 ————

women's leadership that have shaped my own commitment to the recovery of lost traditions as well as to those who have been marginalized by our society and churches because of their race, gender, or sexual orientation.

I dedicate this book to two mentors who taught me first-hand much about Celtic history, spirituality, and soul friendship: Anglican spiritual writer Canon A. M. (Donald) Allchin who invited me to stay one autumn at the St. Theosevia Centre of Christian Spirituality in Oxford, England, to pursue post-doctoral studies in Celtic history and spirituality; and Sr. Benedicta Ward, S.L.G., church historian at the University of Oxford, whose writings introduced me years before I met her to the rich tradition of the desert saints, and who acted as my tutor in my early research and writing. They continue to teach and inspire me with their scholarship and, most importantly, the quality and creativity of their lives.

> March 20, 2001
> The Feast of St. Cuthbert
> St. Paul, Minnesota

o n e

People
oꟻ The Oak,
oꟻ Poetry

> The magicians perform no rites without using the foliage of those trees [oaks]. . . . It may be supposed that it is from this custom that they get their name of Druids, from the Greek word meaning "oak."
>
> Pliny the Elder, Natural History

> A large number of men flock to them for training and hold them in high honor. . . . It is said that they commit to memory immense amounts of poetry.
>
> Julius Caesar, Gallic War

*L*ong before Christianity was divided by the eleventh-century split with the Orthodox Christians and the sixteenth-century Protestant Reformation, one of its most creative churches came to birth. It was made up primarily of numerous small monastic communities in rural areas of what we now call Ireland, England, Scotland, Wales, Brittany, and the Isle of Man. Although not at all cut off from the churches developing on the continent of Europe which were more urban and increasingly more centralized, this early Celtic Church still existed quite independently from the fifth to the twelfth centuries with its own native leadership. It was never united administratively, but its spirituality, common stories, heroic figures, art, music, and great appreciation of landscape, friendship, and kinship ties provided ecclesial unity in a fundamental way. What definitely made the Celtic Church unique was its embracing of so many of the values and beliefs of the pagan culture which had preceded the arrival of Christianity. One of its greatest gifts was the concept and practice of having a soul friend for ongoing support and spiritual guidance. Called by the Irish or Scots an *anamchara* or by the Welsh a *periglour* or *beriglour*, such a person acted in a number roles, including those of mentor, teacher, confidant, confessor, or spiritual guide.

21

One of the most interesting stories from the early Celtic Church in Ireland confirms the importance in one's life of having such an intimate friend:

> A young cleric of the community of Ferns, a foster-son of Brigit's, used to come to her with dainties. He was often with her in the refectory [dining-room] to partake of food. Once after going to communion she strikes a clapper. "Well, young cleric there," says Brigit, "do you have a soul friend?" "I have," replied the young man. "Let us sing his requiem," says Brigit. "Why so?" asks the young cleric. "For he has died," says Brigit. "When you had finished half your ration I saw that he was dead." "How did you know that?" "Easy to say," [Brigit replies]: "from the time that your soul friend was dead, I saw that your food was put [directly] in the trunk of your body, since you were without any head. Go forth and eat nothing until you get a soul friend, for anyone without a soul friend is like a body without a head; is like the water of a polluted lake, neither good for drinking nor for washing. That is the person without a soul friend."[1]

The history of the Christian Celts is filled with numerous examples of soul friendship between women and men, men and men, and women and women, all of whom were changed profoundly by these relationships. Although Western church authorities eventually equated this type of ministry only with the ordained male priest in the sacrament of penance at the Fourth Lateran Council in 1215, such relationships in the earliest days of Celtic Christianity were open to lay people and ordained, women and men alike.[2]

No one knows precisely the historical origins of the *anamchara*. John T. McNeill, for one, believes it to be a racial institution of great antiquity, and associates it with the *acharya,* the spiritual guide or director of conscience, whose functions are described in the Brahman codes of ancient India.[3] This view is not implausible, since some contemporary scholars are convinced that the ancient Celts originated in the East, in the vicinity of present-day India. They point to the similarity between Celtic and Indian music, art, mythology, numbers, language, and attitudes toward sexuality. Some see traces of an Indian link with the Bigoudens in western Brittany who have brightly-colored native costumes of red and orange, and a "not infrequent almond eye."[4] Still, because no hard evidence exists of a connection between the *acharya* and the *anamchara*, there is no way of proving such a hypothesis.

Two sources, however, which can be more definitively traced to the emergence of the *anamchara* as a distinct form of spiritual mentoring are the spiritual leaders of the pagan Celts, the druids and druidesses, and, second, the early Christian fathers and mothers who lived in the desert regions of Egypt, Syria, and Palestine in the third, fourth, and fifth centuries. This chapter will trace the Celtic origins of the soul friend: the pagan Celts and, more specifically, the druids and druidesses, those who were called the "people of the oak" or "people of poetry." Like Native American shamans, these spiritual leaders of the Celts functioned as mediators between the tribes and the spiritual realm, the world of tribal gods, goddesses, and spirits. They taught that the supernatural pervades every aspect of life, and that spirits are everywhere: in ancient trees and sacred groves, rivers, streams, and holy wells, on hills and mountaintops. They valued their families and friends, and considered women to have many of the same rights as men. The Celtic spirituality which they taught is one of the most ancient in Europe, with its inception going back to a people who lived over three thousand years ago. Although these early people received the name "pagan" by later Christian writers on the continent in an effort to depict them as inferior if not outright evil, they should not be seen as lacking in spiritual values or beliefs. This earlier spirituality, at least its best qualities, merging with the expression of Christianity that arose where the Celts lived, can in some ways be compared to the Old Testament of scripture that preceded the writing of the New. For Christians, both books, both heritages make up the Holy Bible, as both pagan and Christian spiritual traditions make up the spiritual heritage and spirituality of the Celts.

The Ancient Celts

In the history of Western civilization, the ancient Celts have, until quite recently, received little attention, largely because, unlike the Greeks and Romans, they did not write anything down until the sixth century C.E. when the Latin alphabet of the

Christian scribes was adapted for the writing of the native Celtic languages. Before that time, all of the Celts' history, knowledge, and lore was kept alive through the oral tradition of the storytellers and other learned members of the tribes. Even the term "Celt" is not a name they used to describe themselves, but comes from the Greek word for them, *Keltoi*. Another word, used by the Romans for them, was *Galli* or "Gauls," from which Gaul or *Gallia*, the larger part of what is now France, took its name, as well Galicia in northwestern Spain, and the country of Galatia in Asia Minor whose people in the Christian era received the Epistle to the Galatians of the apostle St. Paul. (It is interesting to note, considering the inclusivity regarding genders of the ancient Celts that it is precisely this epistle in which Paul posits that in Christ Jesus there are no longer "distinctions" between "male and female" [Gal 3:28].) The ancient Celts themselves left no great written works, such as the teachings of Socrates, Plato, or Aristotle, nor memoirs as those of Julius Caesar or Marcus Aurelius, nor speeches and commentaries like those of Cicero.

Contemporary archaeologists are showing, however, that, even before the rise of the Roman Empire, the Celts, a branch of the Indo-European family from which most of present-day European, Middle Eastern, and Indian races are descended, dominated the center of Europe for centuries from the Black Sea to Spain, from the Mediterranean to the North Sea and Ireland. More archaeological evidence of the Celts' talents and sophistication, such as the Gallic calendar, the advanced agricultural techniques, and the craftsmanship and metalwork which have survived, clearly demonstrates the scale and importance of the Celtic contribution to the formation of European civilization. The names of major cities in modern Europe, such as Paris, Milan, Vienna, London, and Berlin, trace their origin to the Celts, as do the names of such rivers as the Thames, the Seine, the Rhine, and the Danube. In England, the cities of Bath and Wells were originally holy Celtic sites where the thermal waters were used for bathing and making offerings to Celtic deities. Even the site of the beautiful medieval Chartres cathedral in France was once a main Celtic center where the druids are said to have met annually.

The precise origins of the Celtic race are unclear. As already mentioned, some scholars point to the area near India, while others say that Celtic civilization emerged around 700 B.C.E. in the Hallein region of Austria where the so-called Hallstatt culture was born. Another location, discovered by archaeologists at La Tene on Lake Neuchatel in Switzerland, points to the presence of Celts there around the early fifth century B.C.E.[5] The burial mounds at both places have produced a large number of artifacts and images that reveal people who imported luxury goods, especially drinking equipment, from the Mediterranean world, and who appreciated abstract designs in their art which incorporated motifs from nature, such as animals and foliage, as well as human faces. Like the Celts in Brittany, they also were known for and made their wealth from the salt which they mined.

Whatever their actual geographical beginnings, the ancient Celts engaged in a great variety of occupations as warriors, farmers, adventurers, and traders. They were also a nomadic people, given to travel and migration. Wherever they went, they brought with them a certain *Celtic* perception of the world, what Robert O'Driscoll describes as "their belief in the aristocracy of the imagination and the honored place of the poet; their strong feeling for the supernatural, the interpenetration of natural and supernatural, and a veneration for nature in all its manifestations; their ritualistic expression of grief, their sense of the sacredness of place and of a communion between the living and the dead."[6] Other qualities are identified by Aedeen Cremin. "They prized liberty above security," she writes, "loyalty above common sense, and beauty above all things. The beauty of a woman, of a man, of a landscape, of a fine object were celebrated in a myriad of ways, in song, poetry, feasting, and even in death."[7] These qualities of the pagan Celts persisted, as we will see, even after the coming of Christianity.

From the fifth through the third centuries B.C.E., Celtic tribes moved south into northern Italy, west through Gaul and Iberia, east along the Danube into Hungary, Greece, Turkey, and across the North Sea into Britain. By about 387 B.C.E., they had grown so powerful that some of them sacked Rome itself, and by 279 B.C.E. they attacked the Greek oracle at Delphi. Though driven back in Italy, many Celts settled there, producing later Roman authors influenced by their Celtic heritage, among them, Catullus, Cato, Varro, and, not least, Virgil, author of *The Aenead* who was famous for his evocative writings on heroes and nature, two themes dear to the Celts. Much of Gaul, before Caesar's invasions in the 50s B.C.E., contained Celtic tribes. Under the Roman emperors Augustus and Tiberius the remainder of Celtic Europe was subdued. In 43 C.E. the conquest of Britain was initiated, and by 84 C.E. Roman armies reached northern Scotland. Only Ireland remained unconquered by the power of Rome. Due to conflicts with other tribes, including the Anglo-Saxons who invaded Britain in the fifth century C.E. and because of their own desire to be near bodies of water, Celtic tribes eventually settled in those places we now associate with "the Celtic Fringe": Ireland, Scotland, Wales, Cornwall, the Isle of Man, Brittany, and Galicia. During Christian times, in Northumbria or northern England, monks and missionaries from Ireland and Iona passed Celtic spirituality on to the Anglo-Saxons who had settled there, influencing profoundly one of the most powerful abbesses in the early church, Hild of Whitby, and one of the greatest of all storytellers, the Venerable Bede (c. 672-735 C.E.).

Once the Celts had settled down, their society consisted of a number of social classes following a fairly consistent order. The ruling class was led by the kings and sometimes queens of the tribes. As a Latin historian, Tacitus (c. 56-118 C.E.), observed of the Celts in Gaul, "They do not distinguish among their rulers by sex."[8] The warriors and their families were part of this land-owning class, and their primary responsibility was to defend the tribes and enforce the laws that governed them. The next class, the largest, consisted of the serfs, some of whom were free, while others were slaves taken in battle or, like the youthful St. Patrick, kidnapped from foreign shores and held captive far from home. This class was made up primarily of cattle-farmers or shepherds living under the protection of the rulers.

The third main class, small in number but socially very important, were the *aes dana*, Gaelic for "people of learning" or "of poetry." This latter group included poets, historians, experts in genealogy, lawyers, physicians, skilled craftsmen, and the story-tellers of the tribes, the bards. Many of these *aes dana* were also druids and druidesses, advisers to the kings and teachers of the tribes. In fact, according to the Irish historian Michael Richter, "the highest position *(ollam)* of the druids was equal to that of the king,"[9] a position of spiritual authority that would eventually be replaced by the monastic leader or Christian bishop when the pagan Celts had been baptized. All of these *aes dana* were held in high esteem and had the privilege, as did the aristocracy, of travelling anywhere without permission. This respect and the freedom which went with it reveals how much Celtic society valued people of learning, of poetry, and of artistic skills, considering them as essential as any king or warrior to the well-being of their society and culture.

Classical Accounts and Observations

Besides archaeological findings, a primary source for understanding the early Celts is the classical writings of Greece and Rome. These classical writers considered the Celts their enemies and from their perspective "barbarians" (a word connoting "different," "inferior," and "uneducated"). But at the same time they betray in their writings an ambivalent tone: both repulsion *and* attraction, condescension *and* admiration. Despite these somewhat biased and antagonistic accounts, their descriptions of the Celts contain a core of authentic information, much of which is confirmed in the later stories recorded by the Christian Celtic scribes in their monasteries.[10]

Numerous accounts by classical writers over centuries of observation give us insights into what sort of people the ancient Celts were—and perhaps still are today. Greek and Roman observers alike frequently identify them as roving bands of shaggy-haired, mustachioed horsemen whom they both feared for their military prowess and respected for their courage. What both amused and terrified them was the Celts' custom of running or riding naked into battle, wearing nothing but their gold torcs (thick, gold neck-rings) and armlets, carrying only their weapons and shields, and screaming as they ran.[11] Their bodies also were probably painted in bright colors or tattooed. The term for the Irish, "Scotti", may have meant "scarred" or "painted men," and on certain Gaulish coins some faces seem to bear tattoo marks. "Picti," the name of the Celts in Scotland, means "painted ones." Again, there is some ambivalence among the commentators: Polybius describes them in a battle that was fought in 225 B.C.E. as godlike, "in the prime of life and of excellent physique," while another writer, Camillus, to bolster his men as the Celts laid seige to Rome, says that the Celts have only "soft and flabby bodies," and are totally lacking in "hardiness."[12]

The Greeks and Romans, who were shorter, olive-skinned, and dark haired, seemed to admire the Celts for their height, white skin, and fair hair. These physical attributes appear in later Christian art and stories of the saints. In the famous illuminated gospels, the Book of Kells, Sts. Matthew and John are pictured as having red or light brown hair, while numerous angels have golden hair. Jesus himself is portrayed as a strong, warrior figure with long, curly blonde hair and blue eyes. In the ancient Irish stories, the first name of Finn MacCumaill or Mac Cool, as he's called, refers to his fine hair, and, in the hagiography of Findbarr of Cork, he is given the name because of his fair [find] crest [barr] of hair. Classical writers also noted the courage, independence, and physical beauty of Celtic women, and the fierce leadership they provided when fighting against their enemies. Like their male counterparts, they were feared *and* respected. One Latin historian, Ammianus Marcellinus (c. 330-395 C.E.), quoting an earlier author, describes their ferocity in battle: "A whole troop of foreigners would not be able to withstand a single Gaul if he called his wife to his assistance who is usually very strong and with blue eyes; especially when, swelling her neck, gnashing her teeth, and brandishing her sallow arms of enormous size, she begins to strike blows mingled with kicks, as if they were so many missiles sent from the string of a catapult."[13] Considering the references in Irish stories to the presence of female warriors, seers, druids, bards, doctors, and even satirists, as well as the Brehon laws (the most ancient in Europe) which acknowledged women's rights to property, divorce, and greater sexual freedoms, it is clear that the range of roles possible for Celtic women was much greater than that permitted in Greece or Rome.

Admired for their physical appearance, the ancient Celts, male and female, were also loathed for certain of their social attributes. Plato states that they had a reputation for drunkenness, while Aristotle mentions their reckless indifference to danger. Many of their neighbors saw them as quarrelsome, impetuous, headstrong, and, as Julius Caesar once said, "too much given to faction." Caesar was highly accurate in this assessment of the Celts. From a historical perspective, it was this quality that contributed to the Celts' frequently being conquered by outside invaders, including Caesar's own armies in Gaul, and later, in Ireland, by the Vikings, Normans, and British colonists. That same quality, however, can also be seen as a strength, for it reflects the Celts' high appreciation of individual freedoms, loyalty to their tribes, and devotion to their families. All of these traits can be discerned in their lack of tolerance for any type of centralized authority, even among themselves, that might threaten those primary freedoms and loves. This is why, once Christianity came to Celtic lands, the church that was established there had no strong administrative unity, although it did have unity in significant other ways, as we will see.

Certain classical commentators are especially helpful in understanding who the Celts were, and the type of leadership their druids and druidesses provided. Diodorus Siculus, born in Sicily and a writer of Greek history, is a primary resource who provided one of the most extensive descriptions of them in the ancient world.

Diodorus Siculus' Evaluation of the Celts

Writing in his *Library of History* in the first century B.C.E., Diodorus Siculus appears to agree with Plato's comments about Celtic intemperance, and says that "the Gauls are exceedingly addicted to the use of wine." Because they "drink without moderation by reason of their craving for it, when they are drunken they fall into a stupor or a state of madness." Diodorus also says that the Celts are an "exceedingly covetous people" who "amass a great amount of gold, which is used for ornament not only by the women but also by the men. For around their wrists and arms they wear bracelets, around their necks heavy necklaces of solid gold [torcs], and huge rings they wear as well. . . ." He refers to their physical appearance without being able to conceal some degree of awe: "The Gauls are tall of body, with rippling muscles, and white of skin, and their hair is blond, and not only naturally so, but they also make it their practice by artificial means to increase the distinguishing color which nature has given it. For they are always washing their hair in lime-water, and they pull it back from the forehead to the top of the head and back to the nape of the neck, with the result that their appearance is like that of Satyrs and Pans, since the treatment of their hair makes it so heavy and coarse that it differs in no respect from the mane of horses."[14]

Besides their hair, the Celts' clothing, according to Diodorus, is "striking." They wear shirts "dyed and embroidered in varied colors," and breeches, and "striped coats, fastened by a buckle on the shoulder." He mentions, as other commentators do, that many warriors, at least in battle, wear nothing at all, "satisfied with the armor which Nature has given them." Diodorus also comments on a practice of the Celts that he considered especially despicable, their head-hunting: "When their enemies fall they cut off their heads and fasten them about the necks of their horses . . . and these first-fruits of battle they fasten by nails upon their houses, just as men do, in certain kinds of hunting, with the heads of wild beasts they have mastered. The heads of their most distinguished enemies they embalm in cedar-oil and carefully preserve in a chest, and these they exhibit to strangers, gravely maintaining that in exchange for this head some one of their ancestors, or their father, or the man himself, refused the offer of a great sum of money."[15]

This custom of head-hunting was evidently a common practice among the Celts, since the motif of a warrior holding a severed head by the hair is found on numerous Celtic coins, and headless skeletons have been discovered in Celtic cemeteries— from pre-Christian times on through to the Middle Ages. The Celts believed that the soul resided in the head, and that to take another's head home was to somehow obtain that person's spiritual power and wisdom. The busts of famous people some of us have in our studies or living-rooms have similar connotations—though, obviously, less bloody and brutal. The later Christian Celts maintained a respect for the head as well, replacing real heads with the stone carvings of the heads of their saints, as can be seen today on the front facade of Clonfert Cathedral in Ireland. There are also a number of depictions of Celtic saints holding their severed heads in their hands, including St. Trephine of Brittany and her son, St. Tremeur. While Diodorus criticizes the Celts, as did the Romans, for this practice of decapitation, it should be noted that the Romans themselves during their own civil wars beheaded their enemies.

Diodorus is also critical of certain ways Celts expressed their sexuality, relating, for example, how at wedding feasts "relatives and friends take it in turn to lie with the bride." Oblivious or forgetful of his own culture's homoeroticism, he also shows his disgust of sexual behavior between Celtic men: "Despite the fact that their wives are beautiful, the Celts . . . abandon themselves to a passion for other men. They usually sleep on the ground on skins of wild animals and tumble about with a bedfellow on either side. And what is strangest of all is that, without any thought for a natural sense of modesty, they carelessly surrender their virginity to other men. Far from finding anything shameful in all this, they feel insulted if anyone refuses the favors they offer."[16] As in other societies, ancient and modern, in which males are isolated from women for long periods, Celtic men evidently were not reticent in expressing themselves sexually with one another. Other Greek and Roman historians, besides Diodorus, are explicit on this subject, and their comments have a remarkable consistency. Strabo, who died about 26 C.E., wrote about "the young men in Gaul who are shamelessly generous with their boyish charms," and Atheneaus, two centuries later, repeats the statement of Diodorus about the Celts' male "bed-partners."[17] Besides the observations of the classical writers, this appreciation of strong warrior friendships is alluded to in the works of the native Celts, in particular the *Tain Bo Cualnge (The Cattle-Raid of Cooley)* which tells the story of the friendship between two warriors, CuChulainn and Fer Diad, whom CuChulainn describes as "my loved comrade, my kin and kindred. Never found I one dearer. . . . We were loving friends. We were comrades in the wood. We were men who shared a bed."[18]

Not all of male bonds among the Celts, of course, were necessarily expressed genitally, but it is important to remember that ancient peoples did not think in or have strict categories for sexual behavior that we today identify as "heterosexual," "homosexual," "bisexual." The acceptance of homoeroticism and of the fluidity of sexuality was common among ancient peoples, including certain Native American tribes, as it still is among many cultures.[19] The great love between male friends, depicted by Diodorus and the *Tain*, is echoed in the later Christian hagiographies about soul friend relationships: in the expressions of warmth and love between male saints, such as Enda of the Aran Islands and Ciaran of Clonmacnoise, Maedoc of Ferns and Molaise of Devenish Island, Finnian of Clonard and his students Columcille and Ciaran. It also finds resonance in the humorous scene on the bottom panel, north face, of Muiredach's Cross at Monasterboice, Co. Louth, in which two men, wide-eyed and seemingly in earnest, are pulling each other's long beards.[20]

Regarding Celtic women's sexuality, there are numerous stories of the passionate erotic nature of Celtic goddesses, warriors, and queens, but no mention in any pagan writings of lesbian relationships. In an early medieval hagiography of St. Brigit, however, she is said to have had a protégée, Darlughdach (whose name means "daughter of the sun god Lugh"), with whom she slept. The younger woman seems to have been torn between two loves: a certain man with whom she had sex and Brigit herself who wanted her to remain in the monastery. Darlughdach evidently decided to be faithful to Brigit, since she is depicted later as not only being with Brigit when her mentor dies, but herself dying exactly one year later.[21]

Despite the Celtic men's sexual practices, of which he disapproved, Diodorus acknowledges some of the positive attributes of the Celts, including their hospitality: "They invite strangers to their feasts, and do not inquire until after the meal who they are and of what things they stand in need." Diodorus also speaks of their belief in an afterlife, in the eternal quality of the soul, and their great respect for ancestors. When any enemy, for example, "accepts the challenge to battle, they [the Celts] then break forth in a song in praise of the valiant deeds of their ancestors." Celtic women, he says, are unusual, in that they "are not only like the men in their great stature but they are a match for them in courage as well." The Celts, male and female, he concedes, are not without "cleverness of learning." Diodorus also alludes to specific members of the learned class, what has already been identified as the *aes dana*, that class which contained the bard and the druid:

> Among them are also to be found lyric poets whom they call Bards. These men sing to the accompaniment of instruments which are like lyres, and their songs may be either of praise or of obloquy. Philosophers, as we may call them, and men learned in religious affairs are unusually honored among them and are called by them Druids. . . . Nor is it only in the exigencies of peace, but in their wars as well, that they obey, before all others, these men and their chanting poets, and such

obedience is observed not only by their friends but also by their enemies; many times, for instance, when two armies approach each other in battle with swords drawn and spears thrust forward, these men step forth between them and cause them to cease, as though having cast a spell over certain kinds of wild beasts. In this way, even among the wildest barbarians, does passion give place before wisdom, and Ares stands in awe of the Muses.[22]

Diodorus Siculus' reference to the druids, many of whom combined both bardic and spiritual leadership roles, leads us to the one of the primary sources of what eventually developed into the Celtic Christian *anamchara* or soul friend.

People of the Oak, People of Poetry

A great deal of controversy surrounds the druids historically, beginning with their name. Called *drui* by the Irish, *derwydd* by the Welsh, and *dry* by the Anglo-Saxons, the words themselves are subject to various interpretations. Some scholars think the word means "knowledge of the oak," relying upon the comments of Strabo (64 B.C.E.-24 C.E.) and Pliny the Elder (c. 23-79 C.E.), both of whom said that the word "druid" comes from the Greek word *drus*, translated "oak." Another classical writer, Marcus Annaeus Lucanus (39-65 C.E.), although not referring specifically to oak trees, said that the Druids dwelt in "*nemora alta*" (deep groves) and "*incolitis locis*" (solitary places).[23] Pliny, in his *Natural History*, presents the druids as doctors and magicians, and gives us a full-scale description of a druid ceremony which, according to him, normally took place in an oak grove:

> The Druids—that is what they call their magicians—hold nothing more sacred than mistletoe and a tree on which it is growing, provided it is Valonia Oak. . . . Mistletoe is rare and when found, it is gathered with great ceremony and particularly on the sixth day of the moon. . . . Hailing the moon in a native word that means "healing of all things," they prepare a ritual sacrifice and banquet beneath a tree and bring up two white bulls, whose horns are bound for the first time

on this occasion. A priest arrayed in white vestments climbs the tree and with a golden sickle cuts down the mistletoe, which is caught in a white cloak. Then finally they kill the victims, praying to God to render his gift propitious to those on whom he has bestowed it. They believe that mistletoe given in drink will impart fertility to any animal that is barren, and that it is an antidote to all poisons.[24]

For many peoples of the ancient world, the oak was a phallic symbol, and particularly linked with the god of thunder. Although some say the druids wore green robes, symbolic of the oak tree, Pliny obviously has a different view, associating them with white vestments—an interesting feature since, in the early Irish legends, Patrick and his followers, as well as Brigit, are depicted as dressed in white as they traveled across the countryside.

Another classical writer, Pomponius Mela, writing in the middle of the first century of the Common Era, refers, as did Lucanus, to remote places and groves, but also describes the druids as "teachers of wisdom, who profess to know the greatness and shape of the earth and the universe, and the motion of the heavens and of the stars and what is the will of the gods. . . . They teach many things to the nobles of the race in sequestered and remote places during twenty years, whether in a cave or in secluded groves. One of their dogmas has become widely known so they may the more readily go to war: namely that souls are everlasting, and that among the shades there is another life."[25]

Based upon these sources and others, contemporary scholars associate druidry with "people of the oak," "those whose knowledge is great," "people of true vision," or, as Pomponius Mela stated, simply "teachers of wisdom." In those capacities, it would be appropriate to also call them "people of poetry," especially considering what Diodorus said about the poets associated with them, and what Julius Caesar (100-44 B.C.E.), as we will see, wrote. Since the druids themselves preferred to teach everything orally, writing down little, information about them is limited. Numerous classical sources, however, suggest that they were concerned, in particular, with divine or spiritual matters, officiated at rituals and sacrifices, and acted as judges and arbiters in all private and public affairs. One of the main sources, besides Diodorus Siculus, is Julius Caesar.

Caesar gives a comprehensive view of the Celts in his book, *Gallic War*, written about 52 B.C.E., in which he alludes to the customs, culture, and fighting habits of the Celts in Gaul and Britain. He too comments on their physical appearance, how the Celts in Britain "dye their bodies with woad, which produces a blue color, and this gives them a more terrifying appearance in battle. They wear their hair long, and shave the whole of their bodies except the head and the upper lip." He also describes the Celts as *"admodum dedita religionibus"* [very much given to religion], and makes explicit reference to their spiritual leaders, the druids, and the significant roles they performed for the tribes:

> The Druids officiate at the worship of the gods, regulate public and private sacrifices, and give rulings on all religious questions. Large numbers of young men flock to them for instruction, and they are held in great honor by the people. . . . The Druids are wont to be absent from war, nor do they pay taxes like the others. . . . Attracted by these prizes many join the order of their own accord or are sent by parents or relatives. It is said that they commit to memory immense amounts of poetry. And so some of them continue their studies for twenty years. They consider it improper to entrust their studies to writing, although they use the Greek alphabet in nearly everything else, in their public and private accounts.[26]

This regulation and celebration of religious practices and rituals, and the consultation given on religious issues will be taken over by many of the saintly soul friends of the early Celtic Church, as well as the formation and education of the young.

Like Diodorus, Caesar also refers to the druids as reconcilers between individuals and tribes, something for which the Christian *anamcharas* would become known when they advised individuals, including kings, of proper actions and penalties for sins:

> They act as judges in practically all disputes, whether between tribes or between individuals; when any crime is committed, or a murder takes place, or a dispute arises

————— ❧ —————

about an inheritance or a boundary, it is they who adjudicate the matter and appoint the compensation to be paid and received by the parties concerned.[27]

As we will see, the early Celtic saints, including women such as St. Ita of Ireland, are frequently portrayed in the stories about them as hearing confessions and giving out penances not only to members of their own religious communities, but to the laity as well. The *"libri poenitentiales,"* or Penitential Books, that originated in Ireland in the sixth century and that were written to guide soul friends in their role as confessors in the assignment of penances find their origins in the druidic practice, as Caesar says, of appointing the suitable "compensation to be paid."[28]

Caesar also discusses their beliefs, including the soul's immortality and what might be considered the "transmigration" of souls:

> A lesson which they take particular pains to inculcate is that the soul does not perish, but after death passes from one body to another; they think that this is the best incentive to bravery, because it teaches men to disregard the terrors of death. They also hold long discussions about the heavenly bodies and their movements, the size of the universe and of the earth, the physical constitution of the world, and the power and properties of the gods; and they instruct the young men in all these subjects.

Caesar mentions how "they measure periods of time not by the day but by nights; and in celebrating birthdays, the first of the month, and new year's day, they go on the principle that the day begins at night." This approach to time is similar to that held by the Jewish people who begin the celebration of the sabbath on the night before. He also states that all the druids are "under one head, whom they hold in the highest respect," and that once a year "they hold a session in a consecrated spot" in the center of Gaul where the druids' judgments are accepted by all Celts. (This site, as mentioned earlier, was probably near Chartres.) Religious beliefs of the druids, he says, are "believed to have been found existing in Britain and thence imported into Gaul; even today those who want to make a profound study of it [i.e., druidic doctrine] generally go to Britain for that purpose."[29]

Caesar also alludes to a dark side of the druids' spirituality, that of human sacrifice. This practice was evidently common not only among the Celts, but also other ancient peoples, including the Norse, judging by the number of bodies that have been found from the pre-Christian period which reveal forms of ritual sacrifice.[30] Caesar writes:

> They believe that the only way of saving a man's life is to propritiate the god's wrath by rendering another life in its place, and they have regular state sacrifices of the same kind. Some tribes have colossal images made of wickerwork, the limbs of which they fill with living men; they are then set on fire, and the victims burnt to death. They think that the gods prefer the execution of men taken in the act of theft or brigandage, or guilty of some offence; but when they run short of criminals, they do not hesitate to make up with innocent men.[31]

Thus, while admiring some of their distinct qualities, such as bravery in battle and their dedication to the education of their youth, Caesar consistently reveals his critical, if not outright disapproving stance toward the Celts.

All of Caesar's comments, as well as those of other writers mentioned above, provide us with some perspectives on the Celts' spiritual leaders, the people of the oak, of poetry. What Caesar fails to acknowledge, however, is that besides the "druids" there were also women druids or "druidesses." One classical commentator, Vopiscus, says that the Emperor Aurelianus consulted such women in Gaul on the future of his posterity. A woman, referred to as a druidess *(dryadas)* of the Tungri tribes in Belgium is said to have promised the Roman Empire to Diocletian. In Ireland, these druidesses were called *bandruaid*, and more frequently *banfhaith* (seeresses or prophetesses) and *banfhilid* (poetesses), and appear in the ancient legends, including the great epic, *Tain Bo Cualnge*. In Armorica (what is called Brittany today), strong traditions of entire druidical families of both genders were retained.[32] According to some historians, St. Brigit's double-monastery at Kildare was the home of druidesses before the saint's time who, like the vestal virgins in Rome, kept a perpetual fire burning. Whether true or not, Kildare means "the church of the Oak," certainly a name with druidic connotations, and a magnificent giant oak was said to have survived on the site until the tenth century.[33] Kildare was not the only monastic community connected with oak trees. Another key Irish monastery, Derry, founded by St. Columcille, comes from the word for oak in Irish. In a story about the Welsh saint Beuno, he is said to have planted an acorn by the side of his father's grave which "grew into an oak tree of great height and thickness," which had a large branch that grew from it down to the ground. As the medieval hagiographer (who is definitely Welsh) tells the story, "If an Englishman passes between the branch and the trunk of the tree, he shall drop dead on the spot, but if a Welshman does so, he shall be none the worse."[34] Whether in Wales, Scotland, or Ireland, the usual name given to early Celtic churches which were made of wood was *"Duirthech,"* meaning "a house of oak," another sign of the druids' and druidesses' links with the Celtic soul friends.

Druidic Spiritual Beliefs

From the classical sources, the legends and stories of the Celts themselves, and references that can be found in the stories of the saints, it is clear that these druids and druidesses were powerful spiritual leaders in Ireland and in all the lands where the Celts lived. They not only believed in worshipping in sacred oak groves, but in the immortality of the soul, the cult of the head, and the invisible world of the ancestors. For them the physical world was intimately linked with the spiritual, and reality was definitely more than meets the eye. For the ancient Celts and their pagan teachers, druids and druidesses alike, the natural and supernatural realms were inherently connected. This strong awareness of the spiritual realm would eventually evolve into the Celts' belief in fairies and leprechauns whose friendship could bring riches, but whose enmity could cause great mischief, if not outright tragedy. This pagan animism also helped the Christian Celts come to believe in the existence of angels as guardians and soul friends. Wisdom itself was frequently linked with friends and guides who appear in dreams. The historian T. F. O'Rahilly tells of an early Celtic poet who wrapped himself in the hide of a bull, went to sleep, and was aided by "invisible friends" who would answer the questions he had about the future king of his tribe: "A spell of truth was sung over the man and in his sleep he would see the destined king."[35]

The Celts also believed that by consulting the dead a person could receive unexpected guidance. They thought that knowledge could be acquired and healing experienced by sitting or sleeping on the grave of one's spiritual ancestors. Christian Celts took up this practice, as we find in the story of St. Columbanus who was portrayed as travelling to the tomb of St. Martin of Tours and spending the night there in prayer, seeking guidance from the saint from Gaul. Another hagiographical source tells of the sick being laid out on rushes, after bathing in a holy well at Clynnog, near the tomb of the Welshman St. Beuno, mentioned above, where they also spent the night in hopes of being cured.[36]

The earth itself was regarded by the pagan Celts as the source of all fertility, and the great forces of nature (sun, moon, ocean, thunder, and wind) were worshipped as manifestations of the divine. It is no wonder that the later Celtic Christians' theology or understanding of God was so affected by this emphasis, giving God a variety of poetic names linked with nature, such as "Lord of the Elements," "King of the Stars," and "Lord of the Cloudy Skies."[37] The sun ruled the year, they believed, and they celebrated four great festivals in conjunction with its movement: Samhain on November 1 announced the cold onslaught of winter; Imbolc on February 1, the feast of the goddess Brigit, was associated with the lactation of ewes, childbirth, and the beginning of spring; Beltane on May 1, a fire festival in praise of a sun-god, Bel, was celebrated with bonfires on hills for summer's approach; and Lughnasa on August 1 was a harvest feast in honor of the sun god, Lugh.

Besides worshippers of the sun, however, they were also a people who loved darkness, the moon and the stars. The Celtic year was at first measured by the moon. Pliny the Elder, as we have already seen, linked the moon with healing and the gathering of mistletoe. He also identified the Celts as a people who counted the beginning of months and years according to the moon, and believed that night was supposed to precede day. As Caesar implied, their days started not at dawn, but at dusk, that twilight period of liminality when darkness is descending and the world of dreams becomes a potential source of enlightenment. The Celts were known for their love of the moon; some of them, at least in Scotland, planted their crops with a waxing moon in the expectation of a better harvest. In Ireland, to increase the possibility of greater fertility among themselves and fecundity in the land, they are said to have danced an entire night every month under the full moon.

The celebration of their New Year, Samhain, began on the eve of November 1, and was considered a sacred time when the ghosts of the dead, especially those who had died the past year, were more apt to be encountered. This was the time to remember them in a special way by spreading a feast for them at the family hearth or by leaving crumbs for them after a family gathering. In Brittany, at Locronan, "bread of the departed" is distributed even today from house to house in honor of those friends and relatives who have died during the past twelve months. In Ireland, according to a twentieth-century storyteller, chairs and stools were placed around the hearth, and bread and milk left on the table for the people belonging to the house that were dead. "It was said they came back home for that night. Next morning, if there was a track of a foot in the ashes, that was taken for a sign that somebody in that house would die inside the next twelve months."[38] In the stories of the Celtic heroes, this feast was also associated with the time people have special visions and dreams, and warriors celebrate a day of peace and friendship. This originally pagan feast later became in the West the celebration of Halloween, and, because of the Irish church's influence, the universal Christian feast day on November 1 of "All Saints" followed on November 2 by "All Souls." These times of transition, between darkness and light, night and day, dusk and dawn, winter and summer, November and May—all were moments of potential revelation when this world and the unseen world seemed very close.

For the Celts, the landscape was considered filled with a spiritual presence, and, in Ireland at least, every memorable mountain, lake, or landmark was connected with a specific story that gave it its name. Certain geographical locations were spoken of specifically as "thin places" in which people sometimes experienced what seemed to be a thin veil between the world of the living and the so-called dead, and sometimes a blurring of the demarcation of time between past, present, and future. Mountains were identified with the breasts of goddesses, and rivers and lakes were perceived as the homes of gods and goddesses sometimes masquerading as salmon and speaking from the depths. Water, in general, was symbolic of numinosity and regeneration. Holy wells, before they were christianized, were perceived as links between the earth and the underworld. The cult of the Irish goddess Brigit was closely linked with sacred wells—as was the Christian saint. Springs, both hot and of normal temperature, were revered for their medicinal and purifying properties. Objects, some shaped like the parts of the bodies in need of restoration, were thrown into the waters as a way of gaining favor with the healing forces of the gods and goddesses.

Trees with their large roots and branches reaching upward evoked for them the interrelationship of underworld and sky. Their longevity symbolized continuity and wisdom, while their seasonal changes were associated with the cycle of time and with death and rebirth. In Ireland, the most sacred trees were those of the oak, yew, ash, and hazel, and, the Irish believed, all had healing powers and were considered sources of wisdom. It is interesting to note that before St. Kevin of Glendalough finally accepted his call to a more public ministry, he spent a great deal of time hiding in a tree. And the fourteenth-century English mystic Julian of Norwich identifies all the goodness of creation and of God's love with a hazelnut, an Irish symbol of wisdom.

Theiʀ Goðs anð Goððesses

As in other cultures and spiritual traditions, the gods and goddesses of the Celts reflected their values and ultimate concerns. Like the Greek, Roman, and Norse pantheons, the Celtic gods and goddesses governed all aspects of human life, and were considered the Celts' ancestors, not their creators. Unlike the Greeks and the Romans, the Celtic spirits and divine beings were less defined in a strict hierarchical fashion, and more linked with local places. Each tribe seems to have had its own tutelary divinities whose roles which were local were similar to those of other groups or places having different or similar names. With the arrival of Christianity on their shores, local saints replaced these pagan spirits, becoming the new protectors and guides of tribes and individuals, leading to at least one saying popular in Cornwall even today: "There are more saints in Cornwall than there are in heaven." Still, besides numerous spirits and gods and goddesses identified with a local site or tribe, some of the "great" divine beings transcended specific localities.

One of the most ancient Celtic gods was Cernunnos, the god of eros and fertility, healing and renewal, the guardian of the doorway between this world and the so-called Otherworld. Associated with the bard or storyteller, he was also identified as a druidic shaman who is seer, visionary, and healer for the tribe. This Cernunnos appears in a variety of configurations found by archaeologists throughout ancient Britain, Ireland, and Brittany. He is usually represented as wearing the antlers of a stag, and sometimes holding or wearing gold torcs, the prized jewelry of the Celts. Sometimes more animals are present in representations of him than a stag or serpent, leading scholars to describe Cernunnos as "Lord of the Animals." He is one of the most ancient figures of humankind, possibly predating the Celts themselves. There may also have been female equivalents of him, since bronze figurines of goddesses found in France also have antlers.[39]

Another of their great gods was named Dagda or "Good Father" who was said to have a huge club (i.e., phallus) and an inexhaustible cauldron from which "no company ever went away . . . unsatisfied."[40] Some of Dagda's most famous children were Angus, called "the Young God," a Celtic Adonis or god of love who represented eternal youth and masculine beauty, and whose home was said to be the passage-grave at New Grange in Ireland; Ogma, the god of literature and eloquence, whose tongue was supposedly joined by mystical chains to the ears of his listeners; and Brigit or Brighid ("the exalted one"), worshipped by the *filid*, the pagan poets, who considered poetry itself as an immaterial, supersensual flame. The goddess of fertility, poetry, song, and wisdom, Brigit was patroness of the druids and poets, and especially known as the goddess of fire and of hearth. She was said to have two sisters with the same name who were connected with healers, craftspeople, and artists. Brigit also was a goddess of ale which helps account for later depictions of the saintly Brigit creating buckets of it, enough to feed the poor and marginalized, as well as her numerous churches. Even as a virgin saint, she obviously reveals her own fertility through her ability to supply limitless food, milk, and beer to those in need.

———— ❧ ————

In general, Celtic goddesses were more primitive and their personalities more veiled in shadows than those of male deities. These pagan goddesses generally followed two types: one pertaining to fertility and eros, the power of life, and one to destruction and thanatos, the power of death. The first type, the fertility goddesses were depicted in close proximity to rivers, wells, springs, lakes, forests, and animals. These ancient Celtic goddesses, so closely connected with nature, fertility, and healing may well account for the rise of the popular cult of the Black Madonna in Europe in those areas where the Celts once lived.[41] The second type of goddesses, those associated with war, death, and the powers of destruction, were frequently depicted as shapeshifting into ravens or crows, symbolic of death. Like Brigit, some Celtic goddesses came in threes—a triplism or triad that frequently occurs in Celtic mythology and Irish literature. The Celts considered the number three to have special significance, equating it with added power, strength, and divinity. It is no wonder they so quickly accepted the triune God of the Christians when that doctrine was preached.

Possibly the most ancient deity of the pagan Celts, preceding even Cernunnos, was the mother-goddess who went by a variety of names. One was Anu or Ana, Danu or Dana, whose name literally means "she of the water," after whom the Danube River was named. When Christianity came to Brittany, devotion to this pagan goddess was transferred to that of St. Anne, the mother of Mary and grandmother of Jesus. Considered the patroness of Brittany, her shrine at Sainte-Anne D'Auray is a very popular pilgrimage site today where the late-medieval statues portraying the "Holy Family" depict not Joseph, Jesus, and Mary, but a definite matriarchy: St. Anne, Mary, and Jesus himself. Morrigan was another name for the Celtic mother-goddess who in certain legends is described as "a bearer of dreams that tangled in the darkness of her hair." She often took the form of a witch or raven, and had "milk-white breasts" that were scarcely "veiled by silks of saffron laced with gold." When she slept with one of the early Celtic heroes, the two of them "lay in the embrace of life," and "the moon watched over them like the eye of the grey God of the Otherworld."[42] This goddess, whether named Ana or Morrigan, was connected with moon worship, and called *mater deorum Hibernensium* [mother of the Irish gods]. Some scholars believe that the legends describing her as universal mother and oldest of the gods show that Celtic society was originally matriarchal. This could well account for the ancient Celts' high respect for women, as well as the equality and harmony between Celtic women and men that is unique when compared to other peoples in the ancient world.[43] It might also have contributed to Celtic men's homoeroticism, their homosexual or bisexual behavior. This latter trait is one they shared with the men of India, another culture shaped by the strong presence of mother-goddesses and near which, as we've seen, the ancient Celts may have originated.

In retrospect, what becomes clear from our study of the Celts and their druidic leaders is how important they were to the life of their tribes. If we can believe Pomponius Mela, quoted earlier, becoming a druid or druidess involved a formation program of some twenty years, certainly a long and probably rigorous apprenticeship with those who were already spiritual leaders. These mentoring relationships were sources of education not only for those studying to be druids, but for all members of Celtic society. The druids and druidesses handed on to their students what they had memorized, as well as what they had learned from their own experiences. Some of them evidently had strong intuitive senses, and psychic abilities, such as second sight: the gift of being able to see into the future or to keenly perceive matters that others might overlook. Early Celtic literature describes too how the druids had close and affectionate relations with animals and birds. Irish myths in particular tell of the births of their heroes coinciding with those of animals, and how many warriors bore animal names. The druids, it is said, could change themselves into animal shapes, call up dense fogs, make snow fall in midsummer, raise tempests on land or sea, and drive people mad. They also could understand the language of ravens and crows, and believed that these black birds had the ability to impart deep secrets from the Otherworld.

Besides being guides in the spiritual realm, the Celtic druids and druidesses acted in a great variety of leadership roles and functions. They were astrologers, visionaries, diviners, guardians of ancient tradition, seers, seekers of wisdom, healers, protectors against evil, sacrificers, shape-changers, poets, storytellers, and peacemakers. This last function has already been pointed out in the writings of Julius Caesar when he refers to their being reconcilers in the day-to-day life of the tribes.

When conflicts arose between the tribes, they were the ones responsible to somehow mediate the differences. When certain grievances and outright crimes threatened to divide families and tribes, they were the ones who helped discern what might make amends for injuries and injustices. They also acted as "leeches," that is, physicians and healers, who diagnosed illnesses, physical and spiritual, and recommended medicines for both types. As teachers, poets, and bards, these Celtic druids and druidesses, many of whom were married, memorized the genealogies, legends, and spiritual traditions of the tribes, and passed them on to their students and to their own children through the stories they told. Quite literally, they became the living memories of the tribes, links between the ages and between the generations.

The Celtic Christian Soul Friends

In the Christian hagiographies, as we will see, the Celtic saints are often pictured as engaged in some of the same roles and exercises as the druids and druidesses. They frequently seem to share the same powers and use them for their own Christian communities and the glory of God. According to these Lives, the births of the saints were frequently foretold by druids, while some of the greatest saints, including Brigit, Patrick, and Columcille were educated by druid mentors. The latter, Columcille, one of the most famous of all soul friends, addressed Christ himself as "my druid" in his prayers.[44] Though the early Christian legends often pit the druids against the saints in their adult lives, the latter in many ways are portrayed as successors to the druids and druidesses, with the same gifts of prophecy and second sight. Healing especially will also be associated with all of the saintly soul friends, Findbarr of Cork, in particular, being called "a true leech who healed sicknesses and diseases of the body and soul of every believer."[45] Considering that some of the saints' most significant teachers were druids and that they themselves took on similar tribal roles, it is obvious how much those saints treasured what they had learned from their mentors and incorporated that wisdom into their Christian theology and ministries. They did not abandon it because they could not; it was a spiritual inheritance engrained in their minds, hearts, and, on the deepest unconscious level, their souls.

There are other similarities as well between the pagan druids
and the early Christian saints. The druids shaved their foreheads
bare, and wore their hair long at the back, sometimes lightened
by bleaching or possibly dyed in bright colors. Later in the early
Celtic Church the tonsure of the Christian priests which the
Roman clergy and their followers opposed so vehemently was
one which left the hair shoulder-length with a high forehead, as
can be seen today on the statue of St. Aidan on Lindisfarne in
northern England. And there was more. According to the
hagiography of St. Columbanus (c. 543-615), the great Irish
missionary to France and Italy, the Irish missionaries, besides
being accompanied by women, evidently attracted attention by
their somewhat audacious appearance. Carrying long, narrow
writing tablets of wood that were mistaken as swords by the
natives of Gaul, they also wore shoulder-length flowing locks
and painted eyelids.[46] J. M. Clark tells of Irish missionaries to
the continent as not only having long hair but having "tattooed
certain parts of the body, especially the eyelids." He relies upon
a medieval text that says in Latin, *"Stigmata, signa, pictura in
corpore quales Scoti pingunt in palpebris"* [The Irish paint or
tattoo on the eyelids such marks, signs, and paintings as those
(tattooed) on the body]. Clark also describes their tonsure as
going "from ear to ear, that is to say, the front part of the scalp
only was shaved," possibly similar to that of the figure of a Celtic
Christian priest, wearing a brightly-colored cloak, depicted in
the Book of Durrow, at the beginning of the Gospel of St.
Matthew.[47] Very likely the long hair, painted or tattooed eyelids,
and this type of tonsure were carryovers from druidic days.

Above all, the love of learning found in the druidic schools
and the mentoring which the druids and druidesses did became
the foundation of the educational system which arose in the
Celtic monasteries when Christianity took hold. As John Ryan
says about the druids and druidesses in Ireland: "After the
conversion of the country to the Christian faith, druidism died a
natural death, and the boys who in the pagan days would have
spent their youth in druidic studies were placed now under
Christian teachers."[48]

Besides the desert tradition of spiritual guidance which will
be discussed in the next chapter, the Celtic druids and druidesses
had the most immediate impact on the development of the Celtic
anamchara. Though some scholars,[49] like John Ryan, believe

that the druids and druidesses were eliminated by Roman civilization and Christianity itself, these spiritual leaders lived on, rising from baptismal waters as Christian soul friends. Like their druidic predecessors, their spirituality would be closely linked with the landscape. They would build their monasteries in sacred oak groves, on high places, or near the waters of placid lakes or rushing rivers or ocean tides' ebb and flow. They would appreciate profoundly the beauty and transcendence found in the natural world, expressed in early medieval Irish poetry that is evocative of Japanese haiku in its simple, but powerful imagery:

Beautiful spot! the large green of an oak
Fronting the storm.[50]

Soul friends with the people of the oak, their pagan predecessors, the Celtic saints would always carry with them a visionary sense that the natural environment was alive with transcendent power. As one of the early Welsh stories says about Peredur, a prototype of the Arthurian Perceval: "On the bank of the river he saw a tall tree: from roots to crown one half was aflame and the other green with leaves."[51]

TWO

Desert Mentoring and Secrets of the Heart

The two embraced each other and greeted one another by their names, and together returned thanks to God. And after the holy kiss, Paul sat down beside Antony, and began to speak. . . . As they talked they perceived that a crow had settled on a branch of the tree, and softly flying down, deposited a whole loaf before their wondering eyes. "Behold," said Paul, "God has sent us our dinner, God the merciful, God the compassionate."

St. Jerome, Life of Paul of Thebes

An evil thought sheds its danger when it is brought into the open. . . . Its dangerous promptings hold sway in us as long as these are concealed in the heart.

John Cassian, Conferences

In addition to the ancient Celtic druids and druidesses, a second major influence upon the development of soul friendship was the desert spiritual tradition with its emphasis on spiritual mentoring and disclosing the secrets of the heart. Ample evidence exists that Celtic Christians were highly familiar with the desert monks who lived during the third through fifth centuries C.E., and incorporated perceptions of their desert heroes into their own understanding of soul friendship. Literary works about the desert Christians were well-known in the early Celtic Church, including Athanasius's *Life of Antony*, written about 357, the *Life of Pachomius*, composed some years after the monk's death in 346, and the stories of the desert elders found in John Cassian's *Institutes* and *Conferences*, written in southern

49

Gaul in the early fifth century. A fifth literary work, the *Life of Paul* by Jerome, composed about 376, describes the spiritual friendship between two desert elders, the famous Antony and a relatively unknown personality (until Jerome wrote about him), Paul of Thebes. Despite the brevity of this hagiography, the friendship of Antony and Paul seems to have struck a major chord in the lives and hearts of Celtic Christians. While Anglo-Saxon monks in England would identify with St. Benedict (c. 480-550) and the monastic rule which is linked with him, in Celtic lands the two desert friends were the ones especially revered. In Brittany, the monks considered those two men in particular as the first teachers of the monastic and solitary living which they followed.[1]

There is also the artistic evidence, especially that which appears on the high crosses that are scattered throughout the landscape of the Celtic churches. While most of these crosses bear scenes from the Old and New Testaments with some possibly featuring the founders of certain monasteries or aspects of Celtic life, panels with Antony and Paul are found on at least ten crosses in Ireland alone, constituting the largest number of such depictions anywhere in western Europe. Some of the most striking panels where the two men are depicted are those at Monasterboice, Kells, Castledermot, Moone, and on a fragmented high cross in Armagh's Church of Ireland cathedral. The two desert elders also appear on the cross at Kilfenora where they are shown carrying their crosiers, one of which has the Egyptian *tau* shape. In Scotland, the famous Ruthwell cross contains a scene of the sharing of bread between Antony and Paul, and the Nigg cross portrays the two men kneeling, facing each other, seeming to celebrate eucharist together. On the Isle of Man, they appear on one of the crosses at Maughold. A different scene, that of the temptation of Antony in the desert, is found on various crosses, including the south cross at Castledermot, Monasterboice's West Cross, and on one of the crosses at Penmon Priory near Anglesey, Wales. In Brittany, at Locronan, there is a fine statue of Antony in the beautiful church of St. Ronan, an Irish missionary who brought Christianity to the early Breton Celts.

Possibly due to the ancient Celts' love of the sun-god symbolized by an orb, the unusual shape of the Celtic high crosses themselves with a circle supporting the crossbeams may have originally come from Egypt, judging from a fifth- or sixth-century image of an Egyptian jeweled cross that is now displayed at the Minneapolis (Minnesota) Institute of Arts.[2] Found on a sanctuary curtain from a Coptic church, it shows a Christian cross encircled by a large garland or wreath of fruit, a symbol of victory that was given to winners of competition in late antiquity. Many of the illustrations found in the Book of Kells and other early illuminated Celtic gospel books have striking similarities with Egyptian and Syrian art forms, including not only the iconic representations of Jesus, Mary, and the evangelists, but also the use of dots to illustrate them. Even the pigmentation may have come from the eastern desert lands.[3]

All of these literary sources and artistic portrayals point to the influence the desert Christians had upon the early Celtic Church. Extensive travel that was done in late antiquity and the early medieval period would account for the transmission of this desert spirituality. We know from the scripture stories of the early church, relating the missionary travels of Peter and Paul, as well as the travels of later pilgrims to the desert lands, that people in the ancient world were highly mobile. Although travel and communication were certainly not as swift as in our own day, many traveled by horse, camel, chariot, ship, boat, and, of course, on foot.[4] Even before Athanasius wrote his famous *Life of Antony*, he brought the practices of the Egyptian monks to Trier in Gaul during one of his periods of exile. St. Martin (c. 316-397) who became bishop of Tours, in Gaul, established a monastery at Liguge, near Poitiers, possibly the first monastery on Gallic soil, which followed a desert semi-eremetical type of living. When John Cassian moved to Marseilles and established his double monastery, St. Victor's, about 415 he brought with him memories of the desert monks which, when written down, became a basic reference for the emerging Celtic monasticism in Gaul, Britain, and Ireland.

The Spread of Monasticism

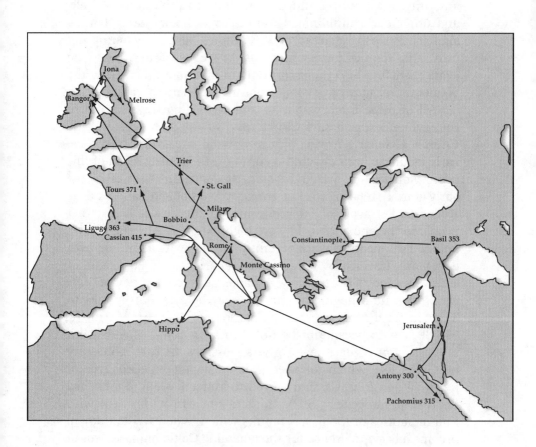

We know too of specifically Celtic travelers and pilgrims who visited the desert lands and carried back stories of their experiences. Adomnan (c. 625-704), abbot of Iona and hagiographer of St. Columcille, wrote an account of the journey to the Holy Land of Arculf, a seventh-century bishop from Gaul. This writing describes the prelate's visits over a nine-month period to a number of holy sites in Jerusalem, Nazareth, and Bethlehem, as well as on Mount Tabor. He obviously saw much, including the holy shroud, and, perhaps most fascinating, "the chalice of the Lord" which became, in later Celtic legends, the Holy Grail.[5] Other Celtic pilgrims visited these holy places and brought back with them the stories of the desert heroes.[6] The Irish, in particular, were known for their frequent travels. The German monk Walafrid Strabo (c. 808-49) refers to them in a book about St. Gall, the companion of the Irish missionary St. Columbanus, as those "in whom the custom of wandering has become almost a second nature."[7] Desert Christians, fleeing the persecutions against them in the fifth century and possibly later when the Moslems took control over the desert regions in Egypt and the Sinai, may have traveled to Ireland and Britain. In a litany from the tenth-century Book of Leinster, there is mention of seven monks from Egypt who died while visiting Ireland who were buried there.[8]

In order to discover more about those desert Christians so highly respected and loved by Celtic Christians and the spiritual mentoring which they did, we will examine here some of the lives and sayings of the desert Christians, both of which, in written form, are considered part of that genre of writing called "hagiography": works whose purpose was to edify and inspire. In this chapter, we will focus upon some key elements and primary themes of the desert Christians as reflected in their stories and wisdom sayings, and how important it was for them to disclose to an elder the inner workings of the heart. This desert spirituality, with its emphasis on encountering God—and oneself—in conversations with spiritual guides and friends affected the later understanding of the Celtic *anamchara*. We will start with an examination of sources regarding the desert Christians and their ministry of spiritual mentoring.

The Desert Made a City by the Monks

During the third, fourth, and fifth centuries of Christianity, numerous people left all they possessed, sometimes including their families, and went into the desert regions of Egypt, Syria, and Palestine. Some were fleeing high taxes, military conscription, or the corruption, complexity, and smoke of city life;[9] some traveled there because of the intermittent persecutions of Christians by the Roman emperors before Constantine (c. 274-337). Others, simply in love with God, were motivated to go there as a result of an adult conversion experience. In imitation of Jesus who had been "led by the Spirit out into the wilderness" (Mt 4:21) and the first martyrs who heroically died for their faith, they desired to find God by living a more disciplined life which the desert would naturally require. These Christians, pioneers of monasticism in both Eastern and Western churches, were mostly laypeople, not clergy, and included women as well as men.

After Christianity became so firmly linked with the rulers of the Roman Empire following the Edict of Milan in 313, many of these laypeople were seeking to escape the politics in which church leaders had become involved, and their increasing fascination with owning property. Hilary of Poitiers (c. 315-367), a theologian from Gaul, was one who condemned this aspect of ecclesial institutions: "What an evil it is, this love of building that possesses you. . . . Safer by far, to my mind, are the mountains, the woods, the lakes. . . . These are the places where, inspired by God's spirit, the prophets spoke. . . ."[10] Another writer from Gaul, Sulpicius Severus (c. 360-420), the author of the famous *Life of St. Martin of Tours*, spoke out against the developing clericalization of the ordained: "Take someone quite inconspicuous either for deeds or virtues, and let him be made a cleric. He will at once broaden the fringes of his clothes, find pleasure in being spoken to, pride himself on the visits he receives, and gad about everywhere. Before, he used to go on foot or ride a donkey; now, he must be proudly drawn by foaming horses."[11] Inspired initially by the stories of the desert elders Antony (251-356) and Pachomius (292-346), these lay Christians desired a more heroic and simpler lifestyle where, according to the patristic writer Origen (c. 185-254), "the air was purer, the heavens more open, and God nearer."[12]

   Living alone as hermits or together in communities under the open skies, the desert Christians eventually became valued as teachers of prayer and facilitators in the healing of spiritual diseases which they called "sins." Their followers respectfully and lovingly called them *abba* ("father") or *amma* ("mother"), or *pneumatikos pater* or *pneumatike mater*, a spirit-bearer who acts as a kind of parent or midwife of souls. A commonly held belief was that a relationship of friendship with these guides could have a major effect on the direction of one's spiritual journey, for, as the gospels said, one person's spirit is very much affected for good or for ill by another's (cf. Mk 8:14-21). They instructed those who came to them not only with words of advice, but more importantly through the spirituality they lived. Theirs was a form of spiritual mentoring that followed the maxim, "Be an example, not a lawgiver."[13] They also taught that it is essential for everyone to speak directly from the heart to another person, and that this self-disclosure is good for the soul. They practiced a form of spiritual therapy that consisted of *exagoreusis*, "opening one's heart," that led to *hesychia*, or "peace of heart." This spiritual practice of these desert guides, united with that of the ancient Celts' druidic mentors, contributed significantly to the rise of the ministry of the soul friend in the early Celtic Church.

   Much of what we know about the desert Christians comes to us from the writings of those who visited them. Towards the end of the fourth century after Christ's death, the "huge silence," and "the great quiet" of the Egyptian desert monks was interrupted by visitors in search of wisdom.[14] Many came to visit the holy places in Jerusalem and Bethlehem, after Helena, Constantine's mother, had begun to build churches at the locations identified with the events in Jesus's life. Latins came from Rome and Western Europe as pilgrims, Greeks from Constantinople and Eastern Europe, Armenians from Asia Minor, and others from Syria and Ethiopia. Some of these pilgrims decided to stay and settle near these holy sites in what came to be called "the Holy Land." Others kept moving further into the Egyptian desert to find guidance from the holy men and women who, already settled, lived alone or in communities. Many came at great personal expense and all at considerable risk, for, as one of them said, "we suffered much on our journey and came very near to losing our lives."[15] Most left no account of their experiences with the desert elders, while others, a very small percentage of the total number of visitors to that region, have. Some of these became famous for their descriptions of what they found.

There was, first of all, Eusebius (c. 260-339) of Caesarea, considered the father of early church history, who visited the Holy Land and witnessed the dedication of the Church of the Resurrection at Jerusalem which Constantine was having built. He incorporated into his *Ecclesiastical History* a section on Origen, who greatly influenced the thought of later desert Christian writers Evagrius (346-99) and John Cassian (c. 360-435). Athanasius (c. 295-373), another famous church leader, visited the desert regions south of the seaport city, Alexandria, where he was a bishop, and became friends with the two desert elders, Antony and Pachomius, pioneers in the rise of monasticism. This Athanasius wrote the highly popular *Life of Antony* which introduced many in the West to desert spirituality. Augustine was one of those profoundly changed by that hagiography, as he describes in his *Confessions*.[16] Others, besides Augustine, were dramatically influenced by the desert monks. Basil "the Great" (c. 330-79), the brother of Gregory of Nyssa (c. 330-395) and Macrina (c. 327-79), journeyed from Cappadocia to visit Syria and Egypt. Based upon what he found, he eventually established his own community with a set of monastic rules that encouraged liturgical prayer, care for the poor, and the training of children in classes attached to his monasteries. Another visitor, Rufinus (c. 342-410), came with his companion, Melania "the Elder" (c. 342-410), a rich, young Roman widow who spent six months at Nitria, located below Alexandria, visiting several desert hermits. Both she and Rufinus founded a double monastery on the Mount of Olives in Jerusalem. Evagrius of Pontus, a disciple of Origen, went to Nitria for two years, and later traveled to the site of Cellia or Cells, near Nitria, where he stayed to become one of the greatest of the Egyptian monks. His writings on desert spirituality influenced Palladius, Cassian, Pseudo-Dionysius, and Maximus the Confessor.

In 385, Jerome (c. 331-420) traveled to Egypt with the wealthy Roman woman Paula (347-404) and her daughter, Eustochium (370-c. 419). These three friends, companions on pilgrimage, also stayed at Nitria and then journeyed to

Bethlehem in 386 where Jerome settled down in a spacious cave to do his own translating and writing—with the support and scholarly help of the two women. In 388, Palladius (c. 365-425), a native of Celtic Galatia who later wrote *The Lausiac History* on the desert Christians, arrived in Egypt and, despite an early episode of poor health which incapacitated him for some time, went on to Nitria and the Cells. One of the most famous of all these visitors, and certainly the person who had a tremendous influence on the development of Western and Celtic monasticism, was John Cassian, who, considering that his birthplace was probably Romania, may himself have been of Celtic blood.[17] Cassian, accompanied by his friend Germanus, journeyed to monasteries in Bethlehem and Egypt in the late fourth century. Based upon this knowledge of the desert from first-hand experience, he wrote his *Institutes* and *Conferences* which the Rule of St. Benedict later incorporated and the monks in the Celtic Church made a part of their lives and their own monastic rules.

All of these early visitors came to listen and observe, hoping to gain insights that would enrich their lives and deepen their commitment to God. One of those who traveled from Jerusalem to the outlying communities astutely expressed it in words that any traveler or pilgrim would understand: "We have come to you from Jerusalem for the good of our souls, so that what we have heard with our ears we may perceive with our eyes—for the ears are naturally less reliable than the eyes—and because very often forgetfulness follows what we hear, whereas the memory of what we have seen is not easily erased but remains imprinted on our minds like a picture."[18] What visitors to these desert regions found there, besides the dangerous summer heat, dry sands, and the great quiet was the vastness of the land. Egeria, a late fourth-century nun, probably from that Celtic region of northwestern Spain called Galicia, uses the adjective "vast" four times on the first pages of the journal which she kept of her travels.[19] That which met many of the visitors' eyes, if they journeyed to Egypt, were untold numbers of monasteries and cells, built there since Antony had entered the desert about 271, and Pachomius had founded his first community at Tabennesi in southeastern Egypt about 320. As a result of these pioneers, "there were monasteries," according to Athanasius, "in the mountains, and the desert was made a city by monks, who left their own people and registered themselves for the citizenship in the heavens."[20] Although numerous other monasteries populated the Holy Land, Egypt was the earliest of the sites associated with the desert Christians and its primary center until a series of raids by military forces of the Emperor in the late fourth century and by barbarians in the early fifth century when many of the monks left. It remained the place that attracted the most attention and produced written records which were to influence the monastic world up to our own time.

In Egypt, three main types of monastic communities and monks existed which corresponded somewhat to three geographical locations. In Lower Egypt, the followers of Abba Antony lived as solitaries and hermits, preferring to follow the eremitic life defined by their leader. Spiritual guidance, when it happened, was done more on a one-to-one basis between a trusted and worthy *abba* or *amma* and his or her protégé. In Upper Egypt, there were those who, inspired by the leadership of Pachomius, lived in large communities, following a cenobitic or communal lifestyle. Spiritual guidance among them had more of a communal dimension in which the entire community offered its assistance, although much personal mentoring still occurred between an elder and his or her protégé. Near and in Nitria emerged the *lavra* or *skete* which to some degree combined the lifestyles of the other two. Here small groups lived with a spiritual father or mother, probably near a church where they could gather for prayers and eucharist on weekends. Other Christians following an ascetic lifestyle settled in Palestine, Syria, and Asia Minor.

Desert Guides and Their Ascetic Spirituality

In addition to the various types of communities, what the visitors found, most importantly, were the spiritual guides themselves. In some ways these desert mentors were very ordinary people, with quite recognizable human attributes and foibles. They also were somewhat extreme (by our standards) in their approach to life: wearing rough clothing (although some solitaries, such as Mary of Egypt, evidently wore nothing at all), and living on a very simple diet of dried bread, fruits, vegetables, and oil.[21] Certainly, they were not in the least "churchy." In fact,

Pachomius's communities at first allowed no priests to join them since they associated priests with what they called a "love of command." There are also occasional stories about desert elders hiding when a bishop approached, fearing that he might want to ordain them. One story relates humorously a discussion between the desert father, John of Lycopolis, and Palladius who was visiting him:

> Then he [John] spoke to me jokingly: "Do you wish to be a bishop?"
> I said: "I already am."
> And he: "Where?"
> I said: "In the kitchen and shops, over the tables and pots. I examine them, and if there is any sour wine I excommunicate it, but I drink the good. Likewise I inspect the pots, too, and if any salt or other spices are lacking, I throw these in and thus season them and eat them. This is my diocese, for Gluttony has ordained me for her child."[22]

While highly conscious of spiritual illnesses, such as gluttony, at the same time they seem to struggle unceasingly with their sexuality. Eros among these Christians never receives a good name, but is most often identified with demonic desires that are to be condemned and definitely controlled. Like the Irish warrior CuChulainn and the Celtic saints, including Patrick, Kevin, David, Cuthbert, Gildas, and even Brigit, some of these desert ascetics soak in cold water overnight. But, while CuChulainn did this to soothe his rage, the desert Christians do it to assuage the power of their eros. A story about the spiritual master, Evagrius, is told by his protégé Palladius: "The demon of fornication bothered him so oppressively, as he told us, that he stood naked throughout the night in a well. It was winter at the time and his flesh froze." Other measures, such as sleepless nights, no bathing, and an even stricter diet than usual, were also encouraged to control what they identified as the "demon of lust" or of "fornication." One monk is said to have "never gone to sleep on purpose, but closed his eyes only when overcome with sleep while at work or eating, so that often a morsel of food would fall from his mouth while he was eating, so drowsy had he become." Another monk, Isidore, never bathed, since that action was linked with the public baths where sexual encounters often occurred between males. Women and boys or young men were to be avoided by the male monks because of their own struggles with "the flesh," while the body, in general, was viewed as an enemy. A story from Palladius provides intimations of this when he describes his stay with Abba Dorotheus who had commanded that he, Palladius, stay three full years with him in order to subdue his "passions":

> He [Dorotheus] used to collect stones in the desert all day long in the burning heat along the sea and to build cells for those who could not build their own, finishing one each year. When I asked him: "What are you doing, Father, killing your body in such heat?" he answered: "It kills me, I will kill it."[23]

In the *Life of St. Hilarion*, by Jerome, we find a similar approach to controlling desires and the attitude towards one's body. According to Jerome, when Hilarion was an adolescent, he went into the desert and was assaulted by salacious images:

> The Devil tickled the boy's senses and excited the fires of passion usual in puberty. Christ's young novice was compelled to reflect upon what he knew not and to revolve in his mind processions of seductive images and scenes which he had never experienced. Enraged with himself, he beat blows upon his heart as if he could destroy the disturbing thoughts by the sheer violence of his attack. "You ass," he said to his body, "I'll see that you don't kick against the goad; I'll fill you not with barley but with chaff. I shall wear you out with hunger and thirst; I shall weigh you down with a heavy burden; through the heat and cold I shall drive you so that you will think of food rather than lust."[24]

Much of this asceticism with its harsh attitudes toward and treatment of the body definitely consisted of a counter-cultural stance to the prevailing attitudes in late antiquity. The predominant culture of the Roman empire espoused the presumed joys of urban living, diverse social interactions and sexual mores, lavish feasts, fine clothes, and all sorts of sensual comforts. Such a culture led to a perpetual and insatiable search for novelty and pleasure, resulting in what even one of the great Roman writers of the first century, Seneca, described as "the dull wasting of a soul."[25] In some ways to counterbalance these cultural extremes, the desert Christians chose their own extreme actions: living in solitary places, fasting from meat and other commodities, abstaining from alcohol, living poorly and simply. They also promoted a celibate lifestyle. Eros and sexuality were to be contained with "purity of heart," unceasing prayer, and, as mentioned, extreme ascetical practices.

Book knowledge too was especially suspect because of its association with pride, indulgence, and sexual temptations. Unlike the Christian Celts, desert ascetics either condemned books (except for the holy scriptures) or found themselves torn between a love of the classics of Greece and Rome and hostility toward them. Jerome, for one, had a dream that continued to haunt him in which he had been flogged at Christ's judgment seat for being a better follower of Cicero than a Christian![26] The one exception in this tradition was Basil who, as noted above, began monastic communities which were frequently located near cities, and that functioned as educational centers. He suggested that Christians should read the pagan classics, but with discretion:

> Cherish the poets when they recount the deeds of good men and words. But if the ancient poets treat of wicked men, avoid imitation (as Odysseus avoided the Siren songs). . . . In all this be like the bees, who as they fly here and there, wisely select the flowers from which to extract the honey. [Like the bees] be selective in what you read from Greek literature and philosophy.[27]

In many ways, this desert asceticism was a highly male-oriented spirituality, much of it influenced by the men who first wrote the stories and wisdom sayings down, but also by their environment. Living in the desert and adjusting to its climate presupposed that a certain discipline was needed, sometimes quite difficult and extreme, simply in order to survive. Images of God and the holy life were necessarily related to this landscape. Desert writers speak of climbing a mountain as symbolic of becoming a holy person—an image used by Dante for his *Divine Comedy*, Thomas Merton for his autobiography, *The Seven Storey Mountain*, and Martin Luther King, Jr. in his last sermon, before being assassinated. If God is found in the heights, as the story of Moses on Mount Sinai suggests, then desert Christians presupposed that to find God we must attempt the journey *up*—and *endure* the hardships and perils along the way.

Another symbol, the ladder, reflects this masculine approach to spirituality. It is an image definitely found in the scriptures: from the dream of Jacob in the Old Testament in which a ladder actually appears (Gn 28:10 ff.) to Jesus' promise in the New Testament to Nathaniel that he would see, if he followed him, "heaven laid open and, above the Son of Man, the angels of God ascending and descending" (Jn 1:51). This ladder imagery was adapted by the desert monks to their own environment. John Climacus (c. 570-649), abbot of St. Catherine, the most famous monastery in the Sinai desert, expounded upon it theologically in his classic, *The Ladder of Divine Ascent*. In this book, each step of the ladder presupposes the acquisition of a particular virtue that supports one's climb upwards. This form of spiritual progress must have been experienced firsthand by the monks of St. Catherine as they built, one at a time, those 3,700 steep stone steps to Mount Sinai that pilgrims use today. The same ladder imagery appears in the works of Plato, Origen, Jerome, Cassian, Benedict, the fourteenth-century English mystic Walter Hilton, Protestant reformers Martin Luther and John Calvin, and Orthodox spiritual writers St. Simeon the New Theologian and St. Isaac the Syrian. Like other images from the desert, the ladder is also found in the stories of the Celtic soul friends. In the earliest extant Celtic hagiography, the *Life of St. Samson of Dol* (in Brittany), the saint himself is compared to a spiritual ladder: "In truth St. Samson had grown so wonderful and, if I may so speak, so ineffable in the work of God, that from day to day, naturally rising as by a spiritual ladder higher and higher to the highest summit of religion, he was seen to emerge, by daily use, renewed and bettered."[28]

What will be found in the Celtic tradition is not so much a God of the heights where one is to leave behind family and friends to find God (as the desert tradition suggests), but a God of the hearth around which stories are told and where people gather for warmth and sustenance; a God who is already present, as friend and companion, in the midst of family, friendships, and ordinary life. Desert asceticism, however, is one that Christian Celts would come to admire and adapt as theirs, precisely because of their own warrior ideals which included rigorous training, difficult initiations, and ongoing endurance, not to mention, in medieval times and beyond, their own acquaintance with persecution, poverty, and suffering. These desert ideals, as we will see, were later incorporated into the spirituality of the eighth-century Celi De reform movement of the Celtic Church, and affected the portrayal of a number of the Celtic saints as solitaires, and most of them to some degree as ascetics.

Still, though the wisdom sayings and lives of the desert Christians reflect a masculine spirituality, and are frequently identified with "Fathers of the Desert" exclusively, such was not the case. From sources that have survived, we know of large numbers of women who lived in the desert regions as both hermits and community members, and who acted as spiritual guides and mentors to those who came to them for help.

Desert Mothers: Sarah, Theodora, and Syncletica

One of our primary sources which recognizes the desert women's leadership is none other than Palladius who was from Celtic Galatia, and thus more sensitive to the contribution of women's gifts. Indeed, his *Lausiac History* begins with a statement that one of his purposes in writing it was "to commemorate women far advanced in years and illustrious God-inspired mothers who have performed feats of virtuous asceticism . . . as exemplars and models. . . ." He goes on to say that not only are men famous "for their strict way of life," but also "holy highborn women, too, who lived the best and loftiest lives." Palladius gives numerous examples in his book of the outstanding women who could be found in the desert, including Paula and Eustochium, friends of Jerome, Veneria, the wife of a count, Theodora, the wife of a tribune, Hosia and her sister Adolia, the deaconess Sabiniana, and others. He calls them "courageous . . . to whom God granted struggles equal to those of men, so that no one could plead as an excuse that women are too weak to practice virtue successfully."[29]

In another important source, the so-called collection of "Sayings of the Desert Fathers," there are mothers too. One was Amma Sarah, a solitary, who lived sixty years beside a river "and never," we are told, "lifted her eyes to look at it," a sign, perhaps, of her humility. Thirteen of those years, she spent fighting the "demon of lust," but she "never prayed that the warfare should cease but she said, 'O God, give me strength.'" On one occasion, almost overcome by this particular demon, she went up to her little terrace to pray. When "the spirit of fornication" appeared in physical form to her and said, "Sarah, you have overcome me," she responded, "It is not I who have overcome you, but my master, Christ." Through these struggles, she became a woman who learned compassion and a wisdom that drew others to her for spiritual guidance. At the same time, despite the cultural and religious messages of her time regarding women, she was not afraid of being assertive. When two old anchorites who came to visit her agreed ahead of time, "Let us humiliate this old woman," she said to them, "If I prayed God that all men should approve of my conduct, I should find myself a penitent at the door of each one, but I shall rather pray that my heart may be pure towards all."[30]

Purity of heart was one of the desert Christians' primary goals, and one that is often discussed by the elders, both women and men. This "purity" was rooted in Jesus' words, "blessed are the pure of heart, for they shall see God" (Mt 5:8), and was equated with moral and spiritual integrity. It was also very much linked with charity, with love of neighbor. It presupposed that if one could empty the heart of vicious and lascivious thoughts, that if one's outward actions were also characterized by unselfish, loving acts, a person would not only experience a new level of freedom in his or her life, but would also be closer to God and more available to truly help one's fellows. Such "purity" brings joy, harmony, and a deep inner peace; its opposite can bring disruptive turbulence. Dante in his *Divine Comedy* compares the lack of purity to a "kind of torment," characterized by "warring winds," a "hellish tempest," and being tossed "hither and thither, up and down . . . by the blast."[31] In John Cassian's writings, this constituted the difference between the "true self" (becoming more like Christ) and the "servile self" (alienated from God and one's spiritual center).[32] Amma Sarah, quite clearly, knew all this from her own experience, and was able to teach others precisely because of what she had learned from these struggles, especially about the importance of centering one's life—and one's heart—in Christ rather than attempting to do it on willpower alone.

The desert women seem to have been highly conscious of the responsibility of mentoring others, especially teaching them about prayer. Some of this, of course, they had learned from the stories of the desert elders Antony and Pachomius. But they also may have been inspired by the *Life of Macrina*, written by her younger brother, Gregory of Nyssa, who was, as we recall, the brother of Basil as well. This fourth-century hagiography is truly amazing, considering Hellenistic culture at the time. In late antiquity when men were primarily identified with philosophy and teaching, it portrays a woman, Macrina, in that role. Like Socrates, she teaches not only by leading an exemplary life, but in the way she prepared herself to die, calling her family and friends around her, and praying as "she traced the sign of the cross on her eyes, her mouth, and her heart."[33] Unlike the story found in Plato's *Phaedo* of Socrates' death in which his dead body, evidently of little consequence, is wrapped in a cloak and left behind, in the *Life of Macrina* her body, after her death, is laid out before the community, and, still luminous, is buried in her parents' grave, next to her mother's.[34]

Another desert mother, Theodora, possibly the same as the one to whom Palladius refers in his writings, lived in a monastic community near Alexandria. According to her wise sayings, she was obviously conscientious of her own roles as spiritual mentor and teacher. As she says, "a teacher ought to be a stranger to the desire for domination, vain-glory, and pride; one should not be able to fool him by flattery, nor blind him by gifts, nor conquer him by the stomach, nor dominate him by anger; but he should be patient, gentle and humble as far as possible; he must be tested and without partisanship, full of concern, and a lover of souls." This lover of souls taught those who came to her about prayer, stating that, through prayer, all temptations "fall away." She also describes "this present age" as "a storm," and says that "it is good to live in peace, for the wise person practices perpetual prayer."[35]

The reference to perpetual or "unceasing" prayer is another major theme of the desert Christians. Originating in the words of St. Paul, "pray without ceasing" (1 Thes 5:17), it was a practice that underwent a great deal of development over time. Among the desert monks, it was linked with *anamnesis*: the conscious, prayerful remembrance of God, the continuing sense of God's presence throughout the day as one works, prays, eats,

—————— ❧ ——————

talks, and rests. They associated this remembrance with the
heart, and to help them maintain this constant awareness of
God, they would repeat verbally or silently a verse from
scripture or a saying that called upon the holy name of Jesus.
This practice developed at St. Catherine's monastery in the Sinai
and at the monastery on Mount Athos in northern Greece, and
was further theologically defined by such writers as John
Climacus, Symeon the New Theologian (949-1022), and
Gregory Palamas (c. 1296-1359). It eventually became the basis
of the refined tradition of "hesychasm" that is so beloved by
Eastern Orthodox Christians and is expressed in the "Jesus
Prayer": "Lord Jesus Christ, have mercy on me," or its variation.
The nineteenth-century Russian spiritual classic, *The Way of a
Pilgrim*, describes how a simple layman who wants to know how
to pray is told to repeat this prayer so often that it becomes a part
of his breathing and the beating of his heart.[36] This devotion to
prayer throughout the day and night, and, in particular to Jesus,
is a strong element that will be found in Celtic monasticism too,
especially in the Celi De movement. The fact that Amma
Theodora recommended perpetual prayer, long before the
practice and its theology had been fully articulated, is a sign of
her wisdom and her own commitment to praying unceasingly.

The third desert mother that appears in the collection of
wisdom sayings is Amma Syncletica (a name that derives from
the Greek term, *synkletos*, which refers to the "heavenly
assembly"). She is one of the most famous of spiritual guides, a
woman who lived for years as a hermit before a community of
women gathered about her. Unlike so many of these female
leaders, her life was written by an unknown fifth-century
hagiographer. It depicts her as "steering her own little boat
attentively with reverence toward God," and bringing it
"undamaged by storms to safe harbor, having placed her faith in
God as her surest anchor."[37] This image of the little boat on the
open sea is a popular one, for it appears in the writings of
Jerome, John Cassian, Fortunatus (c. 530-610), a bishop, poet,
and hagiographer in Gaul, Gildas (c. 500-570), a monk and the
first British historian, and Muirchu, an Irish hagiographer in the
seventh-century who wrote one of the earliest lives of St.
Patrick. All would have been familiar with the sea and the image
of God as a safe harbor or anchor.

Syncletica was born in Alexandria, that seaport city with the beautiful wide harbor, and came from a family of Macedonian lineage. Macedonia is a significant geographical region, probably once Celtic, that had a reputation for women in strong social and religious roles.[38] What is fascinating about this *desert* mother is the fact that she makes frequent allusions to water and sailing. Her most compelling theology is expressed in her numerous references to the sea.

> If you have begun to act well, do not turn back through constraint of the enemy, for through your endurance, the enemy is destroyed. Those who put out to sea at first sail with a favourable wind; then the sails spread, but later the winds become adverse. Then the ship is tossed by the waves and is no longer controlled by the rudder. But when in a little while there is a calm, and the tempest dies down, then the ship sails on again. So it is with us, when we are driven by the spirits who are against us; we hold to the cross as our sail and so we can set a safe course.

[handwritten margin note: Do not doubt in the darkness what God has shown you in the light!]

She compares the soul to a ship that is sometimes "engulfed by the waves without and is sometimes swamped by the bilge-water within." She warns against the bilge-water of thoughts, for these frequently can overflow and "kill the seamen, often when they are asleep and the sea is calm." "Our life," she says, "is a sea," and "we are sailing in uncertainty."[39]

Taking into account these numerous references to water, she probably lived near the sea in her earlier life, observing the ebb and flow of the tide as much as she later would the interior movements of the heart. Yet, contrary to the sailing motif in her words of advice, she cautions, in feminine imagery, against traveling from place to place: "If you find yourself in a monastery do not go to another place, for that will harm you a great deal. Just as the bird who abandons the eggs she was sitting on prevents them from hatching, so the monk or the nun grows cold and their faith dies, when they go from one place to another."[40] This sentiment of Syncletica is reflected in the words of another female spiritual guide from the Celtic Church, St. Samthann, an Irish nun connected with the Celi De movement in Ireland, when she says to a certain teacher who wanted to go abroad on pilgrimage: "If God cannot be found on this side of the sea, by all means let us journey overseas. But since God is near to all those who call on him, we have no need to cross the sea. The kingdom of heaven can be reached from every land."[41]

What is especially interesting in Syncletica's hagiography is her portrayal as a reluctant spiritual guide who does not initially want to speak any words of wisdom to the women who come to her, but only sheds tears and tells them to follow "a common teacher—the Lord."[42] When she does begin to offer spiritual guidance, she seems particularly sensitive to the needs of women, and, though she obviously has a preference for the celibate life, she does not denigrate marriage as numerous patristic writers and desert fathers do. Also, while the latter assail the sin of pride, perhaps a more difficult soul-sickness for men, Syncletica emphasizes despair, and reminds those who are prone to it that "Rahab was a prostitute, but she was saved through faith; Paul was a persecutor, but he became a chosen instrument. . . . Keeping these people in mind, therefore, do not give up hope for your own soul." In her discussions, she addresses both women and men directly, but seems at times especially compassionate toward women—not just those joining the monasteries, but those "in the world":

> Let us women not be misled by the thought that those in the world are without cares. For perhaps in comparison they struggle more than we do. For towards women generally there is great hostility in the world. They bear children with difficulty and risk, and they suffer patiently through nursing, and they share illnesses with their sick children—and these they endure without having any limit to their travail. . . . Since we women know these facts, therefore, let us not be deluded by the Enemy that their life is easy and carefree. For in giving birth women die in labour; and yet, in failing to give birth, they waste away under reproaches that they are barren and unfruitful.[43]

Syncletica's willingness to make her life available to others in care and compassion epitomizes many desert mothers' significant contribution to this spiritual tradition. While there were other women in the desert, such as Mary of Egypt, Pelagia, Thais, and Mary, the niece of Abba Abraham, the three mentioned here provide, in their work as spiritual guides, some balance to the largely male presence that dominates the stories of the desert landscape. Although women may have been perceived as either harlots or hearth-keepers by many of the male elders, and thus as temptations to their ascetic way-of-life, these women showed that love of God, not gender, was the criterion of salvation—and of effective ministry.

Qualities and Gifts

What seems to underlie all the ministries of both desert mothers and fathers was the conviction, first of all, that, as Abba Apollo articulates, "You must prostrate yourselves before brothers [and sisters] who come to visit you, for it is not them but God you venerate. Have you seen your brother [or sister]? says Scripture; you have seen the Lord your God."[44] With this belief that God was truly encountered in their human solidarity with others, they consistently manifested a ministry of hospitality to those who sincerely sought their help. Granted that they highly valued their asceticism and simple lifestyle, but what appears so unusual—and so consistently—in their stories is that these desert people frequently dropped everything they were doing when visitors approached in order to show them hospitality. In one story, two monks went to a certain elder whose custom it was not to eat every day: "But when he saw the brethren, he invited them with joy to dine with him, saying, 'Fasting has its reward, but he who eats out of love fulfils two commandments, for he sets aside his own will and he refreshes his hungry brethren.'"[45]

Sometimes this hospitality even included giving up to guests the cells in which they lived. Seven monks from Palestine who journeyed through the Egyptian desert in 394 tell how the desert figures whom they met "have so much love for each other, and for other monks too, that when, as often happens, many come desiring to attain salvation by joining them, each one hastens to give them his own hermitage as a temporary cell." They describe one *abba*, in particular, by the name of Ammonius who possessed beautifully constructed cells with a courtyard and a well. He gave them all up to a visiting brother while he himself moved to a small cell some distance away. Others he welcomed by inviting them to church for a feast in which each of the new brothers received loaves of bread and other suitable items for their cells.[46] Another story tells of a hermit, also visited by a brother, who says to him, "Forgive me, abba, for preventing you from keeping your rule." The hermit replied, "My rule is to welcome you with hospitality and to send you away in peace."[47]

This quality of hospitality, expressed frequently in the later lives of the Celtic soul friends, was in many ways related to other qualities of equal worth. Pachomius had taught through his words and example that "this is God's love—to take pains for each other," and indeed compassion, along with being non-judgmental, became two essential qualities for spiritual guides.[48] Confrontation was not excluded from any such relationship, but it was always to be done in the context of compassionate acceptance and love. These two qualities are at times specifically recommended in the sayings and the lives. One story is told that the desert fathers used to say, "There is nothing worse than passing judgment," while another story relates how Abba Pastor said, "Judge not him who is guilty of fornication, if you are chaste, or you will break the law like him. For He who said, 'Do not commit fornication,' said also 'Do not judge.'"[49] An additional narrative relates the solidarity felt between a desert father and a sinful brother in spite of the directions of a priest. "A brother sinned," the story goes, "and the priest ordered him to go out of the church; abba Bessarim got up and went out with him, saying, 'I, too, am a sinner.'"[50] Other stories are especially memorable and powerful, expressing in a few words how compassion and being non-judgmental are often qualities closely intertwined: "Some monks came to see abba Poemen and said to him, 'When we see brothers dozing during the services in church, should we rouse them so that they can be watchful?' He said to them, 'For my part, when I see a brother dozing, I put his head on my knees and let him rest.'"[51]

These desert leaders had many other personal qualities that would eventually be identified with Celtic soul friends, such as their affinity with animals, their powers of healing, their respect for dreams, and their belief in the communion of saints. And like the early Celtic saints, they too attracted followers who sometimes numbered only one or sometimes as many as five hundred or more. Many of the desert fathers and mothers whom visitors to the desert consulted could be equated with a depth of insight into human nature that often today is only identified with psychiatrists or therapists. In numerous ways, they could

The gift of mutuality

be described, according to Benedicta Ward, as "the experts of the ancient world in the psychology of the spiritual life."[52] Perhaps one of their greatest gifts was that of mutuality: the paradox frequently found in mentoring relationships that as one gives, one also receives.

Abba Apollo's story reveals much about this experience of mutuality: "Now we saw this man, who had hermitages under him in the desert at the foot of the mountain, and was the father of five hundred monks. . . . The saint quickly became famous as a new prophet and apostle who had been raised up for our generation. As his reputation grew, large numbers of monks who lived round about in scattered hermitages kept coming to join him, making gifts of their own souls to him as if to a true father."[53] Another story mentions the gifts or blessings so often received by spiritual guides from those who come to them seeking counsel. In its own way it also tells how those very guides need the help of others if their own conversion process is to continue. The story, told by Abba John of Lycopolis, is about a monk in his old age who, tested by the assault of demons, begins to think that "he was superior to most men, and that he had attained something greater than others, and having arrived at this opinion he began to trust in himself." Finally, he is struck by his own pretension and hypocrisy, for as "he reflected silently for a moment that although he had counseled others, he had remained without counsel himself. Then his own failure struck his conscience. . . ." This story has a happy ending, one mysteriously revealed in a dream, that teaches all spiritual guides that God's forgiveness and invitation to reconciliation are ultimately greater realities than any of his or her own failures and sins; that this forgiveness is often manifested in the ministries and the gifts from those to whom we have ministered:

> From that time he spent the rest of his life in sorrow. . . .
> He shut himself in the cave, and spreading sackcloth and ashes under him, did not rise up from the ground or cease lamenting until he heard the voice of an angel saying to him in a dream, "God has accepted your repentance and has had mercy on you. In the future take care that you are not deceived. The brethren to whom you gave spiritual counsel will come to console you, and they will bring you gifts. Welcome them, eat with them, and always give thanks to God."[54]

Concerning mutuality, one of the most popular desert writings among the Christian Celts, as we've seen, was that of Jerome's *Life of Paul*. This story of two men's friendship expresses well, through the symbolic action of sharing bread, the beneficial exchange found in relationships of depth that would later be associated with soul friendships.

Paul, Antony, and the Crow

The *Life of Paul* of Thebes was written by Jerome either in the desert of Chalcis in Asia Minor when he was living as a hermit or during his second stay in Antioch before he moved to Rome and became a spiritual mentor to such outstanding women as Marcella, Paula, and Eustochium.[55] His account of Paul, although probably a highly imaginative story, may actually be based upon an authentic tradition in Egypt that such a person existed who was visited and honored by Antony. Jerome begins his narrative by speaking of the persecutions of the Roman emperors Decius and Valerian against Christians in Egypt and the Thebaid. During this period of the mid-third century, he says, Paul, a Christian, was left heir at the age of fifteen to great wealth after the death of his parents. Although he was well-educated, and "of a gentle spirit, and a strong lover of God," Paul's brother-in-law decided to betray the youth to the authorities. The younger man, aware of this possibility, fled into the wilderness where he intended to wait until the persecution had ended. "What had been his necessity became his free choice," according to Jerome, and Paul kept going until he reached a rocky mountain and a huge cave. In this "beloved habitation," Paul offered himself to God, and began to live a life of prayer and solitude with only a palm tree providing him food and clothing. There he stayed, Jerome says, for one hundred and thirteen years.

In another part of the desert, the elder Antony lived, a man of ninety years. Suddenly a thought came into his mind "that no better monk than he had his dwelling in the desert." A dream, however, challenged his mistaken pride: ". . . As he lay quiet that night it was revealed to him that there was deep in the desert another better by far than he, and that he must make haste to visit him." Antony left his cell at dawn the next day, and traveled through the silence of the wilderness, encountering, as he walked, only the scorching heat of the sun and a number of wild creatures. He kept going until he finally reached the cave where Paul lived:

> And the two embraced each other and greeted one another by their names, and together returned thanks to God. And after the holy kiss, Paul sat down beside Antony, and began to speak. . . . As they talked they perceived that a crow had settled on a branch of the tree, and softly flying down, deposited a whole loaf before their wondering eyes. "Behold," said Paul, "God has sent us our dinner, God the merciful, God the compassionate."

The next morning, Paul told Antony that he is about to die, and that the younger man had been sent to bury him. Antony was distraught, "weeping and groaning," and asked Paul to "take him with him as a fellow-traveler on the journey." Only when Paul convinced him to return for the cloak which Athanasius had given to Antony so that Paul could be buried in it, did Antony agree to leave. The younger man set out on his errand, but before he could return with the cloak, the older man died. Antony, in a vision, saw Paul climbing to heaven, accompanied by angels, prophets, and apostles, his face and entire body "shining white as snow." Antony was overcome with grief, and cried out in tears, "Paul, why did you send me away? Why did you go with no leave-taking?" Eventually, with the unexpected help of two lions, Antony buried his beloved friend, and then went back to the monastery, taking with him the tunic which Paul had woven out of palm leaves. Upon his return to the monastery, "he told the whole story to his disciples," and, Jerome adds, "on the solemn feasts of Easter and Pentecost, he wore the tunic of Paul" in memory of his friend.[56]

This poignant story of two men's friendship that takes so long to be made and then is so quickly interrupted (at least on earth) is one that came to be much loved by Christians throughout the early church, including those in Celtic lands. Most likely what these two elders came to represent for them was the mutuality and reciprocity found in friendship, symbolized in the breaking of the bread, a metaphor for the eucharist. What also probably appealed especially to the Celts was the presence of the crow, a symbol both of God's graciousness and compassion in providing food for the two elders, as well as a harbinger of death for the older man. Ravens and crows, the Celts believed, were messengers of death. The story of Paul and Antony also probably revealed to them the paradox of intimate, loving friendships. When someone who is deeply loved dies, communion with that person is not necessarily lost at all, but often strengthened. Depending on the depth of the relationship, it is as if that person's spirit has been passed on to the survivors, integrated into their very core, their spirits, their hearts. In Jerome's story, Antony would always remember Paul, living in his memory, but most especially in his heart.

Time and again desert spirituality focuses on the importance of the heart: *metanoia* takes place there, and purity of heart is a lifelong goal. Repeatedly in the desert stories we find references to the desert elders' ability to read other people's hearts. Abba Apollo, already mentioned, whenever anyone appeared a little downcast in his community, "at once asked him the reason, and told each one what was in the secret recesses of his heart."[57] John of Lycopolis was said to be one of those elders who could read hearts and discern reality more truly because he understood human nature so well, especially his own. Ammonas, a disciple of Antony, in his letters of spiritual guidance, speaks of the "eyes of the heart," and how the gift of discernment of hearts comes only by our requesting such a gift with the "whole heart."[58] Among all the desert writers, John Cassian was the one who most fully explored the human need for disclosing sicknesses and secrets which lie in the heart in order to be free of them—a belief eventually linked with the Celtic soul friend.

Disclosing the Secrets of the Heart

John Cassian's writings on desert elders were among the most influential of all writings about desert spirituality in the early Celtic Church. According to him, a key lesson which he and his friend Germanus learned from their time in the desert was the importance of an elder: a wise, holy, and experienced person who can act as a teacher and guide for an individual or community. Among the many sources of guidance recognized by the desert Christians as helpful to their spirituality, such as reading the scriptures, participation in eucharist, and sitting quietly in a cell, they considered an experienced guide to be,

Cassian says, "the greatest gift and grace of the Holy Spirit."[59] Cassian strongly affirms a belief that the Celtic Christians would later embrace: that God's guidance and wisdom come most often through human mediation, especially, as Cassian says, through the "experience," "sure example," and "spirit" of these desert elders.[60] The honest sharing of what lies within one's heart was an essential aspect of any relationship with such a guide. It was one of the main dynamics in the spiritual mentoring that a younger monk received. This form of spiritual guidance or direction, Cassian's writings make clear, consists of both educative and confessional elements that lead to the type of self-knowledge which not only heals, but frees one to love more fully and genuinely.

The educative aspects of spiritual guidance, Cassian says, had to do with learning discernment. Discernment was "the mother, guardian, and guide of all virtues," *the* virtue that teaches one to recognize differences and to avoid extremes.[61] Along with discernment, education in human nature and self-knowledge was taught, and an elder and student were expected to speak as friends do, openly and honestly acknowledging to each other human struggles and sinful deeds. Mutuality in the relationship was presupposed in "conferences" or meetings between elders and their students. These conferences were a standard method of doing spiritual direction. Many of these sessions evidently began quite spontaneously with a request on the part of the student: "Abba, teach me a word so that I may be saved" or "so that I may live." The "word" given was not necessarily a direct answer, nor was it an extensive list of recommendations for improving one's spiritual life; more often than not it took the form of a simple suggestion for further reflection by the younger person, a prayerful process that might more readily lead the younger person to discover wisdom in his or her own heart, the place where conversion happens (cf. Mt 6:33).

Desert elders, according to Cassian, presupposed that their primary task was not to give advice, but to evoke a response; not to get others to rely upon them for discernment, but to encourage others to rely upon God. Favorite topics of many of these conferences seem to have been sicknesses of soul which they identified with "passions." Desert elders presupposed that before one can get well physically and/or spiritually one needs to first name that which keeps a person sick or in bondage. Such soul-sickness and self-destructive patterns of behavior they called "sin," and spent many conferences describing and analyzing the kinds, origins, and causes of it. All of them, Cassian says, keep a person from true self-knowledge, and are personally harmful to that person's soul and to the community to which one belongs. All must be "laid open by the teachings of the elders." The effectiveness of their meetings, Cassian presupposes, seems to be related not only to the theological insights an elder shares with his or her charges about sins and their remedies, but especially to the elder's willingness to disclose personal struggles and what he or she has learned from them. Such disclosures can be truly educative, not only benefiting the younger, more inexperienced monks intellectually, but actually bringing about healing for them. The elders could explain matters effectively since "they have had experience of numberless falls and the ruin of all sorts of people." "And often," Cassian says, "recognizing in ourselves many of these things, when the elders explained and showed them, as men who were themselves disquieted by the same passions, we were cured without any shame or confusion on our part, since without saying anything we learnt both the remedies and the causes of sins which beset us. . . ."[62] Although Cassian doesn't mention it, the healing brought about by the self-disclosure of the elders may have taken place precisely because the younger monk discovers that he is not alone. It seems that when an elder openly acknowledges his very human struggles to grow in holiness, hope is often born.

As the elders modeled self-disclosure to their charges, so the younger monks were expected to acknowledge their own secrets, inclinations, and woundedness. Throughout Cassian's writings are numerous references to the importance and healing effects of speaking directly from the heart to another person. This self-disclosure was a form of lay confession, since most of the elders and desert guides were not ordained. Before disclosing any sickness or sin to another person, however, Cassian advises that the monk engage in a personal inventory or general examination of his life. "All the corners of our heart," he writes, "must therefore be examined thoroughly and the marks of all that rise up into them must be investigated with the utmost wisdom." Only then will we manage "to destroy the lairs of the wild beasts within us and the hiding places of the venomous serpents."[63]

After this inventory, Cassian recommends that its results and everything arising in the heart be shared with an elder, for "an evil thought sheds its danger when it is brought into the open, and even before the verdict of discernment is proffered the most foul serpent which, so to speak, has been dragged out of its subterranean lair into the light by the fact of open avowal retreats, disgraced and denounced. Its dangerous promptings hold sway in us as long as these are concealed in the heart." Such open and honest confession can help set a person free of all sorts of captivity, for it pulls "into the light from your shadowed heart" the "most loathsome serpent" hiding within. Through the power of such self-disclosure "the grip of this diabolic tyranny" is wiped out and "forever laid to rest." Cassian relates the story of Abbot Sarapion who, when he confessed his dishonest actions to his elder, says: "the enemy never even bothered to revive in me the memory of this urge [to steal] and after this [confession] I never again felt myself moved by the wish to engage in stealing of this kind." When one confesses to "some spiritual person" who is immersed in the "all-powerful words of Scripture" a cure can be found immediately for these "serpent bites." So also "the means of driving the fatal poison from the heart" can be discovered.[64] This healing and the knowledge of self that comes through self-revelation to another can help a person avoid the repetition of self-destructive patterns of behavior that previously characterized one's personality and life. As Alcoholics Anonymous discovered in the twentieth century, Cassian is simply saying that a personal inventory and confession to a reliable guide on a regular basis is good for the body and for the soul. It was a conviction that the later Christian Celts made their own, and associated with the *anamchara*.

The elder's responsibility in receiving another's confession of the heart is to listen without judgment, for, as one of the holy men wisely tells Cassian, "not only must we not denounce the fault which someone has admitted, but we must avoid despising any pain, however slight."[65] With such compassion and deep respect for another's suffering, the elders act, Cassian tells us, as a kind of glass or mirror by which the younger monks "learn both the causes of the sins by which they are troubled, and the remedies for them." Thus, he says, the elders minister to their protégés as "true physicians of the soul," listening to their self-disclosures attentively, and, "by means of spiritual conferences,"

———— ⚜ ————

explaining to their protégés "the causes of the passions which threaten them, and the remedies which heal them," so that they, in turn, might become mature spiritual guides.[66] Considering Cassian's focus on the healing effects of self-disclosure and the important contribution of spiritual guides as "physicians of the soul," it is no wonder that he describes God as a "tender" and "merciful physician" in contrast to the more prevalent desert image of God as found in the heights to whom people must climb.[67]

Cassian's writings had a significant impact not only upon the development of spirituality among the Celtic Christians but upon the evolution of soul friend ministry itself. As James Charles Roy rightly says about one part of the Celtic Church in particular where the *anamchara* originated, "Ireland is truly a child of Cassian, the man who synthesized what he saw in the Egyptian desert and laid it out as a model pathway for those with the strength to pursue virtue."[68]

With his emphasis on disclosing the secrets of the heart, Cassian's works contributed to the emergence of the Celtic soul friend's primary roles as a confessor, teacher, and spiritual guide. What is evident from Cassian's insights is how much they were the result not only of his friendship with the desert monks whom he visited, but with Germanus, his double, his second self, who had traveled with him to the Holy Land. As Cassian acknowledged about that friendship: "each of us would say that we were one mind and one soul living in two bodies."[69]

Friendship and Solitude

When we consider the numerous writings about the desert Christians in their entirety, including Cassian's, two characteristics, seemingly contradictory, consistently appear: the desert Christians' great appreciation of friendship and an equally strong love of solitude. There is much evidence in these written works of the warmth, love, respect, and genuine affection the early desert Christians felt for each other. They embrace each other warmly upon meeting and before they depart. They engage in friendly banter, and yet also seriously discuss the spiritual progress that each is attempting to make. They share their daily work and, at least once a week, celebrate eucharist together. Most of all, they call each other "friends" and root that friendship in Jesus' name and memory. As one of them, Abba Theodore, says so poignantly, "Let us each give his heart to the other, carrying the Cross of Christ."[70] It is this capacity for deep friendships that attracted others to them, giving them the courage to open their hearts and confess their most secret sins. This capacity for friendship and ability to read other people's hearts became the basis of the desert elders' effectiveness as spiritual guides. Abba Helle is typical. Staying with his brothers for three days, he was so loved and trusted by them, we are told, that when he "revealed the secret counsels of each of them, saying that one was troubled by fornication, another by vanity, another by self-indulgence, and another by anger," they could only respond, "'Yes, it is just as you say'."[71] This is why Palladius, as Cassian does with his image of the mirror, compares a wise spiritual guide to a "clear window," and advises people to "seek for meetings with holy men and women so that you may see clearly your own heart."[72]

At the same time, these desert guides, revered for their friendship, hospitality, compassion, and mutuality, also valued silence and solitude, even when they lived within monasteries. Such values were reflected in their deep love for their cells, those very primitive constructions (by our standards) of stone, brick, or wood which they frequently built with their own hands. These cells contained one or sometimes two rooms: an outer chamber for daily living and an inner one for sleeping. Some of them were built in a day; others, more elaborately constructed, took longer. Some were located in isolation; others had companion cells nearby. Sometimes, but very infrequently, both women and men lived in close proximity to each other. (The nun Egeria, for example, reports finding the cells of both genders near the holy shrine of Saint Thecla, a famous female convert of St. Paul. Egeria also tells of seeing some cells that were circular in shape, made out of stone, near the monastery of St. Catherine,[73] perhaps similar to those ancient cells which can still be seen at the Nawamies in central Sinai.) Judging from the information we have, many of the desert cells were without windows. Abba Macarius of Alexandria, for example, lived in some cells which were "windowless, and he is said to have sat in them in darkness during Lent; another was too narrow for him to stretch out his feet in it; another was more commodious, and in this one he met those who visited him."[74] Some, like that of

John of Lycopolis, had a window through which others could receive advice. So much of the spiritual wisdom associated with the desert fathers and mothers was gained in their cells. One of them, as mentioned earlier, tells a younger brother, "Go, sit in your cell, and your cell will teach you everything."[75] Another *abba* warns those who stray too far and too often from their cells: "Just as fish die if they stay too long out of water, so monks who loiter outside their cells . . . lose the intensity of inner peace. So like a fish going toward the sea, we must hurry to reach our cell, in case of staying outside we forget to care for what is inside."[76]

What these stories reveal about the desert Christians is that, despite their love of solitude, or, perhaps precisely because of that love, friendship had a special meaning for them. In cultivating silence and some degree of solitude, they evidently had a greater capacity for and appreciation of friendship itself. What is also apparent from the stories is that their willingness to open their hearts to one another included a willingness to share their cells. Numerous examples are given that their cells were shared with companions, occasionally for only short visits, and sometimes for a lifetime. Palladius mentions in his *Lausiac History* that at Tabennisi, there were "three monks to a cell," and, as the lives of Antony and Pachomius reveal, both of them spent some time living with or in close proximity to an elder or elders who initiated them into the world of desert spirituality.[77] One humorous, but profoundly wise story from the collection of sayings tells of "two old men" who lived together in one cell who had never disagreed about anything:

> So one said to the other, "Let us have one quarrel the way other men do." But the other said, "I do not know how one makes a quarrel." The first said, "Look, I set a tile between us and say, 'That is mine,' and you say, 'It is not thine, it is mine.' And thence arises contention and squabble." So they set the tile between them, and the first one said, "That is mine," and the second replied: "I hope that it is mine." And the first said, "It is not thine; it is mine." To which the second made answer, "If it is thine, take it." After which they could find no way of quarrelling.[78]

This same pattern will typify the Celtic saints, including the wonderful stories of the two soul friends, Brendan and Ruadan, building cells "in a place where they could hear one another's bells on this side and on that,"[79] and Gildas constructing a double cell, "one for him and the other for his companion and disciple, St. Bieuzy."[80] According to Nora Chadwick in her classic, *The Age of the Saints in the Early Celtic Church*, the Celtic *anamchara* was originally someone who, as a companion, shared another's cell and to whom one confessed, revealing confidential aspects of one's life. Chadwick says that the Celtic tradition of spiritual guidance was strongly influenced by the desert Christians, and that the rise of the soul friend in the Celtic Churches was a natural development which may be related to the *syncellus*, "the one who shares a cell" in Eastern Orthodoxy.[81] Considering the cell's importance in desert spirituality as a place where one encounters God and learns everything, to share one's cell with a soul friend, then, is to share one's inmost self, one's life, one's mind and heart. John Cassian shared his cell at Bethlehem with his friend Germanus, a practice common in the east during the fourth century until condemned by monastic lawgivers out of fear that such intimacy leads to homosexual behavior which they abhorred. Cassian, however, in his *Conferences* compares friendship itself to those who by the union of character, "not of place," are joined together "in a common dwelling," a bond that is indissoluble, and that even death cannot break.[82]

Desert Elders and Celtic Christians

Through books and through travel, the early Celtic Church, as it developed, began to incorporate the wisdom of the desert, not only embracing the desert heroes like Antony and Paul as theirs, but eventually depicting their own saints and soul friends as having many of the same qualities and engaged in many of the same activities, including that of spiritual mentoring. All of the stories and wisdom sayings of the desert heroes, and especially the writings of John Cassian, significantly affected how the Christian Celts remembered their saintly pioneers, and how they were eventually portrayed. The early Celtic soul friends too embrace an ascetic lifestyle, eating the simplest of diets and frequently wearing the skins of animals rather than woolen

clothing. They, like the desert elders, value solitude and, in the
midst of many communal and familial responsibilities, seek out
isolated places where they can find "soul-space": room for
developing in silence and in one's depths greater intimacy with
God. They too acknowledge the destructive power of sin and of
the need for confession and forgiveness. Like the desert
Christians, they also recognize God as an intimate companion of
their hearts, longing with a holy desire that their own lives be
transformed from dry clay into fire:

> Abbot Lot came to Abbot Joseph and said: "Father,
> according as I am able, I keep my little rule, and my
> little fast, my prayer, meditation and contemplative
> silence; and according as I am able I strive to cleanse
> my heart of thoughts: now what more should I do?"
> The elder rose up in reply and stretched out his hands
> to heaven, and his fingers became like ten lamps of fire.
> He said: "Why not be totally changed into fire?"[83]

Still, there are important differences. Unlike the desert
Christians who ministered in the barren wilderness of desert
lands, the Celtic soul friends appreciated the beauty of nature
and the powerful pull of the sea. They are found settling near
bodies of water or on land surrounded by the ocean's tides.
Unlike the desert guides who tended to settle in one place for the
rest of their lives, the Celtic saints, with the wanderlust of their
Celtic forebears in their blood, frequently embrace a life of
pilgrimage and of missionary outreach. Unlike the early desert
guides, many of whom were suspicious of classical education
and sought to maintain the primacy of the scriptures in
meditation and prayer, the Celtic saints loved learning and the
life of study, preserving the pagan stories of their native lands, as
well as the spiritual heritage of Greece and Rome.

Despite some of these differences, it was what the desert
tradition taught them about the gifts of friendship and solitude,
of having spiritual mentors and being alone, that Celtic
Christians eventually equated with their own soul friends. The
desert tradition clearly revealed to them that what is learned in
withdrawal, in quiet and solitude, becomes the basis of the
ministry of spiritual guidance itself. This may be the reason why
so many of the Celtic soul friends are portrayed in search
of solitude, settling as hermits in isolated places or as members

of communities on islands off the coasts, like those on Skellig Michael, Iona, Bardsey, Mount St. Michael, and Lindisfarne, or in the middle of lakes, like the early community of Molaise on Devenish Island.[84] This early emphasis on solitude and living alone, attributes of the desert Christians, may well acount for the hundreds of holy sites in Ireland, Wales, Cornwall, Brittany, and Ireland today which carry the name *disserth* (Cornish), *penity* (Breton) or *dysert* (Irish), all of which refer to the term "desert," such as Dysert O'Dea [Desert of God] in western Ireland. In the great quiet of one's cell, of one's heart, one learns to be a spiritual mentor who eventually can share, as Abba Antony says, "the fruits of my experience" with others.[85] When this is done, Abba Copres once said to his visitors from foreign lands, "even the desert can bear fruit."[86]

Having explored the spiritual legacies of both pagan Celts and desert Christians, we turn now to the coming of Christianity to Celtic lands and the rise of the early Celtic Church where soul friendship was born.

Sun's Rays

and

Uncharted

Comets

Meanwhile, to an island numb with chill ice and far removed, as in a remote nook of the world, from the visible sun, Christ made a present of his rays (that is, his precepts), Christ the true sun, which shows its dazzling brilliance to the entire earth. . . .

St. Gildas

The chronicles and records of the times record the picaresque adventures of a great many stray Irishmen, well beyond the byways of traditional pilgrimage routes from Ireland and Scotland to Luxeuil, St. Gall, and Bobbio, to whom many conversions are due. They came and went, as one annalist noted, "like uncharted comets."

James Charles Roy

When Christianity came to the shores of those places where the early Celtic Church arose, in present-day Ireland, England, Scotland, Wales, the Isle of Man, and Brittany in France, the ancient Celts, as we've seen, existed with their own traditions. This Celtic culture and spirituality transcended national boundaries, precisely because the Celts existed at a time before national consciousness and national identity had yet come into being. All of England was originally Celtic before the Saxon invasions, as well as the other lands where the Celtic churches would take root and flourish. What all of these early churches had in common was their close proximity to each other geographically and their shared awareness of being surrounded by water, through their rivers, lakes, and oceans, often as far as the eye could see. The names and descriptions of some of these places attest to this. Brittany, in France, with its long miles of seashore and windswept beaches, was originally called Armorica, meaning "the land facing the sea." The Isle of Man, lying halfway between Ireland and Britain and completely surrounded by water, is named after the mythical otherworld lord, Manannan, and was associated with a mystical isle in the eastern world called Magh Meall ("the Pleasant Plain"). The Venerable Bede describes Britain as an island ("once called Albion") that was remarkable "for its rivers, which abound in fish, particular salmon and eels, and for copious springs." Ireland, "the largest island of all next to Britain," he says, "lies to the west of it," and though it is "shorter than Britain to the north, yet in the south it extends far beyond the limits of that island and as far as the level of North Spain, though a great expanse of sea divides them."[1]

Contrary to Bede's description of the sea dividing these Celtic lands, early Christian literature, including letters that were carried by hand from one person to another, and the hagiographies of the saints that show them frequently visiting each other's monasteries, reveals how extensive maritime contacts were during the period of the rise of early Celtic Church. As the Welsh scholar E. G. Bowen states: "For the student of early western cultures, no longer does the sea divide and the land unite; on the contrary, the seas unite the lands and their shores."[2] The Celtic Church itself was a church of seafarers and voyagers, and the center of influence and activity for early Celtic Christians was the Irish Sea. On it in the early fifth century, St. Patrick was carried, against his will, as a young captive to Ireland from Britain, while St. Columcille in the sixth century left Ireland in his coracle heading into the unknown, possibly fleeing from his past. On the steep cliffs of Wales, overlooking the sea, St. David looked across the waters to Ireland on certain days when the view was clear. Across the same Irish Sea, as Bede relates, numerous scholars, students, and royal family members went to Ireland, a place known in the so-called Dark Ages for its learning and hospitality. On it the Irish monk and bishop, St. Colman, left Lindisfarne and sailed to Innisboffen, a tiny island off the west coast of Ireland, to start over again when the Synod of Whitby in 664 C.E. had rejected so resoundedly his Celtic ideals. At the end of the eighth century, on the same Irish Sea, the Vikings would come, bringing havoc and destruction to Celtic churches and monasteries struggling to survive.

Nora Chadwick refers in her writings to the Irish Sea as "the Celtic pond" on which the coracle (a small Celtic boat made of animal hides stretched over a wicker frame) plied between the shores of southwest Scotland, Ireland, Wales, Cumberland, the Isle of Man, and especially between Wales and southern Ireland. "The barriers were the land masses," she says; that is, "the mountain chains, the rivers, the great areas to be covered by foot, on horseback, with no roads, no bridges, no shops, no ready food or fresh water supplies."[3] Even with those barriers, all the travels of the early Celtic saints on foot, on horseback, and by coracle did much to disseminate a common culture and spirituality, one based on close proximity to bodies of water.

Christianity came to the Celtic lands by water, its stories written on cherished manuscripts, but, most often, carried by word-of-mouth. These stories, first from scripture and then from the desert Christians, had a profound effect on the development of the early Celtic Church, merging, as they did, with the earlier pagan stories and traditions that were already there. From this creative synthesis would come a new form of Christian ecclesiology and spirituality, and a deepened awareness of the need for soul friendships in people's lives.

In this chapter we will examine the coming of Christianity to Celtic lands and the rise of the early Celtic Church, one that was highly influenced by the Irish. This Christian transformation the early British historian St. Gildas (c. 500-570) compares in his writings to the sun-like rays of Christ heating up a chilled landscape, and bringing "dazzling brilliance to the entire earth."[4] It is the same image which St. Patrick, the apostle to the Irish, applies to himself when describing a mystical experience in which, overcome by depression, he sees the sun rising in the sky, a sign, he believed, of his being "sustained by Christ my Lord and that the Spirit was even then calling out on my behalf."[5] This new-found belief in Christ and trust in the Holy Spirit was to change the Celts dramatically, as the spirituality and beliefs of the ancient Celts would affect the expression of Christianity and of the Celtic *anamchara*. The founders of Celtic monasteries and the missionaries who brought Christianity back to the Continent after the barbarian invasions would later be recognized as significant soul friends to the generations who followed them.

———— ✤ ————

Christianity and Gaul

No one knows for certain when Christianity arrived in Ireland, England, Scotland, Wales, Brittany, and the Isle of Man. Some scholars, however, believe that it may have come first to Gaul from the Middle East by way of Italy and then from Gaul to Britain and Ireland. What emerged in those lands where the Celts lived and where Roman culture and institutions were not dominant was a Christian church more monastic than diocesan in its structures, and one that functioned more like an inclusive circle than a pyramid in the way authority was used and decisions made. This Celtic Church was definitely highly influenced by the stories of the desert heroes from which they received their monastic inspiration, as well as the spirituality of the pagan Celts which acknowledged the beauty of landscape and of spiritual ties. This Celtic Church was one that arose, sphinx-like, out of the fires and slaughter of the invading Huns, Goths, Vandals, and Anglo-Saxons who swept across Europe in the fourth century and who, under Alaric in 410, despoiled Rome itself, causing Jerome to cry out in anguish, "If Rome be lost, where shall we look for help?"[6] With the decline of Roman power in the West and the ensuing mass migrations caused by barbarian tribes, not only would Christianity take hold in Celtic lands, but through its missionaries and monastic schools both classical works and the Christian heritage would survive.

The people of Gaul were among Christianity's first converts at a time when most of Gaul, before the Visigoths and Franks invaded it in the fifth century, was Celtic. The Christian faith arrived there possibly as early as the end of the first century, and probably through the two main towns of Vienne and Lyons which served as river ports for trade between the Mediterranean Sea and the Rhine frontier. A letter written by the Christians of those towns is quoted in *The History of the Church* by Eusebius (c. 260-339) in which a rather detailed account is given of the suffering in 177 of fifty martyrs from Gaul. He lists among those who were brave enough to die for their Christian beliefs Sanctus, a deacon from Vienne, Maturus, recently baptized, Attalus "who had always been a pillar and support of the church in his native Pergamum," and Blandina, a "blessed woman" who "grew in strength as she proclaimed her faith."[7] Another early church historian from Gaul itself, Gregory of Tours (c. 539-594), describes how "rivers of Christian blood ran through the streets" during Gallic Christian persecutions.[8]

Judging from the written evidence, by the third century a number of bishoprics existed in the more urbanized areas of Lyons, Arles, Vienne, Toulouse, Rheims, Paris, and Trier. At the Council of Arles in 314, sixteen Gallic bishops were in attendance. In general, considering that only one bishop was present at the Council of Nicaea in 325, and two at the Council of Sardica in 343, it seems that Gallic bishops were not drawn into doctrinal controversies. Some of them, however, were known for their creative theology, and their highly talented pastoral leadership, especially Irenaeus of Lyons (d. c. 200), Hilary of Poitiers (c. 315-367), and Martin of Tours (c. 316-397). Of the three, Irenaeus is known for his theological emphasis on the humanity of Christ, and his beliefs that salvation involves *both* the body and spirit, that suffering can be educative, and that sin is due to the wrong use of freedom. He is perhaps best-known for his assertion that "the glory of God is humanity fully alive."[9] The second, Hilary of Poitiers, whose hymn "in praise of Christ" was popular in the Irish church, is regarded as the first native Celt to make a significant contribution to the entire church's understanding of God. His own pagan Celtic heritage with its respect for triads and triple goddesses, along with beliefs in spirits and mystical experiences, perhaps influenced his important writings on the Holy Spirit and the Trinity.[10]

The third, Martin of Tours, although it is not clear whether he was born a Celt, was originally mentored by Hilary, and went on to become both a bishop and a founder of such key early Gallican monasteries as Liguge and Marmoutier.[11] Both Hilary and Martin were inspired by the stories of Antony and Pachomius, and the desert monasticism of St. Basil which was more dedicated to ministerial outreach than maintaining hermitages and monasteries set apart. Both mentor and student sought to integrate ascetic ideals into their own lives and ministries. The stories about Martin himself, found in the hagiography by his friend, Sulpicius Severus, had a major effect on the development of Celtic Christianity in Britain and Ireland. Scholars point to the influence of Martin's hagiography on the content and style of other Celtic saints' Lives, and the fact that certain early churches in Britain, those at Whithorn and Canterbury, were dedicated to the Gallic saint, revealing his

notoriety there.[12] Though a significant influence on the shape of
the early Celtic Church (as witnessed by St. Martin's high cross
that stands today outside of the restored abbey on Iona), one
could not conclude, as some have, that St. Martin was the
founder of Celtic monasticism. Certainly the writings about the
desert Christians, especially Cassian's, also had a major effect, as
did the leadership of the early Celtic saints themselves.

By the late fourth century, as was typical in other parts of
Europe that had been incorporated into the Roman Empire, the
majority of bishops in Gaul were from aristocratic families who
followed the institutional type of Christianity that was
developing in the West. Educated in classical learning and
familiar with the Roman way of governing, these church leaders
adapted Roman cultural views and practices to the Christian
church, its emerging structures and ministries. From their
perspective, it was only natural to conceive authority as
hierarchical where decisions were made from the "top" down for
those whom one serves, and that women should be excluded
from any effective leadership positions. (Women in late
antiquity on the Continent were subordinate to men, had few
rights and roles outside the home, and were considered, for the
most part, incapable of having genuine friendships with men.)[13]
Like the Roman Empire, the system of church governance was
also based upon having church property divided into dioceses,
headed by bishops, usually in urban areas, that coincided with
the civil provinces created by the emperor Diocletian in the third
century. When desert asceticism and monasticism began to grow
in popularity throughout the empire, especially due to the
writings of Athanasius, Jerome, Rufinus, and John Cassian,
rivalry increasingly arose between the bishops in the cities and
monastic leaders in their monasteries.

Two of the most famous of Gallic monasteries in the fifth
century, besides those established by St. Martin, were the one at
Lerins, founded by St. Honoratus on an island off the Riviera
coast, and St. Victor's in Marseilles, set up by John Cassian in
415. Both monasteries were linked with the development of the
Celtic Church: the one at Lerins, known for its educational
excellence, is associated with a number of the saints, including
St. Patrick, whom hagiographers say studied there; the one at
Marseilles, through Cassian's writings on the desert Christians,
significantly affected and inspired Celtic monastic life, especially
anamchara ministries.

Brittany, Celtic Monasticism, and the Conhospitae

Following the barbarian invasions of 406-407, much of Gaul came under the control of the Franks, Visigoths, and Burgundians, except for Brittany where the Celts continued to flourish. From the fifth through the seventh centuries, this northwestern area of Gaul, originally called by the Romans "Armorica," was overwhelmed with Britons from Cornwall, Devon, and Somerset who were fleeing the invasions of the Anglo-Saxons. The name-change to "Brittany" ("little Britain") took place because so many of these British emigrants settled in that part of Gaul. These Celtic emigrants brought with them their own distinctive social and political organizations, as well as religious traditions and practices which naturally merged with those of the Celts already there. In Brittany, a more monastic type of Christianity took root, influenced to a great deal by the Celtic Churches of Britain and Ireland, which set the Celtic Christians apart from those churches in Gaul that were more Roman. Some of the main areas of disagreement over the ensuing centuries between them had to do with the Celts' inclusion of women in leadership and ministries, the Celtic tonsure of their priests, and clerical celibacy which the Roman church would eventually make mandatory. The Bretons' own distrust of institutions and love of independence, typical of Celtic Christians in other lands, contributed to this ongoing conflict between the more monastic church in Brittany and the Roman diocesan structures.

The seven founders of the Celtic Church in Brittany, as tradition has it, were Sts. Paul, Corentin, Tugdual, Samson, Malo, Brieuc, and Patern.[14] Later hagiographies assert that they were of Welsh and Irish descent. One of the most famous monasteries was at Dol, established by St. Samson who had been born in Wales, traveled to Ireland and Cornwall, and then on to Brittany where he settled in the first half of the sixth century. Other early Breton monasteries named after Welsh saints were St. Paul Aurelius's community at St. Pol-de-Leon, and Dirinon, said to be the burial site of St. Non, the mother of David of Wales. The monastery at Tregiuer was established by St. Tugdual from Cornwall. Gildas, the early British historian, after journeying to Vannes, built a monastery nearby now called St.

Gildas De Rhuys where his tomb is located behind the high altar. St. Budoc, born of Breton parents but educated in Irish monasteries, became a bishop of Dol after Samson, and about 460 founded a monastic school on the island of Lavre.

Specific monasteries and churches linked with the Irish were also built throughout Brittany. Saint-Malo was named after St. Mac Low (later called Malo) who was said to have been a pupil and sailing companion of St. Brendan of Ireland, as well as a guest of Columbanus in Burgundy before settling down in Brittany. Churches dedicated to St. Brendan himself are found in Lanvellec and Tregrom, the latter supposedly claiming to possess his enormous coffin. The picturesque village of Locronan, built on the ancient site of a fertility cult, was founded by a ninth-century Irish saint, Ronan (i.e., *locus Ronani*, "the place of Ronan"). His tomb stands in a beautiful fifteenth-century Gothic church, and is visited by thousands of pilgrims each year. In Landevennec, founded sometime in the fifth century, to be followed by Daoulas around 500, Irish monasticism was dominant for centuries, "a bulwark of civilization and learning where the precepts of Columbanus were upheld and the Irish tonsure worn."[15] There is a story too of an Irish princess by the name of Enora who followed her husband to Brittany, crossing over in a leather coracle. Brittany has legions of Celtic saints and soul friends who live on in the numerous place-names throughout the peninsula. By the end of the seventh century, there were over four hundred monasteries throughout Brittany and all of Gaul, the majority of them with Irish monks.

Besides the monastic sites and churches, another sign of Brittany's "Irish connection" is epitomized in the way certain early Breton priests accepted women as ministerial colleagues. Among the ancient Celts, as noted earlier, women were perceived as equal in many ways to men, a cultural perspective that was carried over to Brittany. According to a sixth-century letter that has survived, two Breton priests, Lovacat and Catihern, were criticized severely by three bishops of the province of Tours for their traveling with women who were called *conhospitae*. In this letter, the practice of women living and ministering with males was condemned:

> Through a report made by the venerable Sparatus, we
> have learned that you continually carry around from
> one of your fellow-countrymen's huts to another,

certain tables upon which you celebrate the divine sacrifice of the Mass, assisted by women whom you call *conhospitae*; and while you distribute the eucharist, they take the chalice and administer the blood of Christ to the people. This is an innovation, an unheard-of superstition. . . . [F]or the love of Christ, and in the name of the Church United and of our common faith we beg you to renounce immediately upon receipt of this letter, these abuses of the table. . . . [W]e appeal to your charity, not only to restrain these little women from staining the holy sacraments by administering them illicitly, but also not to admit to live under your roof any woman who is not your grandmother, your mother, your sister or your niece.[16]

Although married clergy were a common feature of the universal church and, in particular, of the Celtic Church, before celibacy was made mandatory in the West at the Second Lateran Council of 1139, scholars believe that what the Gallican bishops in their letter were objecting to was *syneisaktism*, the custom of ascetic men and women living chastely together.[17] This practice seems to have been particularly widespread in some Christian circles, including the early churches of Britain and Ireland. It may have originated among the desert Christians, a few of whom, while maintaining their celibacy, lived together as husband and wife.[18]

The primary purpose of this intensely intimate type of spiritual friendship or, as it has been called, "spiritual marriage," seems to have been, quite simply, that of men and women offering and receiving mutual assistance and support in their lives and ministries.[19] This is evidently why the two Breton priests, Lovacat and Catihern, were living and traveling with women. They were not the only ones, judging from the frequent references in the Lives of such saints as Scothine and Mel of Ireland, Kentigern of Scotland, and Aldhelm of England, all of whom lived with women to whom they were not married. In an early hagiography of St. Patrick, Bishop Mel lives with a woman precisely for the assistance she offers him with her prayers, and in another life, this one of St. Ailbe of Emly, Ireland, the latter is depicted as traveling with certain women, two of whom are named Brige and Berach.[20] The obvious difficulty with this practice was whether those living together were truly able to remain chaste—and the scandal when they could not. Some people had their severe doubts about the practice, such as Jerome, although he had no cause to condemn it outright, considering his intimate friendships with women in Rome and Bethlehem.[21]

In some ways, from a contemporary perspective, "syneisaktism" can be interpreted as rather bizarre behavior when it is linked, as it was in late antiquity and the early medieval period, with proving one's ascetic stamina. Yet, many people, both in the past and more modern times, have done so. In the twentieth-century, for example, Gandhi is said to have slept with naked young women to prove his sexual constancy and spiritual leadership.[22] In the Celtic Church, a story from the ninth-century *Martyrology of Oengus the Culdee*, tells of the Irish saint Scothine who used to lie every night with "two maidens with pointed breasts" so that "the battle with the Devil might be greater for him." When St. Brendan questioned this practice, and then tried it himself, he could not fall asleep because of his aroused desires. The women with the pointed breasts tell him that he is obviously not as holy as Scothine, for "he who is here every night feels nothing." They, then, recommend that Brendan get into a tub of cold water "if it be easier for thee." Brendan humbly concludes that "it is wrong for us to make this test, for he [Scothine] is better than we are."[23]

Contrary to Brendan's experience, this form of heroic "testing" did not lessen the demands for an end to such relationships no matter how pastoral in intent they may have been initially. Frequent condemnations of it by church councils and detailed prohibitions against it in the penitential books that were written to guide Celtic confessors and *anamcharas* attest to its popularity among the Celts—and its unpopularity with the hierarchy. It clearly was not welcome by the bishops of Gaul—along with other Breton ecclesial customs which were more Celtic, including that a bishop in Brittany, as in Ireland, often resided in a monastery rather than being in charge of a diocese. One example of this is St. Samson of Dol, who combined in his person (as had St. Martin of Tours) both the office of bishop and that of being an abbot of a monastery.

BRITAIN:
The Land of "Heretics" and "Angels"

In Britain, Christianity may have arrived about the same time as in Gaul, probably through the Roman soldiers and administrators who occupied a great part of the country from the first century onwards. Its beginnings there are also vague, but a number of intriguing stories provide intimations of how later writers tried to connect Britain with the early church. One fanciful legend speaks of St. Peter travelling to Britain, carrying the gospel message, while another says that a messenger from St. Paul—or St. Paul himself—were visitors.[24] Perhaps the most fascinating story concerns Joseph of Arimathea, the Jewish leader who, according to the gospels, had asked Pilate for Jesus's dead body which he had placed in his own unused tomb (cf. Mk 15:43-47; Mt 27:57-61; Lk 23:50-53; Jn 19:38-42). In the legends that link him with Britain, this Joseph was said to have been a tin and lead trader who journeyed to Glastonbury (in present-day England) where he planted a thorn from Christ's passion near a small church in sight of the famous Tor. Other medieval stories have Joseph bringing relics, including the Holy Grail, to the same site, a holy place where he and his companions, after their deaths, were said to have been buried.[25] Devotion to this same Joseph is found in Brittany, where it is believed that he was the younger brother of St. Anne and thus the uncle of Mary and great-uncle of Jesus.

In terms of verifiable historical evidence, Tertullian writing about 200 and Origen about 240 allude in their writings to the presence of Christians in Britain, some of whom, as in Gaul, were persecuted for their faith before Constantine recognized Christianity in 313.[26] The Venerable Bede tells of St. Alban, a layman who suffered martyrdom for refusing to worship idols and for protecting a priest.[27] In 314, three bishops of the British church are recorded as being present at the council of Arles, two of them having come from York and London. Their presence shows that the church in Britain, although probably consisting initially of a small number of Christians, was now firmly established along the same lines as that in Gaul. As in Gaul, its clerical leaders were well-educated in Latin culture and from "the romanized urban elite."[28] (It is with these that St. Patrick

---

compares himself in his *Confessio*, and finds himself, in terms of his education, wanting.)

Problems, of course, emerged as Christianity became more established. In 429, Germanus of Auxerre (c. 378-448), possibly a mentor of St. Patrick of Ireland and St. Illtud of Wales (who, in turn, mentored St. Samson of Dol), traveled to Britain to counter the Pelagian heresy. Pelagius, a lay monk, may have been originally from Ireland if some of Jerome's insults against him, equating him with "Irish porridge," are to be taken literally.[29] Contrary to Jerome's views, Pelagius was well-educated and a man of integrity—even his opponent, St. Augustine of Hippo, acknowledged that. Pelagius traveled to Rome, Africa, and Jerusalem with an Irish friend, Celestius, who seems to have had more radical views than Pelagius, but both men were condemned because of their theology. Most of Pelagius' own writings have not survived, but his beliefs concerning the nature of humanity and free will seem to have been more positive than Augustine's. While the latter emphasized original sin and the absolute need of humanity for divine grace, Pelagius stressed that this belief in humanity's total depravity denies humans any ability or incentive to do good through personal choices or actions.[30] As in other ecclesial controversies, those with differing theological views were not always treated respectfully, but rather branded as "heretics" and then condemned. Pelagius suffered that fate. Efforts to eradicate Pelagianism succeeded to some extent in Britain, although the issues raised by Pelagianism would reappear during the Middle Ages and at the Reformation.

Another problem in Britain concerned the corruption of civil and religious authorities as Christianity became more established. In 540, Gildas, the British monk and historian who lived in Wales, Ireland, and Brittany for some time and who preceded Bede by over a hundred years, wrote his main work, *The Ruin of Britain*, which denounced the rulers, secular and ecclesial, of his day. In his preface, he speaks of how these evils, as he saw them, came to be. He describes how the Romans had left Britain to fend for itself after the barbarian invasions on the Continent. Gildas goes on to show his disgust for the Irish and Picts who, he says, were like "dark throngs of worms," raiding the British shores when they were no longer protected by Roman armies. This, of course, was something to which St. Patrick would certainly attest when he was taken to Ireland as a slave.

Unlike Patrick, however, who genuinely loved the Irish, Gildas speaks contemptuously of the Celts. He notes their "greed for bloodshed" and makes reference to their love of being naked, stating how "they were readier to cover their villainous faces with hair than their private parts and neighboring regions with clothes." His writing, although strident, is above all a call to conversion, as Bede's history of the English would later be. He asks (actually demands) of the leaders and people of his day to "be saint-like in all your dealings," and "search out the depths of your heart," leaving behind drunkenness, debauchery, lust, and "evil desire," in order to "be filled with the Holy Spirit."[31]

An important date in the history of Christianity in Britain came in 597 when Augustine (d. 604), the first archbishop of Canterbury, was sent by Pope Gregory the Great (c. 540-604) to evangelize the people in southern England, and to promote the prominence and jurisdiction of that church over the other churches of Britain. According to Bede, this mission to Britain originated in an encounter Gregory had in Rome with beautiful young men who were being sold as slaves:

> It is said that one day, soon after some merchants had arrived in Rome, a quantity of merchandise was exposed for sale in the marketplace. Crowds came to buy and Gregory too amongst them. As well as other merchandise he saw some boys put up for sale, with fair complexions, handsome faces, and lovely hair. On seeing them, he asked, so it is said, from what region or land they had been brought. He was told that they came from the island of Britain, whose inhabitants were like that in appearance. He asked them again whether those islanders were Christians or still entangled in the errors of heathenism. He was told that they were heathen. Then with a deep-drawn sigh he said, "Alas that the author of darkness should have men so bright of face in his grip, and that minds devoid of inward grace should bear so graceful an outward form." When Gregory asked again what the name of their race was, he was told, "*Angli*," which he mistakenly thought meant "angels," and replied, "Good, they have the face of angels, and such men should be fellow-heirs of the angels in heaven."[32]

———— ✛ ————

Augustine was sent to Britain to evangelize these "angels," but the sort of unification that Gregory hoped for took much longer than imagined. In those parts of Britain called Northumbria in the north and Cornwall in the south, along with Scotland and Wales, a more monastic and Celtic type of church had emerged by this time that was unwilling, at least initially, to lose its independence, customs, and identity. Again, a story told by Bede shows something of the conflictual dynamics between the leaders of the more Roman-style church, personified by Augustine, and those immersed in Celtic culture, in this case, representatives of the church in Wales. The latter, consisting of seven bishops, and "many learned men," Bede says, went to meet with Augustine in order to settle disagreements they had over certain practices of the church in Rome:

> As they were about to set out for the conference, they went first to a certain holy and prudent man who lived as a hermit among them to consult him as to whether they ought to forsake their own traditions at the bidding of Augustine. He answered, "If he is a man of God, follow him." When they asked how they could tell this, the hermit replied: "If this Augustine is meek and lowly of heart, it is to be supposed that he himself bears the yoke of Christ and is offering it to you to bear; but if he is harsh and proud, it follows that he is not from God, and we have no need to regard his words." Still desiring clarification, they asked the hermit how they might know whether Augustine was proud or humble. They were advised to let him get to the place of the meeting first, and "if he rises on your approach, you will know that he is a servant of Christ and will listen to him obediently; but if he despises you and is not willing to rise in your presence, even though your numbers are greater, you should despise him in return."

Unfortunately for the good of all, Augustine remained seated, seeming to offer, not hospitality, but a use of power that Celtic leaders interpreted as disrespectful and disdainful.[33]

Whether the story is historically accurate or not, Cornwall did not acknowledge Canterbury's jurisdiction until the ninth century, and the church in Wales not until the beginning of the twelfth century. Northumbria, profoundly affected by the Celtic spirituality brought by Aidan from Ireland by way of Iona and then to Lindisfarne in 635, resisted adopting the Roman-style of church until the Council of Whitby in 664.

Scotland, Wales, and the Isle of Man

Scotland, inhabited by the Picts (the "painted" Celts), had never been conquered by the Roman legions. They had fought off the Roman armies so well, in fact, that the Romans themselves had built a wall (Hadrian's Wall) across the northern part of Britain to keep the Picts contained—and probably to protect themselves from the Picts. According to Bede, these Picts spoke a different language than that of the Britons and Irish. The Picts living in Scotland also were divided, Bede says, into northern and southern groups, separated by "steep and rugged mountains."[34] The southern Picts were converted by Ninian (d. 432) who was said to have been born near Carlisle, close by Hadrian's Wall. Studying in Rome, and then traveling to Tours where he met Martin, he decided to found a monastery in 397 which he dedicated to his spiritual mentor. This monastery at Whithorn called *Candida Casa* (the White House) became an important place for the training of Welsh and Irish missionaries and laity. It may also have been a double monastery, educating both genders.[35] The northern Picts were evangelized by the great Columcille of Ireland who founded, as will be discussed later, his renowned monastery on Iona in 563 and then brought his own Irish spirituality—and extensive talents—to the Picts.

A third major saint of Scotland was St. Mungo, also called Kentigern, who lived during the late sixth and early seventh centuries. Born under scandalous circumstances (his mother was not married), he was raised by St. Servanus, a kindly teacher and mentor, at a place called Culenros where the older man was training other boys for priestly ministry. Eventually ordained a priest and then bishop of Glasgow, Mungo was an effective missionary in southern Scotland and northwest England. He led an ascetic lifestyle, resting on a bed made of stone, sleeping little at night (no wonder!), and stripping naked to plunge into "the rapid and cold water" of the rivers. Mungo also followed the Celtic mode of dress, wearing, as his

———— ❧ ————

hagiographer said, "a garment of leather made of the skin of goats," with a cowl "like a fisherman's." He carried in one hand a pastoral staff "not rounded and gilded and gemmed . . . but of simple wood, and merely bent," and in the other hand, a simple "manual-book" (possibly a rule on how to live the monastic life).[36]

As in northern Scotland, Wales also came under the influence of the Irish during the fourth and fifth centuries when a very considerable Irish colony was established in southwestern Wales, and a smaller and more scattered one in north Wales. Although Wales also contributed to the Irish church (St. Patrick may have come from Wales, and Sts. Gildas and David are said to have made visits to Ireland), Wales between the fifth and eighth centuries also received a large number of wandering monks and missionaries, many of them from Ireland.[37] Some of them may have come, not so much to evangelize as to minister to the pastoral needs of the Irish who were already there. Others may have come simply seeking solitude. There is the story, for example, of St. Melangell, the daughter of an Irish prince who lived about 600, and came to Wales from Ireland, her only purpose being to find a quiet place to pray. Little is known about her except that when a local prince was out hunting rabbits with his horses and dogs, this Melangell protected one of the poor rabbits by hiding it beneath her dress. For thirty-seven years, we are told, she led a solitary life in that place, and

> the hares, which are little wild creatures, surrounded her every day of her life, just as if they had been tame or domesticated animals, through which, by the aid of divine mercy, miracles and various other signs are not lacking for those who call upon her help and the grace of her favour with an inner motion of the heart.[38]

The church which developed in Wales was similar to those of other Celtic lands, distinguished in part, Oliver Davies says, "by its remoteness from major urban centres of organization and population." It was clearly a monastic church, made up of a network of monasteries and frequently headed by bishops or abbots who were often married. It also had its great monasteries, such as the one founded by St. David, the patron saint of Wales, on the western coast, and monastic schools, such as St. Iltud's at Llantwit where Sts. Samson of Dol and possibly Gildas and

David were educated. Because of their geographical and political marginality, the influence of Rome was felt only gradually in Wales. There does not seem to have been, Davies says, any "extensive diocesan and parochial structure of a conventional type in Wales before the twelfth century."[39]

South of Wales, in Cornwall, Christianity arrived sometime in the fourth and fifth centuries, brought by Christians from Brittany and Wales, and especially, according to the French Celtic scholar Louis Gougaud, from Ireland.[40] Cornwall itself, like Scotland, was probably never brought into close contact with Roman civilization as such, except on or near the coast, and the primary influence upon its churches were the Celtic missionaries. This is confirmed in the hagiographies of the Cornish saints which contain numerous references to Welsh, Breton, and Irish saints. Ancient churches in Cornwall are also named after them. The one at Altarnon is dedicated to the Welsh saint, Non, the mother of St. David of Wales, which has, near its gate, a fine Celtic cross that may date back to the sixth century. The parish of St. Hilary, dedicated to the famous bishop of Poitiers from Gaul, has in its church on a hill wonderful scenes from the lives of the Cornish saints painted on the panels of the choir stalls. St. Bridget's at Bridestowe, dedicated to St. Brigit, the Irish saint of reknown, has, behind its altar, the painting of another saint, Francis, who was also affected by Celtic spirituality. Besides churches, the many Arthurian legends, including that of Tristan and Iseault, and the large phallic stone at Fowey, named the "Tristan Stone," point to both ancient and medieval intermingling of Cornish, Welsh, and Breton myths.

The influence of the Irish in Cornwall seems to have been extensive, taking into consideration the large amount of pottery shards found by archaeologists. Many of the Irish came from Munster, the coast immediately opposite Cornwall, and Hayle, the central harbor of the bay of St. Ives, was the port for which they made. The stories about the Irish woman, St. Ia, after whom St. Ives is named, typifies this Irish contribution to Cornish piety and church life. She supposedly came down to the shore from which her friends had already left Ireland for Cornwall, and "when she discovered that she was too late, she was filled with grief." As she knelt on the beach to pray, she noticed a little leaf floating on the water. "Ia touched it with the rod she carried to see if it would sink. Lo! it began to grow larger and larger as she looked at it. Believing that it was sent to her by God, and trusting in him, she embarked upon the leaf and was immediately wafted across the channel, reaching her destination before the others."[41] Again, the kind of ecclesiastical system that developed in Cornwall, at least initially, was definitely more tribal and monastic, thus more "Celtic," with some bishops, as in Brittany, in charge of monasteries. Diocesan bishops were practically unknown to the Celtic world in the days of the early church in Cornwall.

In briefly tracing the coming of Christianity to Celtic lands, the Isle of Man, in the Irish Sea off the northwest coast of Britain, cannot be forgotten. It too, as in Scotland, Wales, Northumbria, Cornwall, and Brittany, was highly affected by the Irish. During the third and fourth centuries, settlers came from Ireland to live, and in the sixth century Irish missionaries arrived. Manx, a Gaelic language, was spoken there, and the old Manx Keills, or cells, are of a similar type to the Irish oratories of the sixth and seventh centuries. Certainly the many place names, dedications of churches, and holy wells are associated with Irish saints of the sixth century, such as Kirk Bride (Brigit) and Braddan (Brendan). This Celtic period, however, came to an end when the Vikings began to plunder during the first part of the ninth century, and then to settle the island, making it an important base with their settlements in Dublin, northwestern England, and the western isles. Despite the Viking invasions, Christianity endured. Its surviving high crosses show the transition from Celtic to Norse influence, with some of the Norse crosses depicting spirits of the land, rarely seen on other Celtic crosses, along with dwarfs, gnomes, trolls, giants, and dragons. Even the Norse gods Odin, Thor, and the trickster-god Loki appear on them.

The Irish Church and Its Golden Age

Last but not least, of course, is Ireland, which was never invaded by Roman armies or influenced significantly by Roman culture. While St. Patrick is credited with bringing the Christian faith to northeastern, central, and possibly western Ireland, beginning in 432, there were certainly Christians living in Ireland, possibly in the south, before his missionary work. Stories associated with Sts. Declan of Ardmore, Ailbe of Emly,

Ciaran of Saighir, Abban of Moyarney, and Ibar of Beg-Eire speak of these spiritual leaders as preceding Patrick. In fact, another missionary, a bishop by the name of Palladius, was sent to "the Irish believing in Christ" in 431 by Pope Celestine who was interested in combating the Pelagian heresy.[42] There are no records telling of what happened to Palladius, but Patrick's mission was highly effective, primarily because of his great love for the Irish people. Through his ministry of spiritual mentoring countless Celts were brought to the Christian faith.

Although controversy over his origins and when he actually lived continues, Patrick most likely was born about 390 near the west coast of England or Wales, and died in northern Ireland, near Armagh, in 461.[43] As is the case of many of the earliest saints, we do not have a great deal of accurate information about him because of the social turmoil of the early fourth and fifth centuries. Still, two autobiographical writings of Patrick's did survive: a *Confessio,* written in his mature years as a missionary bishop, telling the story of his life and defending himself against detractors at home who were questioning his integrity, and a *Letter to Coroticus* in which he protested the captivity and martyrdom of some of his Irish converts by a Welsh chieftain with that name. Patrick's *Confessio,* included in the *Book of Armagh*, is the earliest recorded Irish literature. In it, Patrick tells us that he was born into a Christian family somewhere in Roman Britain, that his father, Calpornius, was a deacon in the early church and his grandfather, Potitus, a priest, and that at the age of sixteen he underwent a horrible crisis. At a time when the Roman Empire was withdrawing troops from Britain in order to protect Rome itself from barbarian attacks, he was captured and taken from his home by slave-traders who had become increasingly more active in the power vacuum. Along with others, Patrick was sold into slavery in Ireland, and possibly taken to the region of County Mayo. While tending sheep and feeling increasingly more isolated and alone, God "made me aware of my unbelief," Patrick says, "that I might at last . . . turn wholeheartedly to the Lord." A captive six years, he finally escaped from Ireland with the help of certain dreams in which a voice guided him to freedom. Then, a few years after his return to his family in England, he had what was to be one of his most significant dreams:

———— ❧ ————

. . . One night I saw the vision of a man called Victor, who appeared to have come from Ireland with an unlimited number of letters. He gave me one of them and I read the opening words which were, "The voice of the Irish." As I read the beginning of the letter I seemed at the same moment to hear the voice of those who were by the wood of Voclut which is near the Western Sea. They shouted with one voice: "We ask you, boy, come and walk once more among us." I was cut to the very heart and could read no more, and so I woke up.[44]

No one knows with any certainty the identity of Victor, although some scholars suggest that he may have been a disciple of St. Martin of Tours.[45] Whoever he was, Victor is obviously significant, considering that only two other figures are specifically named by Patrick in his *Confessio*: his father and grandfather. Patrick interpreted this dream, similar to the one of his hero, the missionary St. Paul (cf. Acts 16:9-10), as a genuine call from God revealing his own vocation. In the seventh century, a monk of Armagh by the name of Muirchu (pronounced "Murra-hoo"), identified Victor, Patrick's dream figure, in his hagiography on Patrick as an angel, a guardian spirit, who guided him throughout his life. By the end of the ninth century, at the time of the Celi De movement, this angel is definitely called an *anamchara*—not only of Patrick, but of the entire Celtic race: "Victor was Patrick's soul friend, and he is the common angel of the Celts. As Michael of the Jews, so is Victor of the Irish."[46]

Though he was possibly educated at Lerins, in Gaul, and thus shaped by the ascetic traditions of Gaul and of St. Martin, Patrick brought with him to Ireland an ecclesiology that was diocesan in organization. Whether this took root at all is questionable, according to Richard Sharpe:

Concerning the first introduction of Christianity and its subsequent expansion, one may well question whether the Irish church has at any stage the appearance of being organized, after the manner that Gregory suggested Augustine should work towards. . . . or whether it was not rather the result of disorganized growth. . . . [T]here is no evidence pointing to a clearly

———— ❧ ————

defined hierarchical structure, no evidence for a canonically recognized metropolitan authority; in short, no sign that growth of the church or its organization were the subject of any form of control. Instead, in the seventh, eighth and later centuries, churches clash with one another in disputes both major and minor without there being any agreed authority to whom recourse might be had.

Instead, Sharpe posits a great deal of diversity and independence:

An essential characteristic of the Irish church, at all times between the earliest evidence and the twelfth century or later, seems to be the very great degree of independence enjoyed by individual churches. . . . Its shape reflects growth *in situ,* local solutions to local needs, and is not an imposed structure.[47]

The sixth century is considered "the Golden Age" in Ireland, the time when the great monasteries arose, headed by powerful abbesses or abbots. These heroic figures were the first to combine the ancient pagan Celtic spirituality of the druids and druidesses with the emerging Christian rituals and desert beliefs, resulting in the important ministry of the *anamchara* or soul friend.

As the hagiographies of the saints reveal, during one's lifetime, a person might have many mentors and soul friends, sometimes beginning at a very early age. St. Findbarr of Cork is typical of many saints, for he had not one, but, according to an early Life, three holy elders to whom he was handed over as a child so that he might learn about Christ in their cell.[48] The pattern found in the stories from the Lives of the Celtic saints is that, after a person has received help from an *anamchara,* he or she goes on to become a soul friend too: someone willing to mentor others out of gratitude for receiving this life-transforming gift. Such friendship did not end with death, for these great heroes of Christianity were considered by the later Celts as true soul friends whom they could call upon daily for guidance, support, and help.

St. Finnian who established a monastery at Clonard about 520 is considered the patriarch of many Irish spiritual leaders, precisely because he tutored and acted as a spiritual guide to numerous early founders of the other large monasteries, such as St. Ciaran of Clonmacnoise and St. Columcille. Finnian, in turn, according to his hagiography, had been mentored from boyhood by a variety of saintly heroes, Foirtchernn of Britain, Caemon of Tours in Gaul, and David, Gildas, and Cathmael, sages of the Celtic Church in Britain, all of whose friendships demonstrate the spiritual connections interlinking Celtic monasteries. The holy nun, St. Ita, acted in a similar capacity as Finnian. She taught so many young men who later became leaders in the Irish church that she became known as the "Fostermother of the Saints of Erin." One of them, St. Brendan of Clonfert, famous for his voyages, frequently turned to Ita for advice throughout his life.

Of all the monasteries of Ireland's Golden Age, the most famous were St. Enda's on the Aran Isles, St. Brigit's in Kildare, St. Columcille's in Derry, Durrow, and Iona, St. Finnian's in Clonard, St. Ita's in Killeedy, St. Brendan's in Clonfert, St. Comgall's in Bangor, St. Kevin's in Glendalough, and St. Ciaran's in Clonmacnoise. Many of the first male founders and abbots of these monasteries, influenced by the asceticism of the desert Christians, were probably celibate priests and bishops. Women founders and abbesses also lived celibate lives within religious communities, a way of life chosen because of the value asceticism placed on virginity, and because, for women in particular, the monastic life offered the opportunity to develop one's intellectual abilities and creative pursuits. It was the only alternative, in fact, to the roles of wife and mother in marriage, or, in spinsterhood the roles of maintaining a household for aging parents and unmarried siblings. The decision to become a woman religious, as the early hagiographies of Sts. Brigit, Ita, and Samthann reveal, was usually opposed by the woman's family (whether it was Christian or not), since that lifestyle so contradicted the values of the Celts' family-oriented culture. As St. Patrick says in his *Confessio* regarding the first female converts in Ireland: "Their fathers disapprove of them, so they often suffer persecution and unfair abuse from their parents; yet their number goes on increasing. Indeed the number of virgins from our converts is beyond counting. . . ."[49]

Unlike the women's lives which were filled with familial, monastic, and pastoral involvements, a number of the early male saints, like Kevin of Glendalough, seem to have had a high regard for the solitary life (possibly in imitation of St. Antony and St.

Martin of Tours) and to have gone to great lengths to maintain it. Perhaps precisely because of that solitude, the male founders appreciated the camaraderie of close male friendships, evidenced in the *Life of Maedoc of Ferns* with its story of the two soul friends, Maedoc and Molaise, who, after a revelation in the forest, kissed each other good-bye and went their separate ways to build their monasteries at Ferns and Devenish Island.[50]

Whether they were male or female, however, or whether they found some time alone or not, the lives of the original monastic founders soon took a different direction, as had the desert Christians', with the approach of numerous followers. Monasteries had to be built to provide food and shelter, spiritual formation, and an education for the communities which sought their leadership. Even on the most isolated islands, such as Skellig Michael, off the western coast of Ireland, beehive huts or cells were frequently shared between two, three, seven, or even more monks. By 600, more than eight hundred monasteries had been founded in Ireland alone. The leaders, both female and male, were frequently more powerful administratively than any bishop, though bishops frequently may have been members of their communities or abbots themselves. Male monastic leaders who followed the first pioneers were either ordained or lay.

Beehive Huts

Many were married, and in some monastic communities the abbacy descended from father to son, as exemplified in the annals, those collections of books which chronicled key persons and events of specific monasteries on their pages. The Annals of Armagh and Louth, for example, list fathers and sons in monastic office in the eighth century: Torboch, abbot of Armagh, at whose command the Book of Armagh was written in 807 in which the writings of St. Patrick were preserved, was said to be the son of Gorman, an abbot of Louth; Torbach's son Aedagan later became abbot of Louth, and went on pilgrimage to Clonmacnoise, taking his son Eogan with him, and died there in 834; Eogan remained at Clonmacnoise and fathered a distinguished line of clerics whose sons eventually returned to Louth for their education.[51] The revered Irish family name, MacTaggert, which means "son of a priest," also testifies to a married Irish priesthood. Whether the abbots were married or celibate, however, the monasteries which they headed had many lay people (known as *manaigh*) attached to them, and were thus definitely family-oriented and dependent on the contribution of the laity.

The original monasteries which the Celts built, in imitation of the desert Christians, were characterized by their austere simplicity and disciplined daily routine. Contrary to the impression one might receive from the ruins which can be seen today at the various monastic sites, there were no great cathedrals nor large numbers of buildings made of rock and stone. Although some monasteries eventually became communities with members numbering in the thousands, at the time of their foundation all began looking more like primitive forts than refined educational and commercial institutions, or probably, as Liam de Paor suggests, "more like a town or village than an integrated architectural unit as was to develop from the Benedictine monasticism of the Continent."[52] Early hagiographies give glimpses into the original layout of these communities. The first buildings were not large communal structures in which hundreds of monks might live, but rather tiny beehive cells built of wood or stone, with the abbot's cell probably slightly apart from the rest. The primitive monastic cell was known as a *clochan*. These cells were usually surrounded by an enclosure or ring-fort made of earth and rocks. A small church, built originally of hewn oak thatched with reeds, would have been an important part of this early settlement where daily prayers were offered. Later, stone would take the place of wood, resulting in various designs, such as those that can be seen today at Kells, Ireland (i.e., St. Columcille's "house") or the Gallarus Oratory on Ireland's Dingle Peninsula. Inside these early structures, one could find a stone altar, sacred vessels for the eucharist, relics (possibly of the monastic founder), and handbells for summoning the community to prayer and meals.

As the monastic communities grew, other buildings might include a refectory where the community ate, a kitchen connected to the refectory for the cooking of these meals over an open fire, and frequently some form of guesthouse for visiting pilgrims and scholars. If a monastery could afford it, a library for precious books might be added. (All books, of course, were precious because of their scarcity and the infinite care which went into their composition.) A scriptorium would be located near the library where manuscripts were written, including the Lives of the saints, and books of the gospels. Sometimes these were beautifully illuminated with pen and brightly-colored inks. A forge or workshop might also be situated inside the stockade, while outside of it would lie the cultivated lands, pastures, rivers, and lakes where the community fished and raised or grew its food and sources of clothing. In the ninth century and later, high crosses with their stories in stone served as visual aids to those preaching a sermon or instructing students or pilgrims about their Christian heritage. Near the high crosses and churches were the graves of the original founders and their followers, mostly lay people who wanted to be buried close to the saints whom they loved.

In the tenth century, tall, circular structures built of rocks called "round towers" also were added to this monastic landscape. The idea for these structures may have originated from early medieval Irish pilgrims traveling in Italy to Rome, for the oldest *campanili* or bell-towers that they might have seen in such places as Ravenna look very similar to those round towers that remain standing in Ireland, Scotland, and the Isle of Man. Ludwig Bieler says that "these towers, by which the Irish landscape is dominated to the present day, must be understood as a specifically Irish version of an early Italian type of campanile. . . . That they, like their Italian models, were originally bell-towers is confirmed by their Irish name: *cloicthech*, 'bell-house.'"[53] Thus, as belfries, they were originally

used to call the monks and lay people to prayer. It is interesting
to note references in early Irish monastic rules to the bells which
were a part of the monks' daily routine. One, in particular, could
refer to the round tower that can still be seen at Glendalough,
the site of Kevin's great monastic city: "A melodious bell, pealing
out over the glen, such is the will of the fair Lord, that many
brothers may be gathered under one discipline."[54]

In times of danger, however, the round towers were also used
as watch-towers and places of refuge when, for example, war
between tribal kings or rival monasteries increasingly occurred,
or when Vikings began to make their raids against the
monasteries in the late eighth century. They were then used as
shelters where the monastic inhabitants could seek protection
by carrying food and valuables into them and closing off the
main entrances which were located high above ground. There
monks might remain for weeks, desperately hoping, no doubt,
that the invaders would go elsewhere before their own supply of
food and water ran out. Not everyone was saved, however. The
earliest mention in the Annals of Ireland tells of "foreigners"
from Dublin attacking the monastery at Slane in 950. These
Norsemen set ablaze its round tower, burnt its founder's crozier
and bell, and, not least, a "large number of people, including the
lector [reader] of the monastery."[55]

Besides these structures associated with communal life,
many monasteries had outlying cells where one or more
anchorites secluded themselves in silence and prayer, or
oratories, such as those found in Ardmore (on the southern
coast of Ireland), Iona (off the coast of Scotland), and on the
Farne Islands in Northumbria that were used as places of retreat
from the active life. The example of the desert fathers and
mothers continued to inspire them. At these early monasteries,
work, study, prayer, and fasting were important aspects of their
daily routine. For communal prayer, the monks, nuns, and
laypeople who chose to join them would gather eight times
throughout the day and night when the bell was rung. The work
would be of two kinds.

> While the seniors were engaged in copying books and
> painting miniatures, or in teaching, the novices were
> doing hard manual labour. They had to fell trees, dig
> out the roots, remove undergrowth, and take away

stones, until a portion of the primeval forest was converted into arable land.[56]

They also had to feed the livestock, care for the sheep, and fish from the rivers or lakes in order to supplement the monastic diet. Gardens had to be weeded, and the orchards tended. Because of the early Christian Celts' respect for the written word, every monastery that was able to afford it had a library that consisted of readings from the classical and patristic writings, and, of course, the Lives of the saints.

Through the seventh and eighth centuries monasteries continued to be built as this distinctive form of Christianity grew in prominence. At a time that historians have called the "Dark Ages" on the Continent of Europe, this Golden Age of Celtic saints was sending thousands of Irish missionaries and pilgrims as far east as Kiev in Russia, and as far north as Iceland. They came and went to continental Europe, according to one annalist, "like uncharted comets."[57] Through the friendships of their leaders and the ministry of their missionaries, this Irish church was in touch with other Celtic Churches in Britain and Brittany, affecting their own development and giving them a distinctively Irish character. This Irish influence can be discerned when we consider the untold thousands of Irish emigrants, missionaries, and soul friends who traveled to Wales, Cornwall, Brittany, and the Isle of Man. It can be seen too in St. Columcille's journeying to Scotland to spread the gospel message to the Picts, in St. Aidan's travel to Northumbria, carrying the torch of Christianity, in Sts. Columbanus and Gall leaving Bangor, Ireland to found monasteries in Gaul, Switzerland, and Italy. Their efforts made it possible for the people of the Continent whose lives had been ravished and libraries destroyed by "barbarians" to continue to have access to the Christian and classical traditions. It is apparent too in the little-known Lives of such hermits as St. Melangell of Wales and St. Selevan at Land's End, as well as the story of St. Ia who traveled to Cornwall on a large leaf (or was it really, like Enora's of Brittany, a coracle?).

All of these celebrated saints and anonymous Christians were bringing into being a unique form of Christianity, the early Celtic Church, a church that brought to Europe and the universal church a love of learning, a knack for teaching, and a unique spirituality and ecclesial life quite different than that

———◦✦◦———

found in other churches. This Celtic Church, located in the landscape of mountains and forests, seashores and lakes, was a church especially marked by its deep love for Christ, Mary, and the saints. As the historian John Hennig says about the Irish, in particular: "In the Western church, no country has made a contribution as wide, as systematic or as varied to the development of the basic pattern of devotion to all the saints as has Ireland."[58]

F O U R

A Church

of

Lasting

Beauty

The Celtic Church of the Age of the Saints, as we see
it in their gentle way of life, their austere monastic
settlements and their island retreats, the
personalities of their saints, and the traditions of
their poetry, expresses the Christian ideal with a
sanctity and sweetness which have never been
surpassed, and perhaps only equaled by the ascetics
of the Eastern deserts.

Nora Chadwick

The simple, fantastic beauty of ordinary things
growing—marsh-marigolds, dandelions, thistles and
grass. . . .

Patrick Kavanagh

The early Celtic Church that included the lands and people just
discussed was made up of churches that were not linked through
administrative structures nor dependent upon a hierarchical
"chain of command." Rather, theirs was a spiritual community
united through a communion of friendships and alliances
between spiritual leaders and their monasteries. Numerous
stories in the hagiographies which portray the monastic
founders studying, working, traveling together, and frequently
mentoring each other reflect how their hagiographers desired to
show that these churches were spiritually connected. Perhaps
the most telling example of this is the site of the church
dedicated to St. Ciaran of Clonmacnoise located right next to St.
Kevin's own church at Glendalough. It testifies not only to the
possibly original soul friendship between the two leaders, but
also to the spiritual link between the two monasteries long after
the deaths of their founders. This is, in effect, what made the

115

Celtic churches one church: the spiritual kinship of the Christian
Celts who shared a common history, common heroes, and, like
their pagan forebears, a common love of poetry and stories. As
Mary Low says about these Celtic Christians, "they had heroes
and heroines of their own, and tended to express themselves
differently: both in terms of church organization and in their
enthusiastic use of poetry and story for religious purposes."[1]

These Celtic churches were not cut off from the more
Romanized churches on the Continent nor the bishop of Rome
(although certain Irish leaders, St. Columbanus in particular,
were not adverse to arguing directly with the Pope).[2] They did,
however, have a preference for the monastic and hermit life.
"The history of the Celtic Church," says Welsh scholar G. H.
Doble, "is largely a history of monks and monasteries."[3]
Although there was certainly much diversity in this early Celtic
Church if one considers the different countries in which it grew
and the differences that developed over the centuries, it
maintained its identity and fundamental unity through its
storytelling, music, art, liturgical and private prayers, all of
which were expressions of its spirituality, a spirituality which
was highly corporate in nature, emphasizing, as it did, the
spiritual bonds of tribe, family, and soul friends.

Some recent writers seem to believe that the designation
"Celtic Church" should no longer be used, preferring instead
"Celtic Christianity." They find the term misleading, as if there
was a specifically Celtic ecclesial institution that was separate
from or in opposition to other churches and the leadership in
Rome in early medieval times. While correctly reacting against
nineteenth and early twentieth-century writers, mainly
Protestant, who equated the Celtic Church with their own
history and aspirations *against* the Roman Catholicism of their
times,[4] some of those who criticize the use of "Celtic Church"
today seem to ignore post-Vatican II ecclesial understandings
that acknowledge the significant influence of culture upon the
development of church entities.[5] Some also seem to believe that
recognition of this diversity in ecclesial, liturgical, and
theological expressions may be contrary to the supposed early
"unity" of the universal church. As the great ecumenist
theologian, Yves Congar, however, posits: "That pluralism
existed in the ancient church and that it exists in the church
today is a fact on which there is no point in dwelling: there were

rites and cultic expressions, theologies, schools of spirituality, traditions and customs, organizations peculiar to a country or socio-cultural area."[6] This would surely apply to the ecclesial reality that emerged in Celtic lands, influenced as it was by the Celtic culture with its Christian monastic emphasis.

Certain critics of the term also seem to recognize solely a largely hierarchical model of church which presupposes that if churches are not united through administrative structures, they do not exist at all. Avery Dulles, in his book on ecclesiology, *Models of the Church*, offers a contrasting view. He argues for a variety of church expressions, each with its own gifts and limitations. One primary model he describes is that of "the church as mystical communion." This model, Dulles says, is expressed in the writings of various theologians throughout the centuries. In Augustine's theology, for example, is found "the image of the body of Christ with particular stress on the mystical and invisible communion that binds together all those who are enlivened by the grace of Christ." This mystical communion presumes that church membership is made up not only of "the earthly" but of "the heavenly" as well. Protestant theologians also provide insights into aspects of this model. Emil Brunner states that the church in the biblical sense is not an institution, but "a pure communion of persons," and Dietrich Bonhoeffer speaks of the church as an "interpersonal community" which he called "the communion of saints." For Roman Catholics, the documents of Vatican II, Dulles suggests, also have an affinity with this model, emphasizing, as they do, community and an image of the church as "the People of God," united through "bonds of creed, worship, and ecclesiastical fellowship."[7]

Besides Dulles, Irish theologian Diarmuid O'Laoghaire, in his own writings on spirituality, describes how one of the earliest themes among Celtic Christians, found in seventh or eighth-century Irish glosses, was that of the church as "the Mystical Body," united in "the fellowship of Jesus Christ": "So we, being many, are one body in Christ, and every one members of one another."[8] Overall, then, the Celtic Church as a "mystical communion" is an historically valid concept and a genuinely authentic theology of the church, especially considering the Celts' own emphasis on the spiritual kinship of soul friends and their love of the saints whom they considered their "first ancestors." As John J. O'Riordan says about the Christian Celts: they always had a "lack of interest in establishing or maintaining bureaucracy," a lack that "must always be seen over against the Celtic preference for friendly person-to-person communication."[9] This was, indeed, the Celtic Church's basic strength, a unity found in their links between soul friends and common spirituality.

This Celtic Christian spirituality was a unique synthesis of ancient pagan and Christian beliefs and practices. Some of its primary characteristics include a dedication to simplicity and small communities, a great devotion to learning, an inclusivity regarding women's leadership, a collaborative and non-dualistic stance, an appreciation of the marginalized, a love of beauty, and, not least, a deep respect for the reality of human fragility and sin that can be healed with the help of a soul friend. These traits of spirituality reflect what Nora Chadwick identifies as the Celtic Church's "lasting beauty," a beauty that can be found, she says, in its gentle way of life, austere monastic settlements and island retreats, and the personalities of the saints. Although I would question the Celtic Church's gentleness and "sweetness," especially if one considers the conflicts and violence of its later history, I agree that this church expresses the Christian ideal with holiness that has "never been surpassed. . . ."[10]

Before considering the beauty of its spirituality, however, let us begin with the Celtic landscape which had such an effect on the particular kind of spirituality which developed among the Christian Celts and the ministry of the soul friend that arose there. If the vastness of the desert profoundly affected the theology and spirituality of the Christians living there, so the landscape of the Celts influenced their character, their understanding of God, and their acknowledgment and celebration of the sacred. Land and a sense of place are continuing themes in Celtic religious writing.

Kinship of Earth and Heaven

Before the saints and soul friends of the Celtic Church, even before the rise of the Celts whom later generations identified as "pagan," there was the land, and the ocean which borders so much of it. The Celts' innate appreciation of beauty certainly had a great deal to do with this landscape: its mountains covered with forests and flowers, its tiny islands and skellig rocks off the shores of lakes and seas, the ocean waters with their ebb and flow of tides. This natural beauty, wreathed so often in mists and fogs, opened the Celts, both ancient and Christian, to the realm of the imagination. It made them receptive to mysticism, poetry, and prayer, as well as to the mysterious language and images of dreams. Located as they were so close to the ocean, the lands of the Celts were watered almost daily by mists and sudden downpours of rain. This weather which changes so quickly and unexpectedly from bright sunshine to the blackest of days contributes to the Celts' temperament, their outlook on life, their character. Some writers have described the Celt, in fact, as "a creature of extremes; his sadness is despairing, his joy is rapture."[11] The same changing weather may also have contributed to their penchant for telling stories. As the storyteller Bryan MacMahon once said in answer to a student's query about the flood of Irish stories, "Oh, it's the rain you know. It turns one to moody reflection, and what else can you do of a long winter's night but tell stories."[12]

Anyone who visits the lands associated with the Celts would agree that they have a common landscape. Wake up in the morning, and look out through the window, and, if you are near the sea, you realize how much they look alike: in springtime one sees green leaves returning to the trees, and fuchsia blossoming in rich colors of scarlet and creamy white; in summer, wild gorse bushes splash the fields and hills with patches of bright yellow, as if from the brush of van Gogh; in autumn, the tops of mountains and hills are encircled with various shades of tan, blue, and purple heather; in winter, cold rain sweeps in sheets across rugged rock formations and deserted beaches. And always there is the smell of the sea, its vast expanse of water, its ever-changing crests of waves. Ruman, a seventh-century Irish poet, refers to the beauty and power of the ocean:

> Full the sea and fierce the surges,
> Lovely are the ocean verges,
> On the showery waters whirling,
> Sandy winds are swiftly swirling,
> Rudders cleave the surf that urges.[13]

For the ancient Celts, a people who have been described in sometimes highly condescending terms as "mere animists," the landscape was inhabited, as we've seen, by multitudes of spirits and by goddesses and gods of nature and of fertility. When Christianity came to Celtic lands, this profound pagan belief in the spiritual dimension of creation was transformed into the Christian belief in the spiritual presence and ready accessibility of God, the angels, and the saints, all of whom, from a Celtic perspective, were not divorced from but closely linked with the environment. A story about St. Columcille alludes to this powerful sense of spiritual presence when it relates why he loved his monastery at Derry so much, located high on the hill where the city by that name was later built:

> For this is the reason why I love Derry,
> For its level fields, for its brightness,
> Because it is quite full of white angels
> From one end to the other. . . .
> My Derry, my little oak-grove,
> My dwelling, my little cell.[14]

For him and other Celts, ancient and Christian, landscape was both luminous, overflowing with light, and numinous, reveling in and revelatory of sacred mystery. Contrary to those of us who live in a culture which has lost its memory and seems to only value the future and the supposedly ever-changing "new," the Celts believed that the landscape itself was filled with echoes of memory, of the eternal.[15] To them, it was immersed in the continuing presence of past lives, and alive with reflections of former times. The Irish writer, John Synge, alludes to this when he says that Celts believe there is a "psychic memory" attached to the landscape and to certain locales.[16]

Spirituality is always necessarily tied to the particular, to a specific place. Ancient peoples, including the Greeks and Romans, spoke of a *genius loci*, a spirit of the place where the divine resides. For the Irish, the word *Dindshenchus* referred to their tradition about places that considered certain geographical locations as having particular significance, often by the names they were given and the stories attached to them. The importance of a specific place where one could grow in holiness and communion with God was recognized by the Celtic Christian storytellers when they portray the saints in search of their "place of resurrection." This belief that a geographical location could become not only the site of a monastery, but the place where one experienced transformation was an important one for the Christian Celts. Though *wanderlust* from their ancient ancestors flowed in their veins, this concept of finding one's "place of resurrection" provided an affirmation of the wisdom that can be gained by staying put, certainly what desert Christians had linked with their cells and Benedictines would embrace with their vow of stability. It presupposed, however, that a person choose wisely where one decides to settle, to plant one's roots, for one's environment can profoundly affect the direction of the soul. The theologian Belden Lane posits that "landscape is a connector of the soul with Being."[17] According to Ralph Waldo Emerson, the place where any person finds his or her self "is the true place, and superior in dignity to all other places."[18] In that context, as the Celts believed, the places people settle can have a transcendent quality and salvific effect upon them; can truly become their own "place of resurrection."

The Celts brought this awareness to the landscape, and their attitude towards it was one of wonder and awe at its profound beauty and effulgence. Noel Dermot O'Donoghue refers to this as "Celtic religious consciousness, Christian as well as pre-Christian," in which "creation does not merely show forth God's glory," but "has its own power, its own presence, its own mystery, its own voices."[19] Influenced by this awareness of nature's mystery, the Irish shared with their later invaders, the Norsemen, what the Norse called *utiseta*, the practice of sitting out under the moon and the stars to listen attentively to the voices of nature, to singing waters and rustling leaves. As the ninth-century Irish scholar, John Scotus Eriugena (c. 810-877 C.E.), states: "every visible and invisible creature can be called a theophany, that is, an appearance of the divine," a belief reflected centuries later in the Welsh poetry of Waldo Williams that there is an "ancient kinship of earth and heaven."[20]

Dimensions of this spiritual kinship are reflected in the stories, poetry, and statements of or about the Celtic saints. St. Patrick, after his return to Ireland as a missionary bishop, encountered at a well Ethne and Fedelm, the daughters of an as-yet-unconverted Irish king. The story is a famous one, and shows how much aware Patrick was of this link between earth and heaven:

Patrick and his clerics went at sunrise to the well called Clebach on the slopes of Cruachain. Fair-haired Ethne and red-haired Fedelm, the daughters of Loiguire son of Niall, went early, as they customarily did, to the well to wash. Beside the well the young women found the assembly of the clerics in white garments, with their books before them. They wondered at the shape of the clerics, and thought that they were men of other worlds or possibly apparitions. So they asked Patrick, "Who are you, and from where do you come?" Patrick said to them, "It would be better for you to believe in God than to inquire about our race." The elder daughter responded, "Who is your god, and where does he live? Tell us about him, how he is seen, how he is loved, how he is found. Tell us if he is youthful or very old; if he lives forever; if he is beautiful; if many people have fostered his son, and if his daughters are recognized by men of the world as dear and beautiful."

Patrick, filled with the Holy Spirit, answered, "Our God is the God of all things, the God of heaven and earth and sea and river, the God of sun and moon and all the stars, the God of high mountains and lowly valleys; the God over heaven and in heaven and under heaven. He has a dwelling both in heaven and earth and sea and all that dwell within them. He inspires all things, he gives life to all things; he surpasses all things. Our God kindles the light of the sun and the light of the moon. He made springs in arid land and dry islands in the sea, and stars he appointed to minister to the greater lights. He has a Son coeternal with Him and, like a son, very similar to His Father. But the Son is not younger than the Father, nor is the Father older than the Son. And the Holy Spirit breathes in them. Father and Son and Holy Spirit are not divided. I desire to unite you to the Son of the Heavenly King, for you are daughters of a king of earth."[21]

The two young women, obviously impressed with Patrick's poetic theology and powerful allusions to nature, immediately were baptized.

St. Brigit too has this awareness. She is portrayed in the earliest Irish hagiography as traveling the countryside in a chariot, preaching to the Irish laity, and communing with all sorts of animals and birds. As her hagiographer says about her, "All the while she praised the Creator of all things, to whom all living things are subject and in whom all things live, as she said, rendering God service."[22] St. Columcille, in a twelfth-century poem associated with him, tells of his joy in communing with nature while listening to the voices and music of the sea:

Delightful to me to be on an island hill, on the crest of a
rock, that I might often watch the quiet sea;
That I might watch the heavy waves above the bright water,
As they chant music to their Father everlastingly;

That I might watch its smooth, bright-bordered shore,
no gloomy pastime, that I might hear the cry of the strange
birds, a pleasing sound;

That I might hear the murmur of the long waves against
the rocks, that I might hear the sound of the sea, like
mourning beside a grave;

That I might watch the splendid flocks of birds over the
well-watered sea, that I might see its mighty whales, the
greatest wonder.

That I might watch its ebb and flood in their course, that
my name should be—it is a secret that I tell—"he who
turned his back upon Ireland";

That I might have a contrite heart as I watch, that I
might repent my many sins, hard to tell;

That I might bless the Lord who rules all things, heaven
with its splendid host, earth, ebb and flood. . . .[23]

Besides these profoundly beautiful references to nature found in the lives of Patrick, Brigit, and Columcille, the "holy trinity" of Celtic saints, there are numerous others, for hagiographers frequently depict the saints (in imitation of the desert heroes) seeking quiet, solitary places, "deserts," as it were, and praying in forests, in ocean waters, on islands and

———— ❧ ————

mountaintops. Mochuda, the founder of the great Irish monastery of Lismore, walks through woods while singing psalms, and Maedoc of Ferns prays "in the recesses of a wood." Kevin of Glendalough, according to one of his Lives:

> . . . was for length of years
> Among deserts in woods,
> And he saw no man,
> Nor did any man see him there.[24]

Soul friends, such as Cuthbert of Northumbria, spent hours praying at night in the cold waters of the oceans, and islands always seemed to attract them, perhaps because they associated them with peace and quiet. Enda taught Ciaran on the Aran Islands, Columcille went to Iona, and Aidan traveled to Lindisfarne, the Holy Island surrounded for much of the time by the tides. Cuthbert himself moved to Inner Farne Island in his quest for the beloved solitude which so often eluded him. Mountains too were places of prayer. As Patrick himself attests, it was on a mountain, possibly Slemish in Co. Antrim in northern Ireland, that he as a youthful slave tending sheep experienced a re-awakening of his Christian faith and "even in times of snow or frost or rain . . . would rise before dawn to pray."[25]

This love of nature, and communion with the beauty and power of the landscape is also alluded to in the saints' love of fishing. Adomnan, Columcille's hagiographer, quoting an elderly monk, Ernene, refers to the latter's fishing "in the fishful River Finn when all at once the whole sky lit up" on the night of the saint's death.[26] Ailbe of Emly, a pre-Patrician saint in Ireland, was exceptionally helpful when there were no fish to catch. Not only did he bless a river in Connacht that was "barren of fish," thus bringing them back to the water, but he showed the local people five places along the stream in which they might catch them again![27] St. Gall, Columbanus's companion in France and Switzerland on his missionary rounds, is depicted in a later hagiography as an avid fisherman who considered the wilderness as "beloved" and like a "royal court." And, unlike many so-called fishermen, Gall did *not* let the big ones get away—at least, according to his hagiographer![28] A Welsh saint, Selevan, who, on his way to Brittany, stopped in Cornwall and decided to stay and live as a hermit, was also said to delight in fishing.[29]

Thus, anyone who reads the stories of the Celtic saints or visits their holy places soon realizes that the landscape is not merely "background" to the lives of these saintly soul friends, but a vital and formative presence, affecting profoundly their spirituality and their understanding of God. This theology is reflected in a medieval Irish litany to the Trinity that addresses God:

O Creator of the elements. . . .
O God of the earth.
O God of fire.
O God of the waters of wonder.
O God of the gusting and blustering air. . . .
O God of the waves from the depths of the ocean.
O God of the planets and of the many bright stars.
O God, creator of the universe and inaugurator
    of night and day.[30]

Oak Groves and High Places

Aspects of the landscape whose elements vividly reflected God's presence and where intimations of God were experienced, sometimes quite viscerally, were, of course, the oak groves and forests of sacred trees. Here, as we've seen, the ancient druids and druidesses had gathered to celebrate their rituals and teach their students about spiritual realities. Here also the later Christian founders would build their monasteries at locations such as Kildare, Derry, and Durrow, whose names specifically refer to oak groves. Here too Irish and Welsh solitaires in the eighth and ninth centuries, probably members of the Celi De Reform Movement who were inspired by the stories of Mochuda, Maedoc, and Kevin, would seek out their own "desert" solitude and write exquisite nature poetry and elegies, with numerous references to forests and the sacred oak trees:

I have a hut in the wood,
None knows it but my Lord;

an ash tree this side, a hazel beyond,
A great tree on a mound enfolds it. . . .

The clear cuckoo sings to me, lovely discourse,
in its grey cloak from the crest of the bushes;
truly—may the Lord protect me!—
well do I write under the forest wood.
Oak, bushy, leafy,
you are high above trees. . . .[31]

Considering this Celtic appreciation of the forests, we can see why St. Bernard (1090-1153), a friend of St. Malachy (1094-1148) of Armagh, once told his students, "the forests will teach you more than books. The trees and rocks will teach you things that the masters of science will never teach you."[32]

Another impressive aspect of any Celtic landscape are the mountains and hills, stretching across certain parts of the countryside, each having its own unique personality and character. In Ireland alone, ringed as it is with them, perhaps some of the most memorable are the Wicklow Mountains surrounding Glendalough, Ben Bulben's golden slopes outside of Sligo, the Mountains of Mourne that sweep down to the sea in the north, the stark beauty of the Twelve Pins of Connemara, and snow-covered Mount Brandon on the Dingle Peninsula. Scotland has its own rich grandeur—from the beauty of the Scottish Highlands to the Lammermuir Hills, from the peaks of Ben Nevis to the Paps of Jura and the heights of Glen Coe. In Wales, the whole region of Snowdonia, to mention only one area, is crowned by the highest mountain in Wales, Yr Wyddfa (Snowdon), which, from its top, has a spectacular view of forests, lakes, and rushing streams.

Like the desert Christians and the Eastern Orthodox Christians who followed them, the Celts had a deep respect for such high places. They considered mountains and hills as locations where one could encounter the divine in a special way. They were (and are) places of light and illumination, when sun's rays at dawn light up the peaks and valleys with translucent depths, and at dusk when the setting sun transfuses everything with a rich panoply of colors, red and gold. Surely, when the pagan Celts first heard the stories of Moses on Mount Sinai or of Jesus teaching on the Mount of the Beatitudes, communing with his spiritual ancestors on Mount Tabor, praying on the Mount of Olives before his death, and being crucified on the Hill of Calvary, they could identify their own landscape with his, and thus more readily embrace his story as a reflection of theirs. It is no wonder that St. Patrick, in an early hagiography, is compared to Moses, and that St. Columcille is said to have prayed on the "Hill of the Angels," located on the western side of Iona.

The Celts' love of mountains, of course, preceded the coming of Christianity. Mountains were sometimes specifically associated with goddesses, as the Paps of Ana or Danu in Ireland suggest. Armagh, before St. Patrick settled there, was called Ard Mhacha [Macha's Height], and dedicated to the Irish goddess of war and fertility by that name. D. D. C. Pochin Mould says that Ireland, in particular, "has a cult of high places and has long cherished the old Celtic custom of lighting hilltop fires at the great seasonal changes of the year, May Day, Midsummer (St. John's Eve), Halloween."[33] Such hilltop fires originated in the pagan worship on the high places, alluded to in an early Patrician hagiography of Patrick which describes the conflict when Patrick lit a fire on the Hill of Slane at Easter, and King Loiguire and his druids on the Hill of Tara were expecting to be the first to do so.[34] Another hagiography, the *Life of St. Samson of Dol*, shows how the high places were linked with the Celtic gods and goddesses of fertility. On his journey through Cornwall, before going to Brittany, Samson is portrayed as finding an idol in the shape of a phallus being worshipped on a mountaintop "after the custom of Bacchantes," possibly a reference to the Celtic fertility god, Cernunnos.[35] In Brittany, especially, high places were linked with the worship of fertility and of the sun.[36]

Early Irish literature is full of stories of encounters with otherworldly creatures on mountains and hills. The Irish hero, Finn Mac Cool, and his band of warriors, the Fianna, spent much of their time hunting near Ben Bulben and enjoying each other's company. A medieval poem, possibly written by a bard disillusioned with the Christian religion, says about Finn and his men:

> dearer to them was the mountain than the church
> sweet they thought the note of blackbirds,
> tinklings of [church] bells they did not think sweet.[37]

———— ❧ ————

The Hill of Tara, the center of high-kingship in early medieval times, was inhabited and honored as a sacred site by a people who lived in Ireland long before the Celts arrived. Croagh Patrick, a popular place of pilgrimage today, was originally the location of pagan worship before it was named after the great missionary.

With the coming of the Christianity, the baptized Celts frequently built their castles, monasteries, and oratories on or near earlier pagan sites, including such high places as those at Armagh and Tara, and at Cashel, the hill of kings and of bishops. Celtic Christians also named certain high places after one of their favorite saints, the archangel Michael: Glastonbury Tor in England; Skellig Michael, off the western coast of Ireland; Mount St. Michael, off Cornwall; and Mont St. Michel of Normandy. These heights, and the hills surrounding them, not only can evoke a sense of awe at the grandeur of the countryside, stretched out in all directions below, but at times elicit the melancholy that sometimes resides so deeply in the Celtic soul, as expressed by a poet from the Hebrides:

On the hillside I recline,
Ever yearning for the lost,
Ever looking to the West,
Where the sun sets in the sea.[38]

The Sea and the Celtic Soul

The ocean itself, as the poem suggests, was never far from the mountains and hills of the Celts. Unlike the landscape of the desert Christians, it was always close at hand. In Scotland, for example, one is always within forty miles of the sea. Of course, if one lived on an island, such as Skellig Michael, the Arans, Iona, Bardsey, Lindisfarne, or Mont St. Michel, the ocean was an intimate daily companion, sometimes a friend, sometimes a foe, depending on the tides and the weather. While a highly masculine spirituality and theology developed in the desert regions, the Celts' closeness to the ocean as well as to other bodies of water counterbalanced for them the masculine emphasis with the feminine, moving them beyond the dualistic one-sidedness that has had such a detrimental effect on

Christian spirituality and ecclesiology. In literature and psychology, the ocean is symbolic of the "collective unconscious," the container of ancestral memories, the cauldron or holy grail out of which flows passion, creativity, a sense of wonder and of adventure. Water itself is a symbol of the "great mother," of the feminine, of the soul, and, for the ancient Celts, of the fluidity of time, space, and sexuality. (Again, it is worth noting that the two exceptions to the desert tradition's highly masculine theology and spirituality were Amma Syncletica and John Cassian, both of whom lived near or possibly traveled on the sea, and were, as we recall, more inclusive in their theology.)

John Healy, a nineteenth-century Irish writer, says that the Irish (and one could presume here all Celts) "had a very keen perception of the grandeur and beauty of God's universe." He goes on to say that "the voices of the storm and the strength of the sea, the majesty of lofty mountains and the glory of summer woods, spoke to their hearts even more eloquently than the voice of the preacher, or the writing on their parchments. . . . Most of all they loved the great sea; it was for them the most vivid image of God; in its anger, its beauty, its power, its immensity, they felt the presence and they saw, though dimly, the glory of the Divine Majesty."[39] Henry Beston, a twentieth-century American of Irish and French ancestry, posits the underlying presupposition of the Celts, that "nature is part of our humanity, and without some awareness and experience of that divine mystery" we cease to be human. Beston refers to what he calls the "three great elemental sounds in nature": the sound of the rain, of wind in a primeval forest, and of the ocean on a beach. "I have heard them all," he says, but "of the three elemental voices, that of ocean is the most awesome, beautiful, and varied. . . . The sea has many voices."[40]

Along with the mountaintops and hills, the forests and sacred groves, the Celts associated sea-voices and the beaches on which the ocean's waves resound with "thin places," those geographical locations where there seems to be only a thin veil between this world and the next, the finite and infinite, the physical and spiritual realms. In these thin places, dimensions of chronological time (past, present, and future) lose their distinctions, and a mysterious presence is often experienced that transcends time. Robin Flower speaks in these terms about his visit to the Great Blasket Island off the western coast of Ireland.

————— ❧ —————

"Standing there," he says, "as the sea-mists crept over the Island and shut out the visible world, I have at times lost consciousness of this present earth and felt the illusion of other presences in the wreathing swirls of cloud."[41] Thomas Cahill refers to this same sort of experience when he describes a seashore scene where naked young men raced horses bareback along the beaches of Clare, Ireland, through the surf at high tide, "looking," he says, "for all the world like their prehistoric warrior ancestors."[42] In some sense, in their naked beauty and vitality, they were Celtic warriors, living, not in the past, but here and now. The soul, the ancestral soul transcends time and space, and is frequently vividly experienced not only in dreams, but in those places which the Celts identify as "thin": boundaries, cemeteries, hilltops, islands.

For most Celts, both pagan and Christian, ancient and modern, the sea and its borders are special places of liminality, possessing spiritual significance.[43] Ancient Celtic poets and bards considered the seashore, the river's edge, the brink of water as always the place where wisdom and knowledge were revealed, the place of poetic revelation, of enlightenment for seers and storytellers. Celtic people also believed that the curragh or coracle, the tiny boat made of animal skins, was a fitting symbol for the frail bark of the soul and its quest for meaning, wisdom, and wholeness, what the Celts call "soul-making." Living so near the ocean, no wonder early hagiographers frequently compared themselves to venturers out in small coracles on the vast sea. Heroes in ancient stories are often portrayed as wanderers, Carl Jung says, "and wandering is a symbol of longing, of the restless urge which never finds its object, of nostalgia for the lost mother."[44] This nostalgia, characterized by a certain wistfulness and longing, may be related to the melancholy mentioned above, as well as to the sighs that seem to come from deep within, from the heart, so often expressed by the native Irish in the midst of conversations. It also finds expression in their writing, poetic and otherwise. As a Gaelic proverb says, "a whole day's rapture is soon forgotten, but a sigh in the night lingers long in the ear and heart."[45]

While the beauty of the landscape with its high places, deep forests, and wide shores washed by the ocean tides spoke to the Celts of the wonder and grandeur of creation, their sighs and melancholy may speak of what is missing, of what's been lost, perhaps of a spiritual vacuum that has not been filled. Early Welsh poetry, with its images from nature, is especially filled with this sense of melancholy. One finds in it frequent references to depression, loneliness, a heart "broken with grief," sadness that "breeds utter despondence," the awareness of sin. One untitled poem speaks of "fairest" summer, tinged with the experience of loss, yet evidently being comforted in some ways by the poet's belief in Christ:

> The beginning of summer, fairest season;
> noisy are the birds, green the woods,
> the ploughs are in the furrow, the ox at work,
> green the sea, the lands are many-colored.
>
> When the cuckoos sing in the tops of the fair trees
> my despondency becomes greater;
> the smoke is smarting, it is plain I cannot sleep.
>
> Since my friends have passed away,
> in hill, in vale, in the islands of the sea,
> in every way one goes,
> there is no seclusion from the blessed Christ.

Another poem, this time focusing on winter and mountain snow expresses a sense of sadness and deep unhappiness, again, within the context of the natural environment:

> Mountain snow, white is the ravine,
> the trees bend at the assault of the wind;
> many a couple love each other
> but never come together. . . .
>
> Mountain snow, the stag is hunted;
> the wind whistles over the eaves of the tower;
> grievous, my friend, is sin. . . .
> Mountain snow, the stag is in the rushes,
> cold are the bogs; mead is in the vat;
> usual for the wounded is lamentation.[46]

James Charles Roy, in his writings, relates melancholy directly to the landscape and the climate, as well as to the "heavy conscience" of the Irish (although, as we see in one of the stanzas quoted above, the Welsh too were quite aware of sin's gravity). "The melancholia of the scenery," Roy writes, "often provides a mere reflection as to the melancholia so starkly apparent, so many times, in the Irish soul. . . ." According to him, it was in Ireland where "the rigors of desert theology remained alive and pertinent longer than anywhere in Europe. One consequence was the development of penance, the idea of admission and atonement for sin, a concept the Celts developed almost by themselves."[47] This consciousness was sometimes intensified by the landscape which was alluded to, above, in the poetry of Columcille contemplating the ocean:

That I might have a contrite heart as I watch, that I
might repent my many sins, hard to tell. . . .

It was also, I would add, what led to the rise of soul friendships, based as they are upon the awareness of the need for a change of heart, and of the need for self-disclosure and support, found in the saying, "anyone without a soul friend is like a body without a head." Or, as a Welsh poem affirms, though it be a "Winter's Day," "fine is a secret shared."[48]

Perhaps one of the most moving expressions of this melancholy, linked with remorse, is found outside the Irish visitor center at Clonmacnoise, in the carved, wooden statue entitled "The First Pilgrim," one of whose hands covers an anguished face, while the other leans on his pilgrim's staff. Whether Irish, Welsh, or whatever race, one can recognize a fellow-pilgrim, weighed down with regret by the sins of the past. Another expression of this human desire for change (and need for comforting) is found in a story from the *Life of St. Samson of Dol*. According to his hagiographer, Samson and his followers had just reached the shores of Brittany for the first time, brought there, we are told, with God as "his guide" and with Christ as his "companion, always and in all things." There, on the beach, Samson encounters a man "making lamentation and ever gazing towards the sea," waiting, as the saint discovers, for divine help and human intervention. Samson asks the man the reason for his lament, and he answers that he has been waiting three days and as many nights for the coming of a helper "from beyond the sea whom God promised me." The helper, as it turns out, is Samson who goes on to heal, with God's power, the man's wife, sick from leprosy, and his daughter, who was possessed by a demon.[49]

Although this story describes the beginning of St. Samson's ministry in Brittany, the man "ever gazing to the sea" represents those who share a Celtic soul. An archetypal figure, he symbolizes both ancient and modern Celts' preoccupation with water, seashores, ocean tides, as well as their mystical connection with all of the elements of nature; above all, their passionate search for God.

He also, quite fittingly, epitomizes the pagan Celts themselves whom, judging from their stories of ancient heroes, were longing for something different, truer, better than their own culture and religious beliefs could offer: forgiveness, healing, transcendence.[50] This is precisely what St. Patrick and other Christian leaders in all their heroic accomplishments and human frailties addressed when they brought the hopeful message of reconciliation to Celtic lands and began to build Christian communities.

The Christian monasteries that were built in the Celtic landscape made up what Irish scholar Liam de Paor has described as a "common ecclesiastical culture."[51] This culture was distinctive in the way it integrated so many of the values and beliefs of the Christian Celts' pagan ancestors, especially regarding kinship relationships with nature, family, and tribe, as well as the ideals of the early desert Christians who valued simplicity of life, discipline, and the need for spiritual guidance in one's life. The Celts' common landscape significantly affected, as we've seen, their theology and their perception of the sacred. It also influenced their art, poetry, music, and dance. This, in turn, shaped the emerging Celtic Christian spirituality that bound individual Celtic Churches together, and became the "ground" or "spiritual soil" out of which soul friendships grew. In the union of Celtic monasteries and churches the spiritual community called the Celtic Church was born, a church united through the soul friendships of its leaders and communities. Some of the traits of this mystical community called the Celtic Church are manifest in various patterns or characteristics of their spirituality.

Simplicity and Small Communities

The first quality of Celtic Christian spirituality is its valuing of a simple lifestyle and small communities, values that had much to do with the rural environment in which Celtic Christians lived, the tribal relationships which they valued, and their deep love of the desert Christians with whom they identified. As we recall, the churches influenced by Roman culture adopted the social structures of the declining Roman Empire as their own, and divided church territory into dioceses, headed by bishops who lived primarily in urban areas. The early Celtic Church, however, was located more often in remote, agrarian areas and influenced by the tribal system of the pagan Celts. While the urban churches came to value large buildings for their communal liturgies, taking as their model what the Romans called a "basilica" (a hall of justice with an antechamber and outer courtyard), the Celtic Church built small churches of wood and, later, stone—materials that they had at hand. Even when the membership in the monasteries increased, the Celtic Christians wanted to maintain greater intimacy among their members. Thus, rather than building larger structures for worship, they continued to construct smaller church dwellings in greater numbers as can be seen today in the ruins of the "seven churches" of Glendalough and those on the Aran Islands. Even this characteristic may have originated with the desert Christians who, according to Orthodox scholar, Gregory Telepneff, built "several small chapels rather than one large central church within a monastic community."[52]

Also, as the churches on the Continent grew increasingly more materialistic, dressing their bishops in fine vestments and having them ride in processions on golden thrones (as described in the *Life of Wilfrid*, the prelate from Northumbria who represented the Roman side at the Synod of Whitby), the Celtic Church valued a more ascetic lifestyle.[53] Their early monastic bishops, such as David of Wales, Aidan of Lindisfarne, and Mongo of Glasgow, dressed simply, clad in animal skins or coarse robes, usually carrying with them on their pastoral visits only a Bible, a walking-stick, and a bell which, as they approached, would be loudly rung to alert the local people. They preferred to walk rather than to ride horses, since horses were associated with wealth and status. Bede tells the story of Aidan giving his horse away to a beggar. The horse had been a gift to him from King Oswine of Northumbria and when Oswine complained of his lack of gratitude, Aidan replied: "O King, what are you saying? Surely this son of a mare is not dearer to you than that son of God?"[54]

The leaders in the early Celtic Church, characterized as they were by intense missionary outreach and an effective pastoral ministry among the common people, ate sparsely and spent long hours in prayer, sometimes immersing themselves in the ocean's frigid waters through the night. Bede perhaps best describes Celtic Christians' dedication to simplicity and their profound integrity when he tells how Aidan taught, like the desert elders, by example, not just words: "The best recommendation of his teaching to all was that he taught them no other way of life than that which he himself practiced among his fellows."[55] As advocated in the Rule of Columbanus, it was a life of simple, yet profound goals, and of a simple daily schedule: "to love God with the whole heart and the whole mind and all our strength, and our neighbor as ourselves;" and to "pray daily, toil daily, and daily read."[56]

A Love of Learning

Reading, knowledge, wisdom—all are related to the second characteristic of Celtic spirituality which was the love of learning. This attribute was one originally linked with the ancient druids and druidesses and the bardic storytellers who transmitted their knowledge through the stories they told under the leafy branches of oak trees or around warm hearths on winter nights. Sites of oak groves, as mentioned earlier, were frequently chosen as the place to construct Christian monasteries. These, in turn, became important centers of education for both monastic members and the laity. Teaching took place, as numerous hagiographies show, through the mentoring that occurred between pupil and tutor, apprentice and soul friend. Students of both genders were often given to the monasteries for formation and education when they were seven years old. This was the traditional age when the Irish custom of fosterage took place; that is, when children of one family were given to another to raise in order to maintain kinship bonds, as well as to reinforce the incentive not to go to war with another tribe (particularly if it was holding in trust one's own offspring).

Subjects that they were taught included scripture, patristic writings, Latin, and even Greek, as well as the classics of pagan Greece and Rome. Virgil seems to have been one classical writer in particular whom the Irish knew directly, judging from their glosses on the Bucolics and Georgics.[57] The latter subjects, we recall, were frequently opposed by certain church fathers and almost all of the desert Christians.

Ireland, in particular, became known for its monastic schools of learning, so much so that it came to be fondly called by later generations *Insula Sanctorum et Doctorum* ("The Island of Saints and Scholars"). Of its numerous schools, John Healy says, "the School of Armagh [which Patrick founded] seems to have been the oldest, and always continued to be one of the most celebrated, of the ancient schools of Ireland."[58] Another of the great northern schools was Bangor, founded by St. Comgall in 558. A large percentage of students who were taught in Ireland were laypeople. According to Kathleen Hughes:

> In eighth-century Ireland the proportion of literate laymen must have been abnormally high when compared with the rest of northern Europe. It is no coincidence that the Irish church was extraordinarily tolerant in her attitude to native secular learning, for the number of boys from the world being educated in the monastery, and of adults in the world who had received a clerical education, would tend to narrow the gap between the church and lay society. Each could sympathize with the other.[59]

Women's communities too, another scholar, Lisa Bitel, says, "were places of learning, keeping books and passing on the scholarly tradition," and obviously educating girls as well as boys.[60]

Not only were the native Irish trained at such schools, but countless others from England and the Continent sailed to Ireland to learn, and to receive the tremendous gift of a free education. Again, Bede is our resource of information:

> At this time [664] there were many in England, both nobles and commons, who, in the days of Bishops Finan and Colman, had left their own country and retired to Ireland either for the sake of religious studies or to live a more ascetic life. In course of time, some of

these devoted themselves faithfully to the monastic life, while others preferred to travel round to the cells of various teachers and apply themselves to study. The Irish welcomed them all gladly, gave them their daily food, and also provided them with books to read and with instruction, without asking for any payment.[61]

Helen Waddell, in her classic on the wandering scholars of medieval Europe who kept learning alive, says that many of them were Irish. She speaks highly of them and equates their love of learning with their love of God. "That fierce and restless quality," she says, "which had made the pagan Irish the terror of Western Europe, seems to have emptied itself into the love of learning and the love of God; and it is the peculiar distinction of Irish medieval scholarship and the salvation of literature in Europe that the one in no way conflicted with the other."[62]

During the eighth and ninth centuries, numerous Irish monks made their way to the Continent, bringing with them their books and desire to teach. Columbanus and Gall founded their famous monastic schools at Luxeuil in Gaul, Bobbio in Italy, and St. Gallen in Switzerland which became the chief centers of religion and scholarship in Europe struggling out of the Dark Ages. These monasteries made a significant contribution to the development of liturgy, sacred music, penmanship, and literature.[63] Alcuin of York (c. 735-804), who had studied in Ireland at Clonmacnoise, became the royal tutor to Charlemagne, and established a palace library in Gaul. Later, as abbot of Tours, he set up an important school and library there. His efforts advising Charlemagne on religious and educational matters led to the Carolingian Renaissance. Learning that had been acquired in the Celtic monasteries and the love of learning which the Irish took with them influenced significantly the cultures of both Anglo-Saxons and Franks. They also left their mark in such countries as Belgium, Holland, and Germany. St. Disibode, one of the Irish wandering scholars, left his name on Disibodenberg, near Bingen, where the famous twelfth-century mystic, Hildegard, later lived and wrote, and was influenced by that rich Celtic spiritual tradition.

———— ❧ ————

Women's Leadership and Gifts

A third quality of Celtic Christianity was its appreciation of women's leadership and gifts. While the other Christian continental churches increasingly isolated women from positions of authority and relationships of friendship with males, as we saw in the Breton church regarding the *conhospitae*, the Celtic Church, influenced by the pagan Celts' belief that women were equal to men and had similar legal rights, encouraged their leadership. Contrary to the prevailing dualistic tendencies found in the Roman culture and churches, and even more so among the desert Christians, the early founders of the Celtic Church "did not reject," according to a ninth century manuscript, *Catalogue of the Saints in Ireland,* "the service and society of women."[64] Women were valued and not ignored, judging from one of the earliest Irish martyrologies, that of Gorman, which lists over two hundred female saints. Monastic communities which arose in Ireland shortly after the death of Patrick in 461 were also headed by women. The oldest monasteries of women recorded in Ireland are those of Brigit at Kildare, Moninna at Killeevy, and Ita at Killeedy. Passing references to quite numerous female foundations in the early period suggest that the great Irish monastic movement was, in fact, pioneered by communities of women from as early, perhaps, as the fifth century.

Leadership of women was not only found in Ireland nor only within women's monasteries. Many of the Celtic Christian female leaders held powerful ecclesial positions in communities consisting of both women and men. These "double monasteries" were evidently a normal feature of the earliest monastic life in Ireland and Britain. The most well-known abbesses over these double monasteries were Brigit of Kildare and Hild of Whitby. The latter was of Anglo-Saxon descent, but was mentored in Northumbria by St. Aidan, and thus very much affected by and in sympathy with the Celtic monks and their spirituality. The origins of these double monasteries of monks and nuns is unclear, although Cogitosus, a monk of Kildare and the seventh-century hagiographer of Brigit, describes the one at Kildare as a double monastery that must have originated at least one hundred years before he wrote. There the monks and nuns lived in separate quarters, but worshipped together in a common church in which the lay people joined them for liturgies. In Britain, during the seventh century, double monasteries were quite numerous, for we know of such establishments at Coldingham, Ely, Repton, Barking, Bardney, Wimborne (Dorset), and Wenlock.[65] This feature of the Celtic and Anglo-Saxon churches the Roman-appointed Theodore of Tarsus did not initially approve, but accepted as the custom of the land when he arrived at Canterbury in 669 to become archbishop, after a plague had wiped out most of the English episcopate.[66]

What is clear from early biographies of Brigit as well as the stories of Hild is that such powerful abbesses exercised an influence on their times that has almost no parallel in later history—except perhaps for Hildegard of Bingen in the twelfth century and Teresa of Avila in the sixteenth. Unfortunately, most of those double monasteries, including the smaller women's communities which were more vulnerable to attack, were destroyed by the Vikings in the ninth century when they laid waste to so much of the Celtic Church's monasteries and artistic treasures.

Reflections of the Celtic Christians' appreciation of women's gifts and leadership can be found in the hagiographies that have survived, especially the Irish. In the earliest, by Cogitosus, Brigit is portrayed as actively engaged in preaching and hearing a man's confession who had turned from a life dominated by lust to embrace a new way of life. In another, Ita gives penances after hearing the confessions of laypeople. In a third hagiography, Samthann is said to possess a marvelous crozier, a symbol of spiritual leadership often associated with a bishop, which worked miracles. (The early Benedictine abbesses at Kylemore Abbey in Ireland are pictured in oil paintings holding large croziers, possibly similiar to hers.) One medieval life even has St. Brigit ordained a bishop by another bishop, Bishop Mel, who was inspired by the Holy Spirit to do so, he says defensively, when asked by an episcopal colleague.[67] Bede the Venerable describes the creative leadership of Hild of Whitby in his ecclesiastical history who, besides being a good administrator, had the insight to encourage Caedmon (d. c. 680), now considered the first English Christian poet, to take his dreams seriously.[68]

Collaboration and Non-Dualism

Another significant quality of their spirituality was the high degree of collaboration between female and male church leaders, as well as ordained people and lay. This, of course, is bound to happen when women are recognized in theory and, most importantly, in practice as full equals with men, made as they are from the beginning in God's image (cf. Gn 1:27), and baptized in the name of Jesus who treated all as equals and friends. Collaboration is referred to in the earliest Life of St. Brigit, written by Cogitosus, when he describes Brigit's pastoral concern for her people, and alludes to the "holy partnership" between herself and the bishop she herself chose, and the imagery of the fruitful vine:

> Wishing to provide wisely and properly for the souls of her people, and anxious about the churches of the many provinces that had attached themselves to her, Brigit realized that she could not possibly do without a bishop to consecrate churches and supply them with various levels of ordained clergy. So she sent for a distinguished man, known for his virtues, through whom the Lord had worked many miracles, who was then leading a solitary life in the desert. Going herself to meet him, she brought him back into her company so that he might govern the church with her in his episcopal rank, and so that none of the ordained would be missing in her churches. Afterwards, he was anointed head and chief of all the bishops; she, the most blessed abbess of all the women. By their holy partnership and with the helping aid of all the virtues, she built her principal church at Kildare. Because of the talents of them both, her episcopal cathedral and monastery spread—like a fruitful vine with branches growing in all directions—throughout the entire island of Ireland.[69]

In Cogitosus's description of the church which existed about a hundred years after Brigit, we find allusions to the double-monastery of both women and men that Brigit originally built, and how the laity were intrinsic to monastic life, including the liturgy. From other descriptions of the early Celtic monasteries, we find that both celibate members within the monastic communities as well as lay people experienced the fruits of collaboration. Education, pastoral care, and liturgical leadership were provided by the monks or religious women; in turn, lay people and their families helped the monasteries grow their crops, manage their farms, fish, plant trees, and keep their bees. All benefited from this mutual sharing of gifts.

This spirituality, with its collaborative qualities, transcended the dualism that would plague Christianity for centuries, up until modern times: the dividing of reality into opposites or distinctions and then labeling or evaluating one side as not only better than the other, but the only true good. Rather than proposing dualities and promoting dualism, Celtic spirituality honored differences and integrated what might seem at first glance (or through long years of religious and cultural indoctrination) as opposites: mind and heart, body and soul, contemplation and action, solitude and community, male and female, people and nature, "sacred" and "secular," human and divine. It shows that perceived differences are not necessarily antagonistic toward each other, but that all may contribute to the richness of the whole. It was a spirituality that recognized the significance of families, of daily work, of the so-called "ordinary" as sacred ground for one's own soul-making.

Appreciation of the Marginalized

A fifth characteristic was the appreciation the Celts had for the marginalized, as well as for the marginalized places in their lives. Celtic Christianity, as Ian Bradley rightly points out, was a faith that emerged at the margins of Britain, continental Europe, and institutional Christianity.[70] The Celts themselves, as we've seen, were originally a nomadic people who experienced little stability and who possessed little wealth. Throughout much of their history, they lived close to nature, close to the elements, and close to God, but also close to homelessness and poverty. Precisely because of this, their Christian spirituality as reflected in the stories of the early saints reveals a sensitivity toward those whose lives, for whatever reason, were considered of less value, and a genuine outreach toward those whom others treated as outcasts. This is especially portrayed in the hagiographies of the Celtic women, and, not surprisingly, most pronounced in that of Brigit's stories.

Many stories tell of Brigit's compassion and of her friendship with the most rejected in her society, especially lepers. Throughout the Brigitine hagiographies that have survived, lepers seeking help from the saint of Kildare make up a major theme. One of the numerous stories tells of a leper whom she gives the best gift of all:

> The same Easter a leper came to saint Brigit and as he was covered with leprosy he asked Brigit for a cow. Not having a cow, she said to him, "Would you like us to pray to God for you to be cured of your leprosy?" He replied, "That to me would be the best gift of all." Then the holy virgin blessed water and sprinkled it on the leper's body and he was cured. He gave thanks to God and stayed with Brigit till his death.[71]

Perhaps the most vivid example of her ministry to the marginalized is the story of her doing what everyone else refuses to do. According to this story, a certain abbess asks her nuns on Maundy Thursday (a special feastday during Holy Week that celebrates Jesus' washing the feet of his disciples, *the* symbolic action of Christian ministry), "Which of you is going to do the washing of the feet today for our old people and our sick?" None of the nuns wanted to do this, so "they made excuses."

> Then Brigit said, "I am willing to wash the poor and sick women." Now there were four sick women in the one house: one a paralytic who was a helpless invalid, the second a possessed woman completely taken over by the demon, the third blind and the fourth a leper. Then Brigit began to wash the paralytic first and the latter said, "O holy Brigit, ask Christ to heal me." And Brigit prayed and at once the woman was healed, the leper cleansed and the deranged nun cured.[72]

Brigit's life and those of the other saints reveal how suffering and oppression have the possibility of leading to compassion and wisdom, wholeness and joy. It may be that, because of their own marginalization, they learned to rely on inner resources for strength and guidance. The Celts, both ancient and Christian, were certainly a people who valued marginal places within themselves: the imagination, intuition, second sight, dreams, visions, tears. Acquainted with grief, they knew that it was important to acknowledge their losses and express their pain openly in order to be healed, eventually, of their sorrows. At their wakes, frequently celebrated in the home of the deceased, life *and* death had a place at the table, the coffin, the bier. Even their art expressed the sometimes "terrible beauty" of marginality, for the most beautiful images and extraordinary poetic passages are not in the main text of such illuminated gospels as the Book of Kells, but in the margins, on the boundaries, where, for them, the sacred and wisdom itself are found.

A Profound Love of Beauty

A sixth quality that can be identified with Celtic spirituality is a profound love of beauty, an intuitive sense and deep love directly linked with the ancestors of the Christian Celts. The Celts had an eye for beauty: the beauty of the body, of the soul, of friendship, of the natural environment. Highly appreciative of the beauty of the landscape, as we've seen, the early Christian Celts built their monasteries in secluded valleys and forests, on the banks of broad rivers, near cascading streams and ocean tides. As J. Romilly Allen suggests, "No one who has visited any considerable number of ancient [Celtic] ecclesiastical buildings can fail to have been struck by the care which the monks took in selecting sites where feelings of religious devotion might be intensified by the contemplation of all that is beautiful in nature."[73] This same sentiment is experienced frequently by those who have visited the valley and lakes of Glendalough, looked across the River Shannon from its banks at Clonmacnoise, watched the crashing waves at Land's End in Cornwall and at Saint-Malo in Brittany, or felt the ocean spray after climbing the rock formations at Giant's Causeway.

In the recognition of nature's beauty in high places or ocean depths, Celts, both ancient and Christian, experienced an outright mystical connection with nature. This sense of spiritual kinship is reflected in their profound respect for the earth and the natural rhythms of body and soul, precisely because they did not see themselves as "lords" over creation, but spiritually, emotionally, and intellectually connected with it. It is found in the belief that their daily lives and work were united with their landscape, as well as with the changing seasons of the year. It is expressed too in their writings. Sun and moon, sea and lake, wind and fire, earth and sky, all have numinous associations in early Irish and Welsh literature, especially as we've seen in their poetry. It is no wonder that references to the elements of wind, storm, rain, and snow, as well as the glorious beauty and warmth of sunlight (when it finally appears!) are found in the stories of their heroes, and that the Christian God had so many elemental names.

Repeatedly in the stories from the Lives of the Celtic saints, we find this kinship with nature: in their awareness that animals are friends, birds have messages, waters can sing, and tree branches have melodies. From this perspective, it is not surprising that St. Gall, for one, when he founded his monastery in a valley between two streams in Switzerland, recalled "the words of Jacob after he had beheld the vision of the ladder and the angels ascending and descending thereon, [and] said, 'Truly the Lord is in this place!'"[74] Patrick Kavanagh, in modern times, echoes this same sense of wonder in his novel, *Tarry Flynn,* whose fictional hero is based upon Kavanagh's own life and mystical beliefs:

> The simple, fantastic beauty of ordinary things growing—
> marsh-marigolds, dandelions, thistles and grass.[75]

The pagan Celts were profoundly appreciative of beauty in all its numerous and diverse forms, reflected in the stories of their ancient heroes' awesome physical beauty, colorful clothing, varied styles of hair, and, of course, their unusual accomplishments. This same love of beauty—and passion for living—were passed on to the Christian Celts, and found expression in the high crosses, illuminated manuscripts, finely-designed chalices, croziers, and saints' reliquaries that can be seen today in the museums of Ireland, Scotland, England, Wales, and France. This love of beauty finds expression too in the Christian Celts' early prayers and hymns to Christ who is described as an "ever young" and "beautiful hero" with a "shapely branch of golden locks," and to Mary with her "twining tress of virgin hair."[76]

In another source, a medieval Welsh text, "The Food of the Soul," which contains highly erotic imagery of Christ, his entire body is described in detail, from his "shining curls of golden yellow hair" to his "slender and noble waist" to his "feet with white, and rounded toes." Obviously written by a poet, Christ's cheeks are compared to the radiance of dawn on a summer's day or "an evening sun setting over a mountain of shining gold, or a bright red wine sparkling through fine glass." His entire face radiates beauty: "So blessed was that face and so fair that no bodily creature of heaven or earth could be likened to it. It was like white snow at Epiphany, or white roses, or lilies, or apple-blossom, or highland gossamer, or fresh shoots, or a splendid sun in the sky, or an evening moon, or the sailors' star, or Venus when it is most beautiful in the firmament, or a summer's sun when it shines most clearly and brightly at midday in June."[77] In later prayers, composed in the Scottish Highlands, Christ is referred to as "the loveliness of all lovely desires," and "the loveliest likeness that was upon earth," as Mary is said to be "of purest fairest beauty, . . . brighter than the waxing moon rising over the mountains."[78]

This same love of beauty is also reflected in the lives of the saintly soul friends, some of whom were known for their physical beauty, including Ita who is described as having "such beauty that has never been seen before nor since," and Mochuda, who was so handsome that "thirty maidens loved him so passionately that they could not conceal it."[79] (It was Mochuda, the founder of the monastery at Lismore, whose own love of beauty affected the direction of his life. According to the story, when he first heard the chanted music of a certain bishop's retinue, he decided to become a monk because, as he said, "I have never heard anything so beautiful as this. . . .")[80]

One of the greatest works of Welsh spiritual literature is the poem "The Loves of Taliesin," which shows vividly the breadth and depth of the Christian Celts' understanding and appreciation of beauty, wherever it is found:

> The beauty of a companion who
> does not deny me his company . . .
> Beautiful too a man who is noble, kind and generous.
> The beauty of berries at harvest time,
> Beautiful too the grain on the stalk.
> The beauty of the sun, clear in the sky. . . .
> The beauty of desire and a silver ring. . . .
> The beauty of an eagle on the shore when tide is full,

Beautiful too the seagulls playing. . . .
The beauty of a proper and perfect wedding feast,
Beautiful too a gift which is loved. . . .
The beauty for a minstrel of mead at the head of the hall,
Beautiful too a lively crowd surrounding a hero. . . .
The beauty of the moon shining on the earth,
Beautiful too when your luck is good.
The beauty of summer, its days long and slow,
Beautiful too visiting the ones we love. . . .
The beauty of the garden when the leeks grow well,
Beautiful too the charlock in bloom. . . .
The beauty of the heather when it turns purple,
Beautiful too moorland for cattle. . . .
The beauty of the fish in his bright lake,
Beautiful too its surface shimmering.
The beauty of the word which the Trinity speaks,
Beautiful too doing penance for sin. . . .[81]

In this poem we see how the ancient Celts' love of the beauty of body, tribe, friendship, and nature is combined with Christian beliefs into an appreciation of another kind of beauty, one far most lasting than any physical beauty: the beauty of compassion, forgiveness, and wisdom; ultimately, the beauty of goodness itself. These very significant qualities Christian Celts found personified in the "beautiful Christ," and in their stories of the saints and soul friends. They came to recognize, as Plato had, that beauty, in all its manifestations, leads ultimately to the source and creator of all beauty, the holy one, God—a God whose immanence is reflected in all of creation. Again, Patrick Kavanagh's poetry captures this profound mystical awareness:

That beautiful, beautiful, beautiful God
Was breathing his love by a cut-away bog.[82]

Beauty, Celtic Christians believed, truly is a reflection of God—and of God's own love of beauty.

To be aware of God's beauty, to experience God's love, these Celts also believed, was to recognize the need for acknowledging in one's own life human limitations, perplexities, and sin.

Perhaps especially in the context of God's overwhelming love, a person can discover "the beauty of doing penance for sin," as the Welsh poem above suggests.

Sickness of Soul, and the Need for a Soul Friend

Grief and tears are manifestations of a seventh quality of this Celtic spirituality: its respect for sin and the desire to heal its destructive power. James Charles Roy, as we recall, mentioned the melancholy and heavy conscience of the Celts, especially the Irish, and how it may have come from the landscape, the weather, the influence of the desert Christians upon them. It may also have been the result of so much of the violence and promiscuity that characterized their society. Whatever the origin, Christian Celts had a sometimes healthy, sometimes overly scrupulous attitude towards sin, but, like John Cassian, they perceived it as a sickness of soul in need of remedies. This awareness was why they valued soul friends so much, and why they advocated frequent meetings with such a person in order to free their lives of insidious and sick patterns of behavior.

One of the most striking Celtic writings on the subject of sin and the need for healing is the "Litany of Confession," attributed to St. Ciaran, one of the Celtic Church's greatest soul friends, and associated with Clonmacnoise which he founded, a monastery known for its spirituality of penance and reconcilation. Invoking God as "rewarder, forgiving, loving, pre-eminent, immense, vast, mysterious," the writer also describes God as "true physician" and "true friend," "marrow of wisdom" and "true life." The Litany goes on to describe the effects of soul-sickness in realistic terms that anyone with a serious addiction would understand:

Come to help me, for the multitude of my inveterate sins
    have made dense my too guilty heart;
They have bent me, perverted me, have blinded me,
    have twisted me and withered me;
They have clung to me, have pained me, have moved me,
    have filled me;
They have humbled me, exhausted me, they have subdued
    me, possessed me, cast me down;

They have befooled me, drownded me, deceived me, and
   troubled me;
They have torn me, and chased me;
They have bound me, have ravaged me, have crucified me,
   rebuked me, sold me, searched me, mocked me;
They have maddened me, bewitched me, betrayed me,
   delayed me, killed me.

And, then, the simple cry and request from the heart comes
at the end of this confession: "Forgive."[83]

Whether the author of the litany was St. Ciaran or not, he
was quite obviously a person aware of human frailties and
human mortality. The Day of Judgment, for him and for all early
Celtic Christians, was not a distant event, but a daily possibility,
especially if we consider how quickly and unexpectedly one
could die then as the result of diseases, plagues (one of which
killed St. Ciaran), battles, or the coming of the Vikings. The
scene of the last judgment, portrayed on numerous high crosses,
including one of the finest, the "Cross of Scriptures" at
Clonmacnoise, was a constant reminder of this, and a challenge
to do something about it. All of this comes through in the closing
lines of the Litany:

> By thy coming again in the day of doom; Grant that I
> may be righteous and perfect, without great dread on
> me of hell or doom, without soreness or bitterness on
> thy part towards me, O Lord;
>   For my sins are blazing through me and around me,
> at me and towards me, above me and below me. Alas,
> Alas, Alas, forgive me, O God. . . .

In the final passage, the prayer seeks a total cleansing, and
also points to what might be an anointing of the body for death:

> From ears, from hands, etc.
> O true God, *tibi soli peccavi*; forgive, forgive, forgive.
> Amen.[84]

For anyone who has grievously hurt another, especially a
loved one, this awareness, and the desire to change, to seek
forgiveness does not necessarily reflect a morbid spirituality so
much as a daily, humble surrender to God, a healthy recognition
of one's own mortality, and of the honest need for soul-making.

Considering this, both clergy and laypeople, at least in their better moments, came to appreciate the gift of tears: those of joy and of compassion, but also those which express repentance, a change of heart, a new, ultimately more realistic picture of oneself. This is expressed in a tenth-century Irish prayer that speaks of contrition for sexual infidelity, anger, jealousy, pride, falsehoods, lying, and greed:

> Grant me tears, O Lord, to blot out my sins;
> may I not cease from them, O God,
> until I have been purified.
> May my heart be burned by the fire of redemption;
> grant me tears with purity for Mary and Ita. . . .
> Grant me tears when rising, grant me tears when resting,
> beyond every gift altogether for love of you, Mary's Son.[85]

This was the context in which soul friendship developed, one of the greatest gifts to the universal church, a tradition based upon the recognition of the need for an *anamchara:* a person who acts as a confidante, teacher, counselor, confessor, or spiritual guide.

The Yearning of the Heart

These, then, are the characteristics of Celtic spirituality, that yearning of the heart for God. They are what united the numerous and diverse Celtic monasteries into one spiritual community called the early Celtic Church. Although this church would eventually, over the centuries, be subsumed into the Roman ecclesial structures and administration, it would never be totally destroyed. For, if beauty, as the Greeks observed, has the power of attracting us or calling us (in Greek, *kaleo* means to call or beckon, while *to kalon* means beauty itself), then the early Celtic Church is still very much alive. The "lasting beauty" of which Nora Chadwick speaks continues to call out to us as an epiphany of God's powerful presence in history and in our own lives.

In the following chapter, we turn directly to those writings which explore the various roles and dimensions of soul friendship as it developed in the early Celtic Church.

F I V E

Songs

of

Praise

*O God of heaven, whoever creates a song of praise
for the saints, great will be that person's glory!*

Oengus the Culdee

*When Christ approaches to converse with the Celi De,
it is not in purple . . . he comes, but in the forms of
the miserable, of the sick and lepers.*

Life of Moling

The main source for our understanding of the Celtic Church's tradition of soul friendship is the hagiographies or Lives of the early Celtic saints. In the Celtic monasteries, constructed near rivers, lakes, and oceans, or deep within woodland areas, hagiographers from the seventh to the thirteenth centuries composed the Lives of literally hundreds of Celtic saints.[1] The flowering of Celtic monasticism which began with the "Golden" or "heroic age" of the early Celtic saints in the sixth and seventh centuries was followed in the late seventh, eighth, and ninth centuries with the writing of these Lives. The Christian hagiographers who first wrote down the stories and legends of the saints drew upon the rich oral tradition of storytelling about the saints which had been kept alive, sometimes for centuries preceding any writing. This earlier stratum of stories had been passed on by pagan and Christian druids, poets, and bards, and by communities and "witnesses" who knew the saints firsthand.

The oldest extant hagiography of a Celtic saint is that of St. Samson, the Welsh bishop who emigrated to Brittany where he founded a monastery at Dol. This Life was probably written in the early 600s at one of the monasteries of the early Celtic Church.[2] A few years later, about 640 C.E., Jonas, a monk from Bobbio, Italy, wrote his famous Life of the great Irish missionary, Columbanus.[3] In Ireland, the first hagiographer known by name is Cogitosus, a Leinsterman who was asked by the community of Kildare in the latter half of the seventh century to write a Life of their foundress, Brigit. Soon after, two other writers, Muirchu, a resident of Armagh and a protégé of Cogitosus, and Tirechan, a native of County Mayo, wrote Lives of St. Patrick. On the isle of Iona off the western coast of Scotland in the late 680s, less than a hundred years after St. Columcille's death, his successor, the abbot Adomnan, wrote a famous Life about that important missionary.

The seventh century, then, was the beginning of Celtic hagiographies which later generations of storytellers would rely upon for their new or expanded versions of saints' Lives. After the seventh century, the eighth and ninth centuries in particular saw the creation of more hagiographies, a number of them influenced, as we shall see, by the Celi De movement. Although the Lives of the Celtic saints which have survived were primarily compiled in the high medieval period (thirteenth to sixteenth centuries), many were written during this earlier period, and almost all contain primitive material that take us back to the earliest days of the Celtic Church, providing insight into the everyday life of Celtic Christians and the type of spiritual leadership they encouraged.

In order to gain a better understanding of these hagiographies and of the soul friends who appear in them, this chapter will explore the historical and literary influences which affected the composition and content of these Lives. In particular, the eighth-century Celi De (pronounced "kaelley day") reform movement will be examined which emphasized the need for soul friends as spiritual guides.

Historical Factors Affecting
The Hagiographies

Certain historical factors had a major influence upon the writing of these hagiographies of the early Celtic saints and their content. The first, of primary importance, is related to the emergence of the written word. Although the Latin language had been introduced to Britain when the Romans had invaded in 43 C.E., the pagan Celts in Ireland had no written language, except for the ogham script which, like a form of short-hand, was evidently used only on stones for markers and memorials. In their oral-based culture, the ancient Celts relied solely upon the spoken word and the highly disciplined memories of the bards and druids to communicate their rich heritage of genealogies, stories, sagas, and poems. With the coming of Christianity to Ireland, Latin became the language of church scholars. Irish ecclesiastical writings up until the eighth century, in fact, are nearly all in Latin. It was not until the late sixth century and seventh century that the Gaelic language (what scholars today refer to as "Old Irish") began to be used. From then on the vernacular grew in popular usage in the monastic schools, and a whole new body of written literature was born. Scribes at the monasteries were the first to write down what had once been strictly preserved orally. Robin Flower believes that the eighth and ninth centuries especially were times of much literary consolidation.[4] Not only were traditions of the earlier ages of the church gathered together in the Lives of the saints, but all sorts of other writings appear for the first time, including law tracts, sagas, heroic tales, and poetry. Out of that creative period, Irish and Welsh literature as we know it today took shape.

Another factor that had its effect upon the writing of the hagiographies was the growth in the size and wealth of the original monasteries which the early saints had founded in the fifth through seventh centuries. At the time the first Lives were written in the seventh century, many of the monasteries had become large population centers where lay and religious leaders received their education and spiritual formation. As we recall from the Venerable Bede's writings, numerous pilgrim scholars from Britain and the continent of Europe came to Ireland to study, frequently traveling to the monasteries and cells of various teachers. Oengus the Culdee, an Irish monk at the monastery of Tallaght, outside of Dublin, writing in the early ninth century, describes this phenomenon in his martyrology: "The cells that have been taken by pairs and by trios are now Romes, with multitudes, with hundreds, with thousands."[5] Those monasteries where the hagiographies were composed were usually large and wealthy communities. They probably had to be, since only the wealthy ones would have given hagiographers time away from other work, a scriptorium or library where they could compose the Lives, and the material necessary for writing in the first place. Each manuscript or illuminated gospel required large numbers of cattle for vellum or sheep for parchment; it is said that the vellum on which the Book of Kells was written cost the monastery one hundred and fifty calves.[6]

Dominating the ecclesiastical landscape of Ireland at that time were federations of monasteries known as *paruchiae*. During the seventh century, three monasteries in particular, those of Armagh, Kildare, and Iona, made claims to widespread jurisdiction and property over smaller monasteries and churches. It is interesting to note that the three earliest Irish Lives to survive are those written by scribes at Armagh promoting St. Patrick, at Kildare describing the wonder of St. Brigit and her double monastery, and at Iona lauding the accomplishments of St. Columcille. Other monasteries imitated their example, so that in the following centuries the country was dotted with a great variety of federations and monastic alliances. Later, as the monasteries grew even wealthier and more ambitious, rivalry between certain monastic families replaced the earlier friendships of the saintly founders, resulting sometimes in open warfare and mutual pillaging.

Hagiographers, of course, were influenced by the political climate of their age, and attempted to trace in the Lives of the early saints these later alliances and sometimes open rivalries— regardless of historical chronology. Mention, for example, in the *Book of Armagh* of the close friendship between Sts. Patrick and Brigit (i.e. "Between holy Patrick and Brigit, pillars of the Irish, there existed so great a friendship of charity that they were of one heart and one mind") clearly reflects alliances between Armagh and Kildare, rather than those two early saints' actual friendship.[7] Historically, it is highly unlikely the two ever met, for, if their biographical dates are at all accurate, Brigit would have only been about seven years old at the time of Patrick's death. The Lives of the Celtic saints also contain references to charters of the early monasteries or visits by certain saints that explain what territories and churches were (at the time the hagiographers wrote) under whose control. An unspoken purpose too of many of the later hagiographers seems to have been to bring *their* saint into contact with as many as possible of the famous early founders and missionaries in order to enhance their saint's reputation and, thus, the reputation of the hagiographer's monastery.

These political considerations were mixed with financial issues. Increasingly, a monastery's economic well-being was tied to its political and religious standing among the other monasteries. During the seventh century there developed, along with the demand for relics of the saints' bodies, the need for shrines and reliquaries in which to place them, as well as sumptuous books and jewelled croziers for the celebration of the saints' liturgical feastdays. This was a period which coincided throughout the universal church with the development of the cult of relics and the increasing popularity of the practice of pilgrimage. When other churches on the Continent were giving special honor to their martyrs, early bishops, and monastic founders, the Celts desired to do the same. They were, however, limited by their own history in which there were few noted martyrs. The Lives of the most well-known of Celtic saints, in fact, show that, though they all faced times of trial and outright persecution, none of them died a martyr's death. They either died in their beds or near them, or in close proximity to their churches or within them: Ciaran and his mentor, Finnian of Clonard, died of the yellow plague; Columcille, Ita, Hild, and David of lingering illnesses; Aidan, apostle to Lindisfarne, died leaning against the buttress of a church; Brendan, at the threshold of a church; Brigit in her monastery after being blessed by a cleric from Rome. It is not that they didn't have the courage for such a heroic form of death. Rather, as John Ryan says about the Irish: though such leaders as Columcille, Columbanus, and others "would have suffered torture and death gladly at the hands of Christ's enemies . . . the opportunities for this were not forthcoming in Ireland until the Norse incursions began at the end of the eighth century."[8] Without many martyrs, Christian Celts naturally turned to those of their own great monastic founders, and thus began to enshrine and display the relics of their first abbots and abbesses. The possession of a saint's Life to accompany, explain, and enhance the relics of that person then became important for each of the major monasteries.

Written stories to explain each founder's uniqueness, personal holiness, and spiritual power became increasingly more commonplace, and added credence to the growing pilgrim trade. These relics and shrines attracted financial support from the "locals" who were considered part of the founding saint's "extended family," whether they liked it or not. The Annals constantly report the circuit of relic shrines during the eighth through the tenth centuries to enforce payment of the saint's tribute. As the practice of pilgrimage became more widespread, many pilgrims also made their contribution to a monastery's wealth. Drawn first by word-of-mouth, they came ever more frequently to the monasteries in search of healing and help, as people had done during the original saints' lifetimes. The Lives which were written describing the saints' holiness and ability to work miracles attracted even larger crowds of pilgrims who brought with them offerings of prayers *and* money. With the increased emphasis at this time on relics and sacred articles associated with the saints, it is clear why there are so many references to bells, books, croziers, stones, and garments which appear in the Lives. Stories about them were obviously included by the hagiographer to explain both to the members of the monasteries and to the throngs of pilgrims the importance of certain relics then on display.

Motivations of the Hagiographers

Almost all of these Lives were written anonymously. Although there is no evidence that any of the hagiographers were women (no woman left her name on any surviving documents), some may have been, since women's communities, no less than men's, were places of learning and of scholarship. St. Brigit's double-monastery at Kildare, in particular, with its increasing wealth and scriptorium would have been one of the most likely places for female scribes to thrive.[9] While the saints' Lives suggest that a considerable number of Celtic women devoted themselves to monastic living in the early Celtic Church, most of the hagiographies which have survived are Lives of male saints.[10] This may be due to the fact that many of the women's communities were absorbed by their male counterparts after the death of their founder or were destroyed by rapacious Vikings who were especially effective in assaulting smaller religious houses. Some were also assimiliated by the Normans who, following their invasion of Ireland in the twelfth century, established their own convents. Patriarchal attitudes which negated the value of women's lives and leadership came to dominate much of the Western church, and this too contributed to the scarcity of stories about female saints. If something is not valued it is soon discarded.

Hagiographers when they set down to write the Lives did so with a variety of motives and, it seems, degrees of willingness. A number of their underlying motivations for writing the Lives have already been alluded to. At the time of an increased appreciation in the Western church for early saints and martyrs and their relics, hagiographers of the Celtic saints wrote to explain the greatness of their own spiritual ancestors and to give credence to their relics. At a time when the larger and wealthier monasteries were vying for political recognition, they wrote to prove their own monasteries' distinctiveness, if not superiority, and probably to prove which smaller churches belonged to whom. At the time when large numbers of monastic members necessarily demanded larger revenues, they wrote to gain financial support from their neighbors and to attract the pilgrim trade to their shrines. These very human and at times self-serving motivations, however, were not the only ones. For many of the hagiographers, a primary motive had to do with their spiritual ideals and theological convictions.

If we look closely at the texts of the writers of the Celtic Lives, a major reason they composed their hagiographies was to present the individual saint as a model and an exemplar of holiness for others to emulate. This motivation is most frequently expressed in the prefaces of the hagiographies, from the earliest to the latest Celtic Lives. Adomnan, writing on Iona in the seventh century, states that he hopes "to place before my reader's eyes an image of his [Columcille's] holy life."[11] Aelred of Rievaulx, in his *Life of Saint Ninian*, written in the twelfth century, speaks of "the desire of many of the wise who have lived before us to commit to writing the lives, the manners, and the words of the saints" in order to redeem them from oblivion, perpetuate their memories, and present "the example of the more perfect life for the edification of posterity."[12] Bernard of Clairvaux, who composed his *Life of Saint Malachy* in Gaul during the closing days of the Celtic Church, clearly expresses his purpose for writing: "It was always considered praiseworthy to record the illustrious lives of the saints so that they could serve as a mirror and good example; they could be as it were a relish for the life of men on earth. In this way they are still alive among us, even after death. They call back to the true life many of those who are dead while they live."[13] Hagiographers, then, primarily wrote the Lives because they believed that the saint whose life they were describing had something important to teach people about holiness, prayer, service, and ultimately union with God.

They also wrote to reveal the Celtic saints as powerful spiritual mentors and soul friends, capable of helping those who turn to them in prayer. They believed that the patron-saint of their monastery was, although dead, very much alive, and that he or she had a spiritual power capable of transforming the lives of those who called upon the saint. Jocelinus, author of the *Life of St. Kentigern,* patron of Glasgow, Scotland, clearly acknowledges this in his hagiography: "where[ever] his memory is held in honor, he [Kentigern] is present as a powerful helper in necessities to those who are placed in tribulations, to those who love him, and trust him, and call upon him."[14] Rhigyfarch, the medieval biographer of David of Wales, states that the saint "performs those works more effectively, since, having laid aside the burden of the flesh and having gazed upon God face to face, he clings more closely to Him."[15] For many hagiographers, this spiritual kinship with the saints was based upon the beliefs of their pagan and Christian ancestors, and, most likely, their own experiences.

Friendship with the saints and appreciation of them as living soul friends had its origins in the pagan Celts' deep respect for the dead. It was also rooted, of course, in the ancient Christian belief that all those who die in Christ live eternally with him. This latter belief was probably accepted immediately by the Celts when they were baptized by Patrick and other wandering saints, precisely because their first mentors, the druids and druidesses, had taught them that the soul was immortal and that their daily life was bounded by a world inhabited by spirits. As we've seen, *Samhain,* one of the major pagan festivals celebrated November 1 at the beginning of the Celtic new year, was linked with the spirits of the dead, and paying honor to them.

The writers of the saints' Lives, immersed in this culture and religious tradition that merged both pagan and Christian beliefs, were, thus, firmly convinced of the efficacy of calling upon the saints. Living in monastic communities, they also knew first-hand about human limitations, angry resentments, petty jealousies, wide ambitions, the proclivity—without compassion—to think only of oneself. Members of a larger society, they were aware too of the precariousness of life, the fatality of yellow fever, the violence of tribal wars, and the persistence of other illnesses affecting soul and body. They naturally turned not only to God, but also to the saints and angels for help, and in that turning, frequently received some form of response. Sometimes that response might have been quite dramatic: perhaps an especially memorable dream that offered guidance and a sense of new direction; perhaps an inner healing of a deep and aching wound or an ability finally to let go, forgive, and move on; perhaps some sort of physical healing that could not be explained by the medicine of their day. Maybe it was simply an experience of things "coming together" for the well-being of the person. Bede describes this as *pulchraque rerum concordia*, a beautiful harmony of events which theologians have named "providence" or "grace."[16] Carl Jung gives the name "synchronicity" to these meaningful coincidences, a psychological term which in no way explains the mystery behind things happening as they do.[17] At other times, the hagiographers may have experienced, as people have throughout the centuries, an almost tangible sense of presence that inspires fear and trembling, wonder and awe.

However varied the experience, when the hagiographers of the Celtic saints sat down to write, many of them did so with conviction that, as their prayers had been heard, so others' might be as well. They did not set out to deceive their readers, but to tell the truth—as they understood that reality from the perspective of their Christian faith and hope.

Literary Sources

In order to tell the stories of the saints and to express the mystery of their lives, a mystery that touched their own, the hagiographers of the early Celtic Church necessarily turned to certain sources. When possible, they relied upon information from living friends and monastic colleagues of the saints themselves. Writers such as Adomnan and Bede refer directly to these "learned and faithful ancients."[18] From these ancients or the oral tradition that they had passed on, hagiographers constructed specific incidents connected with a particular saint that would enhance his or her reputation. Inspired by certain hagiographies in other lands, they frequently borrowed contents directly from them or modeled their own writings upon other works. Those most popular at the time the first Celtic hagiographies were composed were Athanasius's *Life of Antony*, Cassian's *Conferences,* and Jerome's Lives, especially the *Life of Paul*. Another hagiography, Sulpicius Severus's *Life of St. Martin* (of Tours), also influenced significantly a number of early Celtic Lives, including the hagiography of Columcille by Adomnan.[19]

Other writers portray such Celtic saints as Ninian, Columcille, Senan, and Columbanus either learning directly from Martin or praying at his tomb. The obvious veneration of St. Martin in the early Irish church is reflected in the fact that the *Book of Armagh* which includes Patrick's *Confessio* and another Patrician hagiography by Muirchu also contains Sulpicius Severus's *Life of St. Martin*, leading some scholars to conclude that St. Martin's life may have been a model for Muirchu's.[20] That the two Lives are so closely linked surely shows some spiritual kinship between the two leaders.

When Celtic hagiographers began to write down the stories of their own saints, they relied upon these literary sources. The ultimate literary source for all of them, however, was the Bible, primarily the New Testament. Some references are made to the Old Testament, but these tend to be more by way of briefly comparing a particular saint to some Jewish hero than actually full stories. In the introduction of the *Life of Brendan*, for example, the Irish voyager is said to have been like "faithful Abraham, a pre-eminently prophetic psalmist like David . . . , a distinguished sage like Solomon . . . , a lawgiver to hundreds like Moses. . . ."[21] The Lives of the Celtic saints, however, are primarily linked with the stories of Jesus. Celtic hagiographers, immersed in those stories from the New Testament, portrayed each saint not only as an extraordinary person, but above all as an *imago Christi*, a living symbol or image of Christ. Believing, as they did, that Jesus was *the* revelation of both what it means to be divine and to be fully human, they showed the Celtic saints doing in their time what Jesus did in his: healing the sick, feeding the hungry, praying in solitude, having intimate friendships with both women and men, calming the sea, even raising the dead. The Celtic saints' Lives reflect each saint's spiritual kinship with Jesus: how all of them, by uniting their hearts and minds with his, were changed profoundly by Jesus and his story. By implication, it suggested to the readers of those hagiographies how their own spirituality was meant to be shaped, as the saints' lives were, by the life of the beautiful God, Jesus, who was considered to be a primary soul friend.

In addition to this religious pattern portraying the saints as linked intrinsically with the life of Christ, other sides of the saint's personality frequently appear in these early stories. At times the saints seem to be living according to a different standard than that of the Sermon on the Mount. In some of the legends about St. Patrick, for example, we find him cursing his enemies, especially the druids, and in other ways attacking and punishing those who are opposed to him. Other monastic founders, voyagers, and missionaries sometimes employ similar means for maintaining their claims against each other or of vanquishing their foes. These stories in particular reveal the influence of the earlier pagan culture which had its own understanding of what constitutes a genuine hero. Here, in the tales with their sometimes humorous overtones, and in the stories of the saints' kinship with animals and even their potent cursing, we find intimations of how much the Christian hagiographers were often influenced by the ancient pagan bardic storytellers.[22]

According to the pagan Celts, their heroes, both male and female, were people of great physical beauty with unusual magical powers, including the ability to change shapes and even to transcend space and time. They also were flesh-and-blood individuals not only filled with human idealism but susceptible to human error. Once the monks of the monasteries in the seventh, eighth, and ninth centuries began to write down their remembrances of the early saints, they naturally presented them in a guise that the Celtic people would accept, and even expect of any of their heroes, including their religious ones. Thus, certain saints are depicted as having virtues that one might connect with any warrior, such as strength, loyalty, and bravery. Practices such as boasting and reviling one's enemies were included in their descriptions of what the saints said and did. As Kathleen Hughes suggests, "the picture of the saint is infinitely varied," and, according to medieval writer Gerald of Wales, Irish saints in particular were "more prone to anger and revenge and more vindictive than saints of any other country."[23] Not to be discounted here, of course, may also be the Celtic temperament which was alluded to earlier: the Celts' tendency to be a people of extremes, capable of being both blissful and rageful in a short amount of time.

Whatever the saints' depictions or mood swings, the early hagiographers saw little demarcation between ordinary tales and religious ones, and there was often a blending of the two. This blending is clearly evident when we find how frequently hagiographers incorporated into the Lives of the saints certain

folktales which were popular at the time they wrote.[24] Traces of
these folktales appear in the stories of Brendan's voyage to the
Promised Land, Brigit's talented fox at the court of an Irish king,
David's marvelous horse which Findbarr rode across the Irish
Sea, and Kevin's encounter with a fairy-witch. Celtic hagiography
is full of these mythic components, the language of folktales,
fairytales, visions, and dreams.

This "language," related so much to the transforming power
of symbols, was not used to deceive or to mislead readers of the
hagiographies, but to provide them with intimations of the
saint's greatness and assurances that each saint was especially
loved, protected, and guided by God. Throughout human history
the language of symbols has been used not only to describe
mysterious events in the outer world, but also to disclose inner
realities which are sometimes more real—and more
influential—than what can be perceived by the human eye. They
often determine and profoundly shape the course of outer events
as well as the development of character—what the ancients
called, quite simply, the realm of the "soul." Ancient people,
including the writers of the gospels, the fathers and mothers of
the early church, and the Christian Celts themselves did not
invent the great mysteries described in the saints' lives (i.e.,
birth, love, suffering, forgiveness, death, and rebirth). They
experienced them first, and then used the language of symbols in
an attempt to express their awesome mystery to their readers.

The Celi De Reform Movement

Besides the historical factors, religious motivations, and
literary sources already discussed, another major influence on
the composition of the Celtic hagiographies was the rise of the
reform movement known as the Celi De in the eighth century. It
grew in prominence at a time when the Celtic Church was
increasingly being challenged by the leadership of the church in
Rome and her sympathizers, and when the Vikings were
beginning their raids along the coasts, and then farther inland.
Regarding the Norsemen, the first attack in Ireland occurred in
795, and the worst "drowning" or destruction of sacred books
took place from 830-870—about the same time as the Celi De
movement was growing in popularity. The Vikings did not limit
their attacks to Ireland, but ravaged many of the monasteries of
the early Celtic Church throughout Wales, Scotland, England,

Brittany, and the Isle of Man. These incursions, along with the assimilation of the Celtic Church that will be discussed later, surely contributed to monastic hagiographers' desire to preserve, through their writing, what they perceived to be a threatened heritage.

Another unsettling development in the early ninth century was the rivalry between some of the monasteries which resulted, at times, with them actually going to war with each other. In 807, for example, there was a battle in Ireland between the monastic family of Cork and the community of Clonfert, "with a great slaughter of the men of the church and of the noblest of the *familia* of Cork." In 817 a war between the community of Taghmon against the house of Ferns resulted in four hundred persons being slain. In 824 the community of Kildare was plundered by Tallaght. One of the most violent men, Feidlimid, king of Cashel who reigned from 820-847, not only killed the monastic families of Clonmacnoise and Durrow in 833, but in 836 attacked the oratory at Kildare and imprisoned its leaders.[25] At the time many people, clergy and laity alike, were obviously alarmed by this ecclesial development, and what they perceived to be a lack of genuine leadership throughout the early Celtic Church. They also were concerned about the loss of their original founders' ideals. Anytime Christians are disillusioned or dissatisfied with the Christianity of their day, they naturally ask the questions, "Where is God?" "How do we recognize and express the sacred?" and, "Who models for us the holy life?" Bede the Venerable, writing in Northumbria at this time, was at least implicitly asking these questions as he wrote his great work *Ecclesiastical History of the English People*. His portrayal of such saints as Aidan, Hild, and Cuthbert as exemplars of the holy life provided his readers with his own answers to those questions, his own theology of what constitutes effective ministry, authentic church life, and meaningful spirituality. Bede, however, though surely the most outstanding, was not the only one desirous of reform. Other individuals and communities throughout Ireland and the Britain whom scholars have identified as "Culdees" or Celi De (a term which means "friends" or "servants" or "people of God")[26] were likewise disenchanted and in search of renewal.

The Celi De movement originated in Ireland at the very time more lives and martyrologies were being written down. It gave

———— ✤ ————

impetus to the growing devotion to the saints and the emphasis upon soul friend relationships. This movement consisted of both lay people and ordained, many of whom were married, who wanted to recover the lost traditions of their spiritual ancestors, and thus bring new life into their own churches and monasteries.[27] Much of their inspiration was found in the ascetic ideals of the desert fathers and mothers, expressed in the stories of Athanasius, Jerome, and John Cassian, as well as those told about St. Martin of Tours in which Martin, like the Celi De, is called "a friend of God."[28] Although some of the more conservative Celi De leaders would probably not have admitted it, much of it also came from the spirituality of their pagan forebears who appreciated the native beauty of the land, the realm of the spirit world, and the druids' teachings and mentoring.

Both desert and pagan Celtic heritages came together in the Celi De's beliefs that simplicity was a virtue to cultivate, that the solitary life had special advantages, and that a spiritual guide or *anamchara* was especially helpful for the enrichment of one's life. In their appreciation of poverty, they sought a more ascetic lifestyle; in their respect for scripture and theology, they advocated the revitalization of monastic studies; in their commitment to prayer, they espoused both liturgical reform and long hours on one's knees; and, in their love of nature and the natural environment, they built hermitages in isolated areas, near lakes and among the forests of oak and pine. In order to show their commitment to this reform and their respect for the desert Christians, some of their monasteries even took the name *dysert* (meaning "desert" or "retreat"). The large increase, in fact, during the late eighth and ninth centuries in the rise of anchorites and hermits can be associated with the Celi De. The records of the movement which have survived clearly demonstrate, however, that it was not only in solitary retreats that the Celi De improved their souls, but with the help of confessors and spiritual guides called soul friends.

A number of reputable scholars, including Robin Flower, Ludwig Bieler, Padraig O'Fiannachta, and Peter O'Dwyer are convinced that this reform movement had a major effect on the spiritual writing of the times, on religious devotion, monastic renewal, and Irish and Welsh literature, especially the beautiful nature poetry that began to be written. They also believe that the

earliest religious works written in Irish were the product of the
Celi De, and that this reform movement affected the writings
and content of the monastic rules, penitential books, and
hagiographies.[29] Other scholars believe that the Celi De affected
ecclesial art, including the high crosses which are still visible
throughout Ireland, Scotland, Wales, and England. In Ireland,
before the Celi De, the high crosses were relatively simple
creations, but with the reform movement and its dedication to
recovering its spiritual heritage, the spirals and interlacings
found on the earliest crosses, such as those at Ahenny, began to
give way to figured scenes found on the high crosses of Durrow,
Moone, Kells, Clonmacnoise, Castledermot, and Monasterboice.
These scenes depict not only figures from the Old and New
Testaments, as mentioned earlier, but also the Celi De's own
exemplars and mentors, the desert Christians and Celtic saints.

Concerning the hagiographies themselves, three themes
which appear frequently in the writings of the Celi De are
specifically expressed in the Lives which were produced during
this time: first, the advocacy of spiritual disciplines, especially
solitude, prayer, and simplicity of life; second, a profound
devotion to the saints; and, third, a belief in the value of an
anamchara not just when one wants to confess or seek advice
concerning serious sins, but for one's ongoing spiritual
development. When the hagiographers wrote about the early
Celtic saints, they naturally emphasized those aspects of
spirituality and ministry which resonated with their own. They
were not, however, simply inventing these elements. Those
themes and practices were already there as gifts from their
ancestors, pagan druid and Christian saint alike. Their
emphasis, of course, affected the hagiographies which were
written later or revised.

The chief leaders of this reform movement in Ireland were
Maelruain (d. 792), the founder, abbot, and bishop of the
monastery of Tamlachta (Tallaght), and Dublittir (d. 796), abbot
of Finglas. The monasteries of Tallaght and Finglas were known
as "the two eyes of Ireland," possibly because of the clear vision
of spirituality which they advocated.[30] Other monasteries in
Ireland especially associated with the movement were
Clonmacnoise, Louth, Lismore, Terryglass, Clonfert, Ferns, and
Clonbroney. Samthann (d. 739), abbess of Clonbroney in Co.
Meath, evidently had a significant influence upon the

movement's rise since, in writings linked with Tallaght, she is
portrayed as an early soul friend of Maelruain. In a separate Life,
probably written at the end of the eighth century or the
beginning of the ninth, she seems to epitomize Celi De reform
when she is described as a "Servant of God" committed to
outreach to the poor and poverty herself (i.e., "She refused to
possess lands and never had more than six cows").[31] One story,
in particular, compares her care for a poor leper to St. Martin of
Tours, revealing Martin's popularity among Celtic Christians,
especially the Celi De:

> One day the holy Samthann rose very early and heard
> the voice of a certain leper at the other side of the pond.
> He was asking in a loud voice to be brought across the
> water. Responding to his wishes, the holy virgin guided
> a boat with her staff and brought him across. Since he
> was complaining of his poverty and lack of clothing,
> she gave him a cow with a calf and her cloak, as though
> she were another Martin [of Tours]. When she asked
> him from where he had come, he said that he had come
> from holy Ultan's monastery. The cow and calf which
> that leper received were later found in the cattle-shed
> where they had previously been and there was no sign
> of any tear in holy Samthann's cloak.

Samthann was also a person who believed that charity begins
at home, with those we live and work, since it was said about
her: "She was extremely careful in her charity to all but
especially to those of her own household."

Above all, Samthann is portrayed by her hagiographer as a
woman of prayer, as someone who knocked frequently "at the
doors of divine mercy." There are many references to her
prayers for the liberation of hostages and captives. (Clearly, this
seizure and exchange of hostages was a common political
practice of her times.) As a result of her dedication to prayer, we
also find Samthann identified not only as a pray-er, but as a
teacher of prayer: someone, according to a story in her Life, who
is asked by a monk in what position it is best to pray—lying or
sitting or standing? She wisely replies, "We must pray in every
position." This commitment to prayer was a quality highly
valued by the Celi De. The manner of her death also reflects the
esteem others had for her, including her God:

On the night on which she gave her soul to heaven, the holy abbot Laserian . . . saw with his eyes wide-open two moons, one of which came down to him. Remembering his request to her that she bend towards him when she was going to the heavenly kingdom, he recognized that she was in the form of a star. And he said: "Well done, faithful servant of God, Samthann, because you are now about to enter the joy of your Lord and Spouse." Thus she disappeared, ascending to heaven where she enjoys eternal life for endless ages. Amen.[32]

At least two other figures were key leaders of the Celi De reform in Ireland: Oengus the Culdee and Maeldithruib. Both men were mentored by Maelruain when they were younger, and each contributed a great deal to the reform's popularity. Oengus was born in the mid-eighth century and died March 11, 824. A story from the preface of the *Martyrology of Oengus* which he composed at Tallaght expresses his great appreciation of soul friends, his devotion to the communion of saints, and perhaps some of the motivation for his work:

Once upon a time, Oengus set forth from his hermitage in Munster in order to find Maelruain in Tallaght for his soul friend. He saw a grave in the church and all over it were angels climbing up to heaven. So Oengus asked the priest of the church, "who has been buried there?" "A certain wretched person who lived near this place," replied the priest. "What good has he done?" Oengus asked. "Truly, we did not see any good done by him," the priest said, "except that on lying down and rising up he recounted the saints of this world." "O God of heaven," Oengus exclaimed, "whoever creates a song of praise for the saints, great will be that person's glory!"[33]

Oengus's martyrology, put together about 800, contains a number of significant references to the *anamchara*, including the famous lines spoken by St. Brigit that "anyone without a soul friend is like a body without a head; is like the water of a polluted lake, neither good for drinking nor for washing."[34] The martyrology itself is a concrete expression of the reform movement's love of the saints, and its respect for the leaders and

---

heroes of Christian faith, including Oengus's own mentor and guide, Maelruain, whom the martyrology calls "the splendid sun of the Gaels' island." Oengus's soul friendship with his teacher, whose feastday was July 7, evidently lasted a lifetime, for he tells us that visiting Maelruain's grave "heals the sighs of my heart," and he continues to pray to him for guidance:

> May my tutor bring me unto Christ
> Dear beyond affection
> By his pure blessing
> with his heart's desire.[35]

What is the source of a Christian's power to bring about transformation in the church and world? According to Oengus, in his martyrology's prologue:

> This is the [true] strength—
> Great love of Mary's Son.[36]

A collection of memorabilia which were written down at Tallaght after Maelruain's death often mentions Maeldithruib (d. 840), the second student of Maelruain's who was called "anchorite and sage of Tir da Glas [Terryglass]." This collection also has frequent references to "sons of life" or "children of life" or "servants of God," phrases which the Celi De applied to themselves and which appear in the hagiographies of such saints as Ciaran, Findbarr, and Samthann, as well as other Celi De documents.[37] In one story about Maeldithruib from this collection, he asks his mentor Maelruain "whether it was enough to recite fifty psalms, if there happened to be instruction along with them?" Maelruain replies that he considered the recitation of all the psalms in the Bible "not too much of a task."[38] In another story about a conversation between Maeldithruib and Maelruain, the younger man finds that his teacher affirms the need for his followers to listen to the yearnings of their hearts—yearnings or wishes, in fact, that contain the central ideas of the Celi De movement:

> Maeldithruib said to Maelruain: "I have long had four
> very dear wishes. My first wish was to read and to cast
> my eyes over whatever sacred reading had come into
> the country. Another dear wish of mine was that,

wherever there is a household of the holiest men in this country, I might attend to those saintly people and earn their blessing. My next wish was that I might attain my fill of conversation with you. And the last was that I might earn the blessing of your people here, both those that we should discourse with and those we should not." Maelruain responded to him: "Our saintly friend, Fer da Chrich, said to us, speaking of such things, 'Let the good desires of their hearts be granted to the sons of life, for they will be rewarded according to the results those desires bring about.'"[39]

Much of what is known about the Celi De took place at the monastery of Tallaght, located just south of Dublin. It was from there that the movement spread in Ireland to Tipperary, Cork, Kildare, and Westmeath, and from Ireland to other parts of the Celtic Church in Northumbria, Scotland, Iona, and Wales, including Bardsey Island off the Welsh coast.[40] In Ireland, the Celi De seem to have lasted longest in the monastery of Terryglass in Co. Tipperary where Maeldithruib had retired when he left Tallaght. Tallaght itself, dedicated to God and St. Michael, was a gift from a king of Leinster to Maelruain in 774 at the time when, as the *Martyrology of Tallaght* states, "Maelruain came with his relics of martyrs and virgins to Tallaght."[41] Three famous documents of the Celtic Church originated there: the *Stowe Missal*, the *Martyrology of Tallaght*, and the *Martyrology of Oengus*. Another document, quoted earlier regarding Maeldithruib, is simply entitled "The Monastery of Tallaght," and was first translated by scholars E. Gwynn and W. Purton in 1911. Besides the Rules of the Celi De associated with Maelruain, this document provides the fullest explanation of the Celi De spirituality which Maelruain espoused.[42] All of the writings seem to have been, as reform movements are, closely tied to the personality and ideals of the founder.

Aspects of Celi De Spirituality

Certain stories give intimations of the spirituality which Maelruain passed on to his followers, and, through them, to the Celtic hagiographers. Two stories in particular allude to Maelruain's ascetic disposition. The first story, relating the

———— ❧ ————

practices of abstinence and fasting at Tallaght, is similar to the description of St. David of Wales in the twelfth-century hagiography by Rhigyfarch:[43]

> Not a drop of beer was drunk in Tallaght during Maelruain's lifetime. When his monks used to go anywhere else, they would not drink a drop of beer with anyone they happened to meet. However, when they went a long distance, they were allowed to drink. Not a morsel of meat was eaten at Tallaght in his lifetime either unless it were a deer or wild swine. What meat there was at Tallaght used to be consumed by the guests. Then Dublitir [of Finglas monastery] came to Maelruain to urge him to grant his monks relaxation on the three chief feasts [Christmas, Easter, and Pentecost], even if it were not allowed after nor before those days. Maelruain replied: "As long as I shall give rules, and as long as my injunctions are observed in this place, the liquor that causes forgetfulness of God shall not be drunk here." "Well," said Dublitir, "my monks shall drink it, and they shall be in Heaven along with yours." "Anyone of my monks who listens to me and keeps my Rule," Maelruain replied, "will not need to be cleansed by the fire of Doomsday, because they will be clean already. Your monks, however, will perhaps have to be cleansed by the fire of Doom."[44]

A second story describes Maelruain's aversion to music. This personal quality and the story itself are very similar to those found in the *Life of St. Brendan* whose monastery at Clonfert was one of the main places in Ireland of the Celi De. In the Tallaght document:

> Maelruain did not approve of listening to music. There was a certain piper, Cornan, who lived in Desert Lagen, and he was an anchorite. They called him Cornan of the Glen, a man of grace. Presents used to be sent to him from Maelruain. He said once to Maelruain's monks, "I would be entirely happy if I could play a tune for the cleric." Then Maelruain answered, "Tell Cornan, these ears are not lent to earthly music so that they may be lent to the music of Heaven alone."[45]

The impression, thus, is given that, although Maelruain surely was a charismatic individual or he would not have had such a profound effect on the reform movement, he must have been a difficult person with whom to live. Despite the apparent rigidity (by our standards) of Maelruain and some of his monastic practices, there are intimations of pastoral sensitivities. In the same Tallaght writings everyone is told to regulate his own diet "for the course of nature differs in each person." Maelruain also allows thirsty students to drink water when they need to do so. He says too that the rigor of the rule does not apply to the infirm or elderly. The principle of moderation in all things, including the recitation of the divine office is enunciated in the sayings, "Different folk for different hours," and "according to each person's infirmity."[46]

There are other references to the lifestyle which Maelruain's monks embraced when they came to live with him: a strict diet, long hours in prayer, many genuflections, and standing long hours in water "for the purpose," the Tallaght document says, "of crushing and subduing desires and longings; or else as an additional labor of piety."[47] Cross-vigils, praying for an extended period of time with one's arms outstretched in imitation of Christ hanging on the cross, were also highly recommended. The scene of Moses with his arms being held up by Aaron and Hur, pictured on the west face of the top panel of Muiredach's high cross at Monasterboice, provides an example of what this must have looked like—although it gives no idea of how extreme the pain was when practiced by oneself, without the aid of others.

Another aspect of Celi De spirituality at Tallaght and elsewhere included great respect for and outreach to the poor and to strangers—a trait rooted in the earliest and deepest strains of Judeo-Christian spirituality. This characteristic of hospitality to the poor and to lepers, as well as to pilgrims and strangers was a constant attribute of the Celi De. One story from the *Life of St. Moling*, an abbot of Ferns and a prolific poet, is very similar to the one found in St. Martin's Life.[48] Here it reflects Celi De's values as well as that reform movement's obvious knowledge of and identification with Sulpicius Severus's stories. It describes how the devil, disguised as a youth wearing a purple garment, came to the saint who asks who he is. The devil says, "I am Christ, the son of God." "This is not possible," said Moling: "when Christ approaches to converse with the Celi De, it is not in purple . . . he comes, but in the forms of the miserable, of the sick and lepers."[49] Both stories, one from Martin's life and one from Moling's, may have originated in the desert Christians' admonishment to be always discerning about the devil appearing disguised as an angel of light.

In terms of Maelruain's own community at Tallaght, he is portrayed as telling his monks that any food left over from their meals (which must have been quite meager anyway) was to be given to the poor, "for they [the poor] have nowhere to go to beg anything." His followers frequently ate only gruel. A story in the Tallaght writings about the origin of gruel reflects not only this dietary asceticism, but also certain ecological implications that might be appreciated today:

> There was once a great gathering of the saints of Ireland at Mag Lena. This is what brought them together: they were grieved that penitents died on bread and water in the days of the elders who lived before them. They fasted against God on account of this. Then an angel came to them and said, "Wonder not if the bread and the water cannot sustain penitents today. The fruits and plants of the earth have been devastated, so that there is neither strength nor force in them to support anyone. Falsehood, sin, and the injustice of men have robbed the earth's fruits of their power. When men are obedient to God's will the plants of the earth retained their proper strength. At that time water was no worse for sustaining anyone than milk is today." Then the angel told them to mix some meal with their butter to make gruel, so that the penitents should not perish when the water and bread did not suffice to sustain them.[50]

Another characteristic especially connected with Celi De spirituality was their great respect for the dead (like their pagan ancestors) and the communion of saints. Maelruain strongly recommended to his followers the practice of remembering the dead and praying for them. The effectiveness of such prayers is expressed in the form of a wisdom saying and an admonition:

> There is nothing that a person does on behalf of one who dies that does not help that dead person, whether it be vigil or abstinence, or reciting intercessory prayers

or almsgiving, or frequent blessings. Maedoc and all his monks were a full year on bread and water to obtain the release of the soul of Brandub mac Echach. Sons ought to do penance for the souls of their departed parents.[51]

Most of the hagiographies of the Celtic saints end with requests to God or to the saint directly that the writer and those who read the life will someday be united with all of the saints in heaven—a wish, surely, of Oengus the Culdee.

Considering all of this, perhaps the Celi De spirituality espoused by Maelruain and expressed in the hagiographies composed at the time of that reform movement is most succinctly summarized in this one line: "Spare diet, early rising, frequent prayers, and loving gaze fixed on the friends that lie in the churchyard beneath your feet."[52]

This loving gaze, of course, was probably most pronounced when a soul friend was one who was buried there.

Soul Friendship and the Celi De

The theme of soul friendship, found in numerous Celtic hagiographies, is frequently mentioned in the Tallaght writings of the Celi De.[53] The practice of seeing an *anamchara* on a regular basis seems to have been expected of all committed Christians, both clergy and laity, at the time of that reform movement. Maelruain advocated that this consultation with a soul friend should occur at least once a year: "This we received from Maelruain: To consult one's *anamchara* once a year regularly, if he be at a distance; if he be nearer, however, to consult him oftener."[54] When spiritual direction and confession are specifically related to the giving of a penance (a practice not limited to priests, as we've seen), Maelruain recommends the performance of the penance which has been agreed upon. He also saw the value of full and honest self-disclosure, and expected it when a person confessed. This principle is enunciated in a story about a soul friend named Helair:[55]

This is what Helair did in the matter: at first he had received many [penitents], but he ended by sending them all away, because he saw that their penance was not zealously performed, and also that they concealed their sins when making confession. After that he finally refused to receive anyone at all for spiritual direction. However, he would sometimes allow holy persons to consult with him.[56]

Maelruain's expectations presupposed that individuals not go from one soul friend to another, since that practice could result in superficial relationships and possibly a great deal of confusing advice. Anyone who seeks a new spiritual guide or confessor should do so only after terminating the previous relationship he or she had, as Maelruain inquires of one of his students, "Did you ask permission of those whom you left before coming here?"[57]

A story, involving a married couple with ten sons who were living under the spiritual guidance of a soul friend by the name of Eocha ua Tuathail, clearly expresses how both lay people and clergy could benefit from having an *anamchara*. As the story unfolds, a layman is murdered, and, after his death, certain other lay people ask the question, "What did it avail him to live virtuously?" Eocha, the murdered man's soul friend, goes at once to see Dublitir, the abbot of Finglas monastery:

> Dublitir told him to distribute half or a third of the layman's substance to the poor, and that one of his sons should offer to God his body and soul, and for seven years should observe on his father's behalf the penance his father would have performed. He also recommended that the man's wife should do penance on her own behalf and on her husband's for the same period. When all of this was done, his son and wife came to communion seven years later. That night the layman appeared to Dublitir, seven years after his death, with shining countenance and glistening raiment. Then he gave Dublitir a blessing for the help that had been given him, and said to him, "This night the Lord has taken pity on me and has brought me out of hell to the kingdom of heaven." Afterwards, he appeared the same night to Eochu and to his wife and son and blessed them, telling them the same.[58]

A similar story is told in the *Life of Ita* about her uncle who dies and goes to hell and is also saved by the penitential practices and prayers of his sons who are counseled by Ita, their aunt. (Although hell may seem a horribly unjust punishment for both men, especially since they apparently raised families of committed Christians—judging from their willingness to undertake severe penitential practices for the sake of their fathers—church theologians at this time had not yet developed the concept of a *temporary* place where expiation for one's sins can be made [i.e., purgatory], and thus portrayed people as going either directly to heaven or hell.)[59] Besides revealing the efficacy of prayers and penitential practices for the dead, both stories confirm the value of having soul friends.

There are, however, in the Celi De documents intimations of what many today might describe as prejudice to the laity, particularly women, directly connected, it seems, to sexuality. According to the Tallaght document, a garment received from the laity was considered unclean, and had to be washed before use in the monastery. It also states that lay people involved in spiritual guidance had certain sexual and dietary restrictions imposed upon them. For a male, sexual intercourse with one's wife, for example, must be avoided for a time: "If one of the laity accepts spiritual direction, he is to keep himself from his wife three nights a week: Wednesday night, Friday night, and Saturday night; Sunday night too if he can. And when a woman is in her monthly sickness, a man ought to keep away from her."[60] Women generally in the Tallaght writings are portrayed as sources of temptation, for they are said to have stronger sexual desires than men ("a third part as strong again in women as in men"). They are to be avoided especially when they are menstruating. Even nuns were not to receive communion during menstruation for they were considered "unclean" at those times. In one part of the Tallaght document on Maelruain, a saying attributed to St. Samthann, "let him [Maelruain] bestow no friendship nor confidence upon womankind," follows immediately a beautiful story about Maelruain's soul friendship with her:

> There was a certain itinerant peddler in Munster in the time of Samthann, who used to carry greetings from her to the "sons of life" [Celi De] in that country. Once she called him to her and bound him not to add to nor take away a single word that anyone should say to whom he was sent. Then she said to him: "Say to Mael Ruain for me," said she, "that he is my favorite among the clerics of the South, and another thing you will say

to him: ask, does he accept women for confession and
will he accept my soul-friendship?" The peddler took
his message. But when he told him that he was
Samthann's favorite, he rose at once and raised both
hands as in a cross-vigil and gave thanks to God. When
the peddler asked him next whether women took
counsel of him and whether he would accept
Samthann's soul-friendship, he blushed down to his
breast, and made three genuflections, and fell silent for
a long time. Then he said: "Tell her," said he, "that I
will seek counsel from her." Then the peddler told all
those sayings to Samthann, and she said: "I think," said
she, "something will come of that youth."[61]

Since we know that Maelruain's formation was so positively
influenced by Samthann, and by at least one other nun, a
woman from Coill Uaithne who taught Maelruain, he says, the
practice of saying the Our Father after every fifty psalms he
recited, it is especially ironic that he should quote Samthann
concerning the undesirability of female soul friends. Some
scholars, including Kathleen Hughes, say that these explicit
references to women, especially the supposed statement by
Samthann *against* women, are later revisions of an original
text.[62] They may well be; they may also simply reflect the
increased influence of ascetic and monastic ideals throughout
the Western church, especially upon the followers of Maelruain
who identified so closely with the desert Christians. These
ideals, which in effect denigrated sexuality and equated the
married state and, by implication, women as serious
impediments to holiness, resulted in the revisions of certain
sacred writings and documents. It also affected other devotional
practices of later centuries. Medieval churchmen in Durham,
England, for example, limited the visitation of St. Cuthbert's
grave to only males, warning that the saint would not tolerate
the presence of women, when, as is apparent in the *Life of
Cuthbert* by Bede, Cuthbert himself clearly had strong and
intimate friendships with women—as was true of his spiritual
mentor and inspiration, Aidan.

It seems likely, then, when we consider the effect of the Celi
De movement upon hagiographers (at least as expressed in the
Tallaght documents) we find a mixed heritage. On the positive
side they name an ancient mentoring practice found in the lives

of the original Celtic saints; they reveal a deep appreciation of soul friends, living or dead; they emphasize the importance of such a practice for the deepening of one's spirituality. How seriously they took that practice is apparent in another source attributed to Maelruain, the *Rule of the Celi De,* which warns: "Any person who does not reverence the rule of the soul friend is not in harmony with God or man; it is not lawful, therefore, to give him communion, or to sing his intercession, or to bury him in the church of God. . . ."[63] At the same time, on the negative side, the Tallaght writings reveal increasing separations between clergy and laity, women and men, sexuality and spirituality—perhaps precisely because the Celi De movement was so deeply influenced by the desert Christians who, unlike the Celts' pagan ancestors, did not have, for the most part, a positive appreciation of their sexuality and were highly suspicious of women.[64]

Despite this ambivalent heritage of the Celi De, few movements in the history of Celtic Christians had such a major effect on monastic life and literature. That literature included the Lives of the early Celtic saints which were frequently written or revised at those Celi De monasteries. As Peter O'Dwyer says, "the great literary collections produced before A.D. 1200 were executed in monasteries which either had members of the reform or were connected with them in some way."[65] Thus, the Celi De, the friends and servants of God, made a significant contribution to the Middle Ages' devotion to the saints. Although they themselves disappear from history by the fourteenth century, their legacy endured with the flowering of a spirituality throughout the entire Western church that appreciates the help of a spiritual mentor or guide and the genuine human need for experiences of healing and reconciliation.[66] Deeply affected by the history, culture, and religious milieu of their day, Celtic hagiographers included so many references to the *anamchara* in the Lives of their saints because they believed in its value, most likely because they themselves had personally benefited from having a soul friend.

Taking into account the texts which have survived, most of the writers of Celtic Lives, whether influenced by the Celi De movement or not, seem to have considered their writing and work, like dedicated iconographers today, a matter of sacred

———— ❧ ————

trust. They hoped to act as an icon to their contemporaries and to succeeding generations: painting the picture of a saintly hero, mediating a sacred presence, helping readers encounter in their own lives the *living* reality of the saints. Although surely some pride and egotism were involved as the hagiographers set to work on their compositions, it seems negligible, especially since most of the Lives were composed anonymously. Even those hagiographers who put their names to the texts, such as Cogitosus, Muirchu, Bede, and Rhigyfarch, at least *tell* the reader of their own unworthiness, inexperience, or lack of talent— although this may have been more of a polite custom than felt conviction. What is clear from their own words, however, is that they believed the saints to be leaders, mentors, teachers; most of all, living soul friends capable of giving spiritual help. It was this theology and the spirituality in which it was rooted that finds expression in the Lives of all the Celtic saints. Like Oengus the Culdee, the hagiographers were convinced that to write about the saints was in effect to sing their praises, and, in so doing, they hoped someday to find their own place in the communion of saints.

S I X

Soul Friendship
and
Soul-Making

For no one can raise up one who is falling beneath a weight unless he bends himself that he may reach out to him his hand; and no physician can treat the wounds of the sick unless he comes in contact with their foulness.

Tripartite St. Gall Penitential

They confessed their sins to Cuthbert, confided in him about their temptations, and laid open to him the common troubles of humanity they were laboring under—all in the hope of gaining consolation from so holy a man. They were not disappointed. No one left unconsoled; no one had to carry back the burdens he came with.

Bede the Venerable

Like the desert fathers and mothers, Celtic Christians knew from firsthand experience that the soul, to know itself, must gaze into another soul; must speak from the heart to be heard by another heart. The popular saying linked with St. Brigit which was reaffirmed by the Celi De movement asserted the belief that everyone was expected to have an *anamchara* or soul friend, a relationship with a spiritual guide or mentor that often began as early as the age of seven years.[1] In a warrior culture that was famous, or rather infamous, for its taking of heads in battle, as well as one that believed the soul resided in the head, to say that someone without a soul friend was "like a body without a head" was to use imagery every Celt would understand, one which obviously implied the grave seriousness of such a situation. Without even considering the Christian sacramental dimension of this relationship, from the pagan perspective alone, going

181

without a head meant quite literally the loss of one's soul! The Celtic Christian belief about soul friendship implied something similar: being without a soul friend could have the same terrible consequences.

Soul friends, then, were considered in the early Celtic Church as a very necessary part of spiritual growth, what pagan philosophers, such as Plato and Aristotle, and early church writers, such as Augustine, associated with magnanimity or "greatness of soul."[2] To nourish this "greatness" a person needed to develop, with the help of another, patterns in his or her life and spirituality that would contribute significantly to spiritual health, holiness, and wisdom. This was a lifelong process, one intimately related to "soul-making": seeking healing and reconciliation with God, others, and oneself in preparation for one's death. This latter event Christian Celts equated not only with the anguish of dying or the grief of watching someone else die, but with *natalis dies*, a day of birth, of new life in Christ and intimacy with God; hence, a passage not only of sometimes unmitigated grief, but also of great joy. As Celts, they took both life and death seriously, with wonder and gratitude, and saw the interrelationship of one with the other. They believed that the best preparation for dying was precisely in how well one lived each day, one day at a time. It is no wonder that soul friendship was eventually linked in the Hebrides with being a midwife of the soul, facilitating the transition from this life to the next, and particularly with women, music, and the celebration of mystery:

> In the days of the old Celtic Church, the Death-croon was chanted over the dying by the *anamchara*, the soul-friend, assisted by three chanters. Later on, the rite passed into the hands of *seanairean a' bhaile*, the elders of the township, and the *mnathan-tuiridh*, the mourning-women, the latter eventually developing into a professional class, whose services could always be obtained for a consideration. In more recent times, the *bean-ghluain*, the knee-woman, the midwife, was also the *bean-tuiridh*, the mourning-woman, and as friend of the folk in the coming and the going of life, was regarded with the greatest veneration both by young and by old. To this day the knee-woman of the isles chants her runes and celebrates her mysteries in the

houses of birth and death, but always with closed doors—metaphorically, at any rate.[3]

Relationships of soul friendship, of having a confessor or spiritual mentor, arose at a time when the church on the continent had come to rely almost exclusively upon a reconciliation process that was reserved for serious sins alone, such as murder, adultery, or apostasy. What had developed into a formal and somewhat highly ritualized rehabiliation process was also very public, although it often began with a personal confession or acknowledgment of sin and remorse to a bishop or priest at which time a suitable penance would be mutually agreed upon. The penitent then would be enrolled with others in an *ordo paenitentium* or penitential group. These penitents (again, because of what was perceived to be the seriousness of their violations) would often be expelled from the Christian community and its eucharist until they were considered ready to return, once they had done the assigned penances. These penances could include severe restrictions on their freedom, sexual expression, and personal comfort. Along with the cropping of one's hair and the wearing of special penitential garb (hence the origins of the phrase "sackcloth and ashes"), fasting, prayers, and celibacy were commonly prescribed. When satisfaction was finally considered to have been accomplished, the penitent could be welcomed back into the community. Sometimes this public reconciliation ceremony took place on Maundy Thursday during Holy Week in some formal ritual which might include absolution or the imposition of hands by the bishop in the presence of the entire congregation.[4] Needless to say, this rehabilitation process, because of its severity, was often limited to a once-in-a-lifetime experience, and was increasingly not used unless a person had to do so.

What emerged in the early Celtic Church was something altogether different, a practice more associated with healing, ongoing conversion, and spiritual guidance than of public punishment (although that too could occur at times). In the Celtic practice, there was no order of penitents nor any public ritual or ceremony; privacy was assured and confidentiality was to be maintained at all costs. Nor was the confessor necessarily an ordained person. As in the desert tradition, confession was often made to monks, ascetics, and women known for their holiness. Among Celtic Christians, the lines separating confessors who were priests and those who were not ordained were by no means clearly perceived. The presupposition behind these encounters was that a soul friend would act more as a spiritual guide than a judge; more as a healer and a friend (hence the name "soul friend") than a disciplinarian. As Oscar Watkins, an early twentieth-century scholar, has said:

> The outstanding significance of the Keltic monastic systems of Penance for the student of the history of Penance is that whereas on the continent of Europe the rule throughout the West is public penance and public reconciliation, in the Keltic procedure the public character has been taken away from penance and reconciliation alike. The change is of momentous importance. It marks the beginnings of the modern revolution in penitential procedure.[5]

It also marks, with its emphasis on personal guidance and discernment, the beginnings of the professions of psychology and psychotherapy where respectful attentiveness is given to the psyche or soul.

To gain a better awareness of the various dimensions of soul friendship as it developed in the early Celtic Church, we turn in this chapter to two primary sources specifically describing the *anamchara*: the penitentials and hagiographies of the saints, many of which were significantly influenced by Celi De spirituality and values.[6] What we will find in them are two categories of soul friendships: first, the more formal role of confessor, a description found in the penitentials, and eventually connected exclusively with the ordained male priesthood; and, second, the more personal, intimate friendship relationships of great affection, depth, and longevity, characterized by dynamics of true mutuality. In practice these roles quite frequently may have overlapped, but, as we will see with certain women's hagiographies, even the more formal role was definitely not limited to men nor to priests.

The Penitentials and Pastoral Roles

Besides the hagiographies of the saints, to which we will return later in this chapter, another source for coming to understand the meaning of soul friendship is that of the *libri poenitentiales* or penitential books. These books originated with the Irish Christians, although other churches later wrote their own. The penitentials were designed to offer assistance to soul friends in their roles as spiritual guides and confessors so that they, in turn, could be more effective in their reconciling work with monks, nuns, and laypeople. They were primarily pastoral in intent, written both as a guide to confession and an instrument for educating the confessor. With their listing of sins and their required "remedies," they were meant to help name sins and sicknesses in order to have the wounds caused by them healed, and to restore to greater harmony a person's relations with God, the church, society, and oneself. Their underlying theology was that confession is good for the soul, and penance is a good medicine for healing. They also employed medical imagery, as John Cassian had done in his writings, when describing the soul friend as a "physician of souls" who attempted to make the right diagnosis in treating the illness caused by sin. Jesus himself, who compared himself to a physician (Mt 9:12, Lk 5:31), was their model; union with him was their goal.

While the penitentials usually consist of a description of sins with their assigned penances, the *anamchara* was to make some prudential discernment, taking into account the expected holiness of the individual. Penances were frequently more severe for clergy and nuns, and more lenient for children and first-offenders. Often in the penitentials, a dark side seems to have taken over, especially regarding eros and sexuality, and the healing element of confession and spiritual guidance lost sight of. The original intent, however, was always that of providing pastoral care for both clergy and laypeople. From the earliest times lay people formed an important part of the Celtic monasteries, as has been noted, and in that context "the penitential literature was shaped and fashioned," Hugh Connolly says, "and therefore it was quite natural for authors to distinguish between penances for clerics and those for the laity."[7]

Unlike the public forms of penance that had developed in other parts of Europe, participation in these encounters was not only for serious sins, but as a way of continually examining progress (or lack thereof) in one's spiritual life. The saying attributed to Brigit as well as to St. Comgall, Columbanus's teacher at Bangor, that "anyone without a soul friend is like a body without a head," suggests the assumption that confession and penance were normal for all Christians.[8] Although many of the penitentials seem to presume that only priests were acting as soul friends, we know that non-ordained people, including women, probably used the earliest ones in their roles as *anamcharas*. As often happens, "when once the hierarchy began to patronize and imitate the books, . . . they were regarded as solely for the use of priests."[9]

An important aspect of the early Celtic penitentials was the assignment of some penance that might help repair and heal the harm that those sicknesses of soul had caused. This "tariff system," as it came to be called, most likely originated with the teaching of the druids and druidesses who, in their roles as spiritual mediators of tribes, recommended certain actions for wrongs done. While certain patristic writers such as Pachomius, Basil, and Cassian refer to the practice and value of confession which they learned from the desert monks, there is no specific reference in those writings to penances being assigned the penitent. That seems to be uniquely an Irish contribution, derived from the druids who, as we recall from the writings of Caesar, revealed to him that they exercised "justice in both criminal and civil cases."[10]

Christian soul friends, many of whom were educated by the druids or who may have once been druids or druidesses themselves, prescribed what they considered to be healing remedies, some of which were quite drastic, depending upon the offense. Sometimes to heal the wound or to address the injustices caused by one's sins, a soul friend might recommend going on pilgrimage to Jerusalem or other holy sites. He or she might even suggest, as happened to St. Columcille when he left Ireland for Iona, leaving one's homeland never to return. This latter penance was an especially difficult hardship for Celts since they valued highly their families and tribes as well as the beauty of the landscape that they called "home." As St. Columcille himself expressed it: "It is the parting of soul and body for a person to leave his kindred and his country and go from them to strange, distant lands, in exile and perpetual pilgrimage."[11]

The earliest penitential documents of the Celtic Church that have survived were those that were written in Wales in the early sixth century: the *Preface of Gildas on Penance*, decrees of the synods of North Britain, the *Grove of Victory*, and the *Excerpts*

From a Book of David (the patron saint of Wales).[12] Although they are not in the genre of the *libri poenitentialies*, they are considered "proto-penitential" texts. In addition to the principles of Cassian, those writings linked with Gildas and David seem to have influenced the first Irish penitential, that of St. Finnian of Clonard.[13] Numerous other Irish penitentials followed, teaching about soul friendship, not by means of stories, as the hagiographies do, but through their references to the roles and responsibilities of the *anamcharas*. Unlike the hagiographies, these books reflect much more the strict ascetic ideals of the desert Christians and patristic fathers. They do not reveal the more personal dimensions of soul friend relationships which can be discerned in the hagiographies, as we will see. In the examination of the penitentials, we will only concentrate upon those which provide some insights into the *anamchara*. Even though Gildas's "Preface" on penance is not, strictly speaking, a penitential, we will briefly examine it here because it was so influential.

The *Preface of Gildas on Penance*, of sixth-century Welsh origins, begins with the statement: "A presbyter or a deacon committing natural fornication or sodomy who has previously taken the monastic vow shall do penance for three years." Already we have an intimation of how much the penitentials seem to concentrate upon sex and controlling what they considered to be abhorrent sexual behavior. One of their most striking features, it seems, is what Pierre Payer describes as "the breadth and detail of their treatment of human sexual behaviour."[14] While this can have a positive side in promoting the containment of erotic energies, the obsessive quality of the penitentials regarding eros and sexuality is apparent. Gildas's document on penance reflects his own unhappiness with what he perceived to be sexual license, and as noted earlier, his outright disgust, in particular, with the Irish in this regard. The document itself recommends that the penitent "at all times deplore his guilt from his inmost heart. Above all things let him show the readiest obedience." This obedience implies listening to his confessor "lest his soul perish utterly from lacking so long a time the celestial medicine" (i.e., participation in the eucharist). Other sins are identified: drunkenness, carelessness, stealing—all offenses against the monastic community that must be confessed, according to Gildas, to the abbot. A fellow-monk should "first admonish the offender to confess alone to the abbot the wrong he is doing. Let him be found not so much an informer as one who truly practices the rule."[15] As is clear, Gildas is writing for members in the monastery whose confessor is usually, it seems, the abbot himself.

The *Penitential of Finnian*, the most ancient Irish pastoral guide, seems to have been written by St. Finnian, the sixth-century founder of Clonard, and soul friend to so many early Irish church leaders. Although, like Gildas's, there is no specific mention of the *anamchara* in this document, penance is portrayed as less of a juridical function of getting rid of sin, and more of a healing process for moving beyond sin's destructiveness. Penance is seen as a remedy; sins were healed by the practice of virtues. Its opening lines (*after* condemning bestiality, homoerotic behavior, fellatio, and fornication) turn to repentance and making amends: "If anyone has sinned by thought in his heart and immediately repents, he shall beat his breast and seek pardon from God and make satisfaction, and so be whole." This penitential proceeds to state a fundamental belief that "sins can be absolved in secret by penance and by very diligent devotion of heart and body." Sins, especially those of wrath, envy, backbiting, and greed, "slay the soul", it says. But whatever the sin (and many are enumerated), weeping and tears can help, as can prayers by day and night, and imploring God for forgiveness.

What is especially recommended in this document is the principle of "contraries": a belief, advocated in the writings of John Cassian, that remedies can be found not by concentrating on the spiritual illness to be eradicated, but on its opposite. Thus, if a person hopes to be freed of certain faults or sins, rather than focusing attention and energy upon eliminating the vice, one instead seeks to develop its opposite virtue.[16] The *Penitential of Finnian* relies upon Cassian when it states, "But by contraries, let us make haste to cure contraries and to cleanse away these faults from our hearts and introduce heavenly virtues in their places: patience must arise for wrathfulness; kindliness, or the love of God and of one's neighbor, for envy; for detraction, restraint of heart and tongue; for dejection, spiritual joy; for greed, liberality." Other actions are also wisely recommended: "contributing for the redemption of captives;" spending money "fruitfully on the poor and needy;" receiving pilgrims into "our houses;" visiting the infirm; ministering to those "in chains." Though Finnian does not explicitly describe the confessor in these penitential encounters, by the way he ends his work, he obviously is advocating attributes, through his personal example, that one might expect from a soul friend, such as reliance upon scripture and elders, and, most importantly, love: "These few things concerning the remedies of penance, my dearly beloved brethren, according to the pronouncement of scripture and to the opinion of very learned men, I have tried to write down, compelled by love of you."[17]

The *Penitential of Columbanus* was probably composed by Columbanus himself after he had left Bangor and settled at Annegray and Luxeuil in Gaul. While it is highly indebted to Finnian's penitential, Columbanus's differs in that the role of the confessor or spiritual guide achieves special prominence. Influenced by the Celtic warrior culture of which he and his family were a part, Columbanus viewed life as a battlefield, with penance, confession, and other disciplines as necessary weapons against the foe, the Devil.[18] Early in the penitential, he speaks of what he calls "the common sins" of murder or sodomy, and lists others that require the penitent's confession, such as stealing, perjury, striking one's brother, drinking and vomiting, and defiling oneself (i.e., masturbation). Recalling Cassian's contraries, he advises the confessor to prescribe the following: "The talkative is to be punished with silence, the restless with the practice of gentleness, the gluttonous with fasting, the sleepy with watching, the proud with imprisonment, the deserter with expulsion; let each suffer exactly in accordance with his deserts, that the just may live justly." Then he turns to a description of the healing role of the soul friend:

> Diversity of offences causes diversity of penances. For doctors of the body also compound their medicines in diverse kinds; thus they heal wounds in one manner, sicknesses in another, boils in another, bruises in another, festering sores in another, eye diseases in another, fractures in another, burns in another. So also should spiritual doctors treat with diverse kinds of cures the wounds of souls, their sicknesses, [offenses], pain, ailments, and infirmities. But since this gift belongs to few, namely to know to a nicety all these things, to treat them, to restore what is weak to a complete state of health, let us set out even a few

———— ✺ ————

prescriptions according to the traditions of our elders,
and according to our own partial understanding, for we
prophesy in part and we know in part.

The imagery is very much in line with the theology of
Cassian and other desert figures: that sin is a sickness, a wound
of the soul, and needs special attention. But Columbanus also
goes on to include (as is clear from the above statement) more
than a soul friend being attentive to sin, but also to the
penitent's pain, ailments, and infirmities. Thus, any worthy or
competent confessor or spiritual guide must be sensitive to the
total person who comes to him or her, and attempt to discern
fitting remedies that will benefit the whole person. The great
Irish missionary also affirms, as other desert writers had
recommended, including John Cassian, the value of knowing
"the traditions of our elders," of not acting alone, but drawing
upon their wisdom for any decisions or recommendations that
should be made. Columbanus clearly presupposes that this
discernment and seeking counsel from wise confessors and
elders is a necessary aspect of Christian spirituality.

Finally, in the short paragraph quoted above, Columbanus calls
the confessor's attention to his or her own humility: the *realistic*
comprehension of oneself and of one's abilities. Whatever we
know, Columbanus says, is "partial understanding;" hence, our
reliance must all the more be on God, the ultimate guide of souls.
Though he goes on to provide a lengthy list of more sins which he
thinks need acknowledgment if they have been committed,
Columbanus does not further elaborate on the ministry of the
confessor. He does, however, posit that all confessions should be
made "carefully" in preparation for eucharist, and as a way of
healing the heart: "For it is better to wait until the heart is healed,
and becomes a stranger to offence and envy, than rashly to
approach the judgment of the throne" (the altar and the body and
blood of Christ).[19]

Columbanus's penitential was highly influential, as was the
author of it. Historians tell us that it became the model for later
compilations of Frankish and English penitentials, while St.
Columbanus and his missionaries were responsible for the shift
of the Celtic system of penance to the European continent. This
movement of Irish monks, with their Bibles and penitential
books, "worked a revolution," according to James Kenney, "in
the penance-discipline of Continental Europe."[20]

The *Penitential of Cummean* is one of the most comprehensive of the Irish penitentials, with its main content focused upon penances grouped according to the eight capital sins formulated by John Cassian. Fortunately, it begins well with a "Prologue on the Medicine for the Salvation of Souls" in which its opening lines "tell of the remedies of wounds." From its inception, then, this penitential places in the forefront an interpretation of sins as "wounds" and, like the penitential of Columbanus, the role of the confessor as a "physician of souls." What follows in it is a presentation of sins that fall under the broad categories of Cassian: gluttony, fornication, avarice, anger, dejection, languor, vainglory, and pride, with an added section on "petty cases," "the sinful playing of boys" (primarily sexual in nature), and "questions regarding the [eucharistic] host." Much of the space is given to two sins in particular: fornication and pride, although "the sinful playing of boys" receives a sizable amount as well—betraying a preoccupation with male sins of the flesh and of the spirit. Still, suitable contraries are also presented with each category of sins. In terms of dejection, for example, "he who long harbors bitterness in his heart shall be healed by a joyful countenance and a glad heart;" under "languor," it is advised that "the idler shall be taxed with an extraordinary work, and the slothful with a lengthened vigil."

Specific advice is also given to the confessor who, as a healing physician, should attempt to diagnose sins adequately as well as assign appropriate remedies:

> But this is to be carefully observed in all penance: the length of time anyone remains in his faults; what learning he has received; by what passion he is assailed; how great is his strength; with what intensity of weeping is he afflicted; and with what oppression he has been driven to sin. For Almighty God who knows the hearts of all and has bestowed diverse natures will not weigh the weights of sins in an equal scale of penance. . . . Whence a certain man, wise in the Lord, said: "To whom more is entrusted from him shall more be exacted." Thus the priests of the Lord, who preside over the churches, should learn that their share is given to them together with those whose faults they have caused to be forgiven.

The preceding passage strongly advocates that the soul friend view any offense or sickness of soul with compassion and pastoral discernment. The penitential goes on to recommend that whether one acts as an exhorter, a teacher, an inspirer, the confessor should lead the other person "to penance, correct him of his error, amend him of his vices, and make him such that God is rendered favorable to him after his conversion." Such a reconciling ministry is extremely important, Cummean implies, with great responsibilities; one that needs to be rooted in prayer and humility.[21]

Cummean's penitential was much circulated on the Continent during the eighth and ninth centuries which also saw the promulgation of numerous other penitentials. What emerges in so many of them are four types of roles that are associated with the confessor or spiritual mentor: being a judge, a physician, a discerning guide, and a teacher. Although the first role, that of being a judge who responds to another's sins by assigning a penance, seems to take precedence, at least in some of the language and certainly the framework in which the penitentials were written (i.e., the listing of sins and their penances), those other roles, taken together, really change the nature of the confessional encounter with an *anamchara*. On the part of the penitent, they are much more than simply receiving a judgment; they can become an opportunity for spiritual healing, discerning the nature of one's spiritual illness, and learning how to integrate into one's life ongoing conversion and reconciliation. Such encounters imply on the part of the soul friend numerous pastoral skills: listening, discernment, teaching, challenging.

One other role also can be found in at least some of the penitentials that has not, as yet, been named: that of being a fellow-sufferer or, to use the language of Carl Jung, of being a wounded healer, a person whose own sins, sicknesses, and limitations are a source of learning and compassion.[22] This role presupposes, as Cassian recommends in his writings and which some penitentials designate, the importance of humility, a knowledge of self rooted in Christ and in a spirituality of reconciliation. Again, the way some of the penitentials are written, with their emphasis upon the sins of the penitent, this aspect of soul friend ministry seems to get lost. But, I would suggest, this underlying theme or role is there in most of them.

One penitential, in particular, which reflects this wounded-healer ministry, explicitly moving away from an emphasis upon the sinfulness of the penitent to the sin (and grace) both confessor and penitent share is the *Tripartite St. Gall Penitential*. This penitential was composed about 800 C.E. and is linked with the famous monastery founded by St. Gall in Switzerland. In it one finds a moving testimony of what the soul friend's approach should be in any confessional encounter or relationship of ongoing spiritual guidance:

> As often as we assign fasts to Christians who come to penance, we ourselves ought also to unite with them in fasting for one or two weeks, or as long as we are able; that there be not said to us that which was said to the priests of the Jews by our Lord and Savior: "Woe unto you scribes, who oppress men and lay upon their shoulders heavy loads, but you yourselves do not touch these burdens with one of your fingers." For no one can raise up one who is falling beneath a weight unless he bends himself that he may reach out to him his hand; and no physician can treat the wounds of the sick unless he comes in contact with their foulness.

Every soul friend, it goes on to imply, needs to be compassionate and non-judgmental, since both confessor and penitent make up a corporate body:

> So also no priest or pontiff can treat the wounds of sinners or take away the sins from their souls unless in view of the pressing necessity he brings solicitude and prayers and tears. Therefore it is needful for us to be solicitous on behalf of sinners, since we are "members one of another" and "if one member suffers anything all the members suffer with it." And, therefore, if we see anyone fallen in sin, let us also make haste to call him to penance by our teaching. . . . Therefore, as we said above, the bishop or presbyter ought to humble himself and pray with sadness and moaning and tears, not only for his own fault, but also for those of all Christians, so that he may be able to say with the Apostle Paul: "Who is weak and I am not weak; who is scandalized and I am not on fire."

Preparation for this ministry, the penitential makes clear, is rooted in prayer, and, whether one is a bishop or priest (or layperson), one's fundamental role is that of being a humble mediator:

> When, therefore, anyone comes to a priest to confess his sins, the priest ought first to pray by himself in the secrets of his own heart: Lord God almighty, be propitious to me a sinner, to make me, on behalf of sinners and those who confess their sins, a worthy mediator between You and them. And You who desires not the death of sinners, but that they should be converted and live, accept the prayer of Your servant which I pour forth before the face of Your Glory, for Your servants, male and female, who desire to do penance; that You may both release them from their sins for the future and keep them unharmed from every offense.[23]

The early penitentials with their dual purpose of counsel and correction eventually transformed early medieval life among Christians of Britain and continental Europe, primarily through the Irish missionaries. Brittany, in particular, seems to have been central in the dissemination of the *libri poenitentiales*.[24] Private penance eventually took the place of the public forms, and spiritual guidance was seen as accessible to everyone. In Ireland, especially, all good Christians were expected to make use of a soul friend on an ongoing basis. Thus, like the Celtic monastic rules, the penitentials did more than just punish sins; they also provided a forum for the giving of counsel and of spiritual advice, and spread the practice of people relying upon soul friends for their spiritual growth. These private encounters with soul friends became a significant turning point not only in early medieval spirituality, but in the rise of penance as one of the seven "great" sacraments of the universal church before the Reformation.[25]

This growing awareness of the need for confession and spiritual guidance, reflected in the prayers and poetry of the times, affected the daily spirituality of the people, making them more conscious that conversion, forgiveness, and reconciliation was everyone's responsibility, as in the early church when St. James admonishes, "Confess your sins to one another and pray for one another, that you may be healed" (5:16). It also offered them an alternative to the constant cycle of vengeance and violence that their pagan ancestors were caught in, with seemingly little hope of transcending. Confession and encounters with soul friends, however, offered a message of hope that one can break out of this vicious cycle. Christianity, of course, presupposes that this is not something that is accomplished by oneself or by one's own willpower, but with the help of God, a soul friend with whom one can take an honest look into soul and heart, and a loving, supportive community of people united in their love of God, Christ, and the saints.

While the penitentials provided some description of what might be considered the "professional" roles of confessors and spiritual guides, the hagiographies of the saints confirm these roles, as well as reveal the more personal aspects of such relationships. In them we can find less of an impression of someone sitting in judgment, however compassionate he or she might be, and more of a spiritual companion on life's journey.

Soul Friendship in the Hagiographies

The hagiographies of the Celtic saints, as we've already seen, provide a wealth of information about soul friendship and its immersion in the everyday life and spirituality of the early Celtic Church. They reveal how common soul-friend relationships were between men and men, women and women, and women and men, and, as the story of Brigit and the young cleric shows, the importance of everyone having a soul friend, including the laity. As is true of hagiographies in general, not everything they contain can be considered historically accurate or "factual" according to today's standards. Still, contemporary scholars are increasingly aware that there is much more historical information in them than once realized. Lisa Bitel, for one, states that "hagiography, written by and for monks, provides more evidence for the study of Irish monasticism than any other type of source, written or material."[26] Hagiographies, as suggested earlier, were primarily written to honor a saint and his or her monastery, and, as such, are filled with images, symbols, and mystical numbers that had special meaning for ancient peoples. Like dreams, this "language" of myths was considered capable of revealing eternal truths of wisdom that far surpass so-called

—————— ❦ ——————

"facts." In turning to these early Lives for more of an understanding of *anamchara* relationships, this symbolic language will be relied upon to discern sometimes hidden meanings regarding soul friendships that can be found in the saints' hagiographies.

In those hagiographies, the early soul friends are portrayed by the monastic storytellers in a great variety of ministerial roles. Some, like Patrick, Brigit, and Columcille, are clearly depicted in their lives as shamans, healers, and spiritual guides to the tribes, as the druids and druidesses had once been. A great many, such as Finnian, Ita, and Aidan, functioned as teachers and tutors to both younger students and adults, gathering people about them, and making a very significant contribution to the continuity of the Celtic legacy. Many of them, including Findbarr, David, and Hild, were powerful founders of monasteries, a role that surely involved good communication and administrative skills. As in the case of Brendan, Columbanus, and Samson of Dol, a large number were missionaries and pilgrims, willing to live an extremely harsh lifestyle, far from friends and kin, bringing the gospel to pagan lands. Many of these soul friends were mystics and visionaries, like Samthann, Maedoc, and Cuthbert, who prayed intensely and had intuitive abilities to read the future, and more importantly the heart. All of them were pioneers, reconcilers, and confessors who, despite very active lives, valued their times of solitude, and, especially in their last days, the opportunity for soul-making.

Though not many hagiographies of female saints have survived, we know from those which have (as well as the stories in the men's Lives that refer to women in the early Celtic Church) that some of the greatest and most competent of the soul friends were Irish women, such as Brigit of Kildare, Ita of Killeedy, Samthann of Clonbroney, Moninna (or Darerca) of Killeevy. Not only were these women excellent teachers, administrators, spiritual guides, and preachers, but they also functioned as confessors. Their participation in so many ministries makes sense if we take into account not only that the pagan culture of the Celts had a deep appreciation of women's capabilities, but also that women were the prime supporters of Patrick when he returned to Ireland as a missionary-bishop.

Still, it is important not to over-romanticize women's participation in the early Celtic Church or their place in Celtic society. Besides fighting against poverty, plague, and all those ills that faced the people of their times, men and women alike, many Celtic women also had to fight prejudice and outright resistance to their choice of lifestyle and leadership—despite the encouragement of saints like Patrick. In certain stories which are found in the hagiographies, we can see how much opposition such women as Ita and Samthann received when they chose to be baptized and to remain virgins for Christ's sake. As noted earlier, both pagan and Christian Celts evidently still perceived women's primary roles as those of spouse and mother. In those Lives of Brigit written later than Cogitosus', we find her constantly asserting herself against the taboos of illegitimacy and the disgust and outright opposition of certain men: her natural father, her brothers, and a wealthy man who attempts to keep her from building a monastery at Kildare.[27]

Frequently male church leaders, recognized for their holiness, are in fact the most obstinate. This is apparent in the story from the *Life of St. Senan* about Canair the Pious (d. 530) who had to confront a "good man" about his exclusivity and unwillingness to collaborate. In the inclusive theology that she presents to him, we find perhaps the first Irish feminist:

> Canair the Pious, a holy woman of the Benntraige of the south of Ireland, set up a hermitage in her own territory. There one night, after nocturnes, she was praying, when all the churches of Ireland appeared to her. It seemed as if a tower of fire rose up to heaven from each of the churches. The highest of the towers of fire, and the straightest towards heaven was that which rose from Inis Cathaig [Scattery Island]. "Fair is Senan's cell," Canair said. "I will go there, that my resurrection may be near it." She went immediately, without guidance, except for the tower of fire which she saw continuing to blaze day and night until she arrived. Now, when she had reached the shore of Luimnech, she walked upon the sea as if she were on smooth land until she came to Inis Cathaig. Now Senan knew that she was coming, and he went to the harbor to meet and welcome her.

"Yes, I have come," Canair told him.

"Go," said Senan, "to your sister who lives on the island to the east of this one, so that you may be her guest."

"That is not why I came," said Canair, "but that I may find hospitality with you on this island."

"Women cannot enter on this island," Senan replied.

"How can you say that?" asked Canair. "Christ is no worse than you. Christ came to redeem women no less than to redeem men. He suffered for the sake of women as much as for the sake of men. Women as well as men can enter the heavenly kingdom. Why, then, should you not allow women to live on this island?"

"You are persistent," said Senan.

"Well then," Canair replied, "will I get what I ask for? Will you give me a place to live on this island and the holy sacrament of eucharist?"

"Yes, Canair, a place of resurrection will be given you here on the brink of the waves," said Senan.[28]

Another story, this one from the medieval *Book of Lismore*, tells of a Celtic "gospel-nun" (those under guidance of a soul friend, probably a member of the Celi De), and how she too has the courage to challenge an abbot about his prayer life. The prayer called the *Biait,* referred to here, was Psalm 118 which was believed to have special power to help those who had died:

Mael Poil Ua Cinaetha, the abbot of the monastery of Cill Beagain, had been discussing astrology with another monk. Afterwards in his sleep he saw coming toward him a gospel-nun who had died six months before. She complained bitterly. "How are things there, woman?" he asked. "Much you care," said she, "discussing astrology and not saying prayers for my soul. Woe to you!" "What prayers do you want from me, woman?" he asked. "The *Biait*, of course," she said, "the *Biait* after the *Biait*, the *Biait* on the *Biait*, the *Biait* beneath and above the *Biait*." She said this all in one breath, demanding that the *Biait* be recited often for her. So there are no prayers for the dead, except for the Mass for the Dead, that is held in greater honor by God than the *Biait*.[29]

Women's persistence evidently paid off. Despite the opposition of their families, Ita and Samthann did become nuns, and, despite the conflict with the landowner, Brigit succeeded in building her double-monastery at Kildare. St. Senan, as the story shows, was converted (quite dramatically) by Canair's courage and forthrightness. And, although we don't know what happened regarding the anonymous gospel-nun's complaint, we can deduce that the abbot, finally, responded positively to such an apparition in his sleep—or faced the prospect of additional nightmares.

Women as Confessors

Women's leadership as confessors is perhaps one of the most interesting roles depicted in the hagiographies if we take into account how the sacrament of reconciliation in the Roman Catholic church is limited to male priests, and, on the other hand, how many women of all denominations are now sensing a call to be spiritual directors or guides, very much in line with the origins of the ministry of the *anamchara* and of the sacrament itself. In hagiographies of the Irish saints, all four female leaders mentioned above are linked in some way with confession and penance. Brigit is portrayed in one story as responsible for the repentance and confession of a small boy who had stolen, killed, and then eaten a goat that did not belong to him.[30] In another story, she and St. Brendan confess to each other, not necessarily their sins, but their devotion to God—which is certainly a fitting subject that can be a part of any ongoing relationship of spiritual mentoring.[31] St. Samthann, as we've seen, was an excellent and effective confessor of the Celi De, and soul friend to Maelruain, one of their chief founders. In another story about her from her Life, she is shown in dreams providing guidance to a member of her community, as well as confrontation to a "lord of the woods" which results in his repentance. One can presume that the man, as frightened as he was, will eventually make his confession, if not to her, to some other soul friend:

> Another time when the servant of Christ [Samthann] wished to build an upper storey for the sisters' dwelling, she again sent the prioress Nathea with workmen into the forest of the Connacht men for pine trees. When they had spent three days looking for these

and could not find them, they grew tired and wanted to return home on the fourth day. As they slept that night holy Samthann appeared in the dreams of Nathea and said: "Cut to the roots the willows in the bog and there you will find sufficient pines already cut." When day broke, they did as she had commanded and they found the pines they wanted. The lord of those groves, however, upon seeing such a supply of pines, said: "You cannot have these trees unless you buy them." Nathea said: "We will willingly pay for them." On the following night, holy Samthann appeared to the owner in a dream and in a threatening voice said: "O man, why do you try to withhold God's gifts?" And after that she struck his side with a stick and said: "Miserable man, unless you do penance, know that you will die soon." Next morning that man was filled with repentance and gave them the wood without any question of payment. All the people of the neighborhood praised Christ in holy Samthann, and supplied sixty yokes of cattle for transporting the wood to the monastery.[32]

A third female leader was Moninna (also called "Darerca") of Killeevy, who founded her monastery at the beginning of the sixth century. Her Life includes two stories associated with her role as a confessor. In the first story, she is depicted as both encouraging the confession of another nun *and* being the recipient of it. According to her hagiography, she and her nuns are stopped at a flooding river, unable to cross. Aware that one of her company is a thief, she tells her companions the following: "My sisters, observe and be aware that it is in retribution for our sins that this inundation prevents our passage. Let us therefore examine our consciences, so that if we are at fault through any transgression of ours, we may confess it duly and be relieved from punishment." This approach, very much reflective of that found in the penitential of St. Gall, not so much shames the other person as it encourages full self-disclosure which is evidently what happened:

And at this one of the sisters answered her and said: "As I was leaving the monastery, I saw garlic drying, and I carried off one bunch, which I thought to belong to us." St. Darerca [Moninna] said to her: "Bring it back immediately to the place from which you took it. For we should no more take away the smaller items than the bigger ones, without the permission of those with whom we left the larger." And when the nun, obeying the command of her superior, returned the bunch of garlic to the place they had left, the river reduced its flood to its former level and allowed the nuns to pass.

The second story found in Moninna's hagiography tells specifically of men who have stolen food from one of the nuns making their confession to the saint:

> Those robbers, after they had stolen the food, were confused by the power of God so that they lost the track they were following, and they wandered, lost, for three days in woods with which they were very familiar. At length they came to their senses and understood that they had to make good the wrong they had done; and they promised to do whatever penance the judgment of the holy virgin should impose on them if they found the right way. And since God is quicker to show mercy than condemnation, once they had acknowledged their fault, He opened their eyes, and showed them the way to the monastery, which was close by. When they arrived at the monastery, they presented themselves to the holy virgin and returned what they had stolen; and, throwing themselves down, they humbly begged forgiveness and voluntarily offered themselves to perform such penance as might be imposed. And they renounced robbery and returned to a life of amendment.[33]

The fourth female confessor is St. Ita, the sixth-century abbess of the monastery in County Limerick called Killeedy (which means cell or church of Ita). Some historians say that it was a double-monastery—which may be true, since in her hagiography there is mention of priests at her convent who wonder where she was when she had miraculously visited Clonmacnoise to receive eucharist from "a worthy priest." Her own pupils, as we recall, were many of the future leaders of

Ireland, one of whom was the famous Irish voyager, Brendan of Clonfert. Known as the "Fostermother of the Saints of Erin," she is also described by her hagiographer as "a second Brigit" from whom many laymen received guidance and advice. Judging from the churches and chapels in Cornwall with which her name is linked and the ancient litanies on the European continent which invoked her help, including one by Alcuin at the court of Charlemagne, she was as well known in Britain and western Europe as in Ireland.

Ita's name derives from her thirst (*iota*) for holiness, a quality, along with compassion, that may have been what drew so many women to join her monastery and many families to send their sons to her. Ita's Life contains numerous stories about her various ministries. She is depicted as an effective healer, a role verified in Celi De writings, including the *Martyrology of Oengus,* in which she is described as healing a grievous disease.[34] In her hagiography, Ita also is someone who ministers to the dying, an intriguing role, considering how soul friendship, at least in the Hebrides, eventually became associated with this form of pastoral care. One story, in particular, describes Ita's hospice-like ministry:

> The holy abbot, Comhganus, when he knew that the time of his death was approaching, asked Ita to visit him. When she did, he said to her: "I am to die soon of this disease and I ask you in the name of Christ to place your hands on my lips and to close my mouth at the hour of my death. I know from the angel of God that whenever you place your hands on those who are dying, the angel of the Lord will immediately bear his soul to the kingdom of God." Ita said to him: "O holy father, what are you saying? Only a sinful man should say such a thing. God will reward you greatly and you will be glorious among God's saints. What do you need from me?" St. Comhganus said: "I speak truly. Because of what I have asked, no demon will dare to come near us on our journey, or to accuse us in any way." St. Comhganus then left this world accompanied by choirs of angels, and what he had requested, Ita accomplished.

As in Moninna's hagiography, certain stories in Ita's Life depict her as an effective confessor who hears the confessions of both her monastic community and of laypeople outside of it. According to these stories, women as well as men seem to have had difficulties with chastity and sexual continence:

> A nun who had been under Ita's charge committed fornication, and on the following day, Ita called her to her and said to her: "Why did you not care, sister, to guard your virginity?" She, however, denied that she had committed fornication. Ita said to her: "Did you really not commit fornication yesterday in such-and-such a place?" The nun saw immediately that Ita could prophesy about things past and present. She admitted the truth and was healed, doing penance according to Ita's command. Another virgin, living far away from Ita in the province of Connacht, secretly committed adultery. Full of the spirit of prophecy, Ita knew this, and ordered St. Brendan to bring the nun to her. St. Brendan made the woman go to Ita. Ita then described to her, among other things, how she had conceived and given birth to a son. When the woman heard her sin from Ita's mouth, she made a fitting penance. Her soul was restored to eternal salvation, and afterwards she led a holy life.

No wonder, as the Life says, "because of this, all of Ita's community and many others who knew of her prophetic power respected her, whether she was absent or present." They also were probably much more dedicated to guarding their own virginity!

Another story shows Ita's compassion toward a murderer who seeks forgiveness and reconciliation from her, and her commitment to keeping promises as a true soul friend would:

> A certain man killed his brother, and touched with remorse, he came to Ita and did penance according to her command. Ita, seeing his devout heart, said: "If you obey my words, you will not have a sudden death, but you will go to eternal life." It happened afterwards that he went with his chieftain to fight, for he was a soldier, and the battle went against them, and he was killed. When Ita heard that, she said: "I promised that man that he would have a happy end to his life because he listened to my advice." She said to her attendants: "Go,

find him in the devastation, and call upon him in God's name and mine. I believe he will rise and meet you." They did as she said, and the dead man rose from the battle as if he had never been killed. He ran towards those who were searching for him and came with them to Ita. Afterwards everything turned out as Ita had promised.

Yet another story shows her patience in waiting for a man finally to change his ways:

> . . . A great battle was waged against the people of Ui Conaill by many enemies. That people asked Ita, their patron, to gain God's help against the great forces of their enemies. Ita, having pity on them, asked God, saying: "Blessed Trinity and inseparable Unity, Father, Son, and Holy Spirit, help my few unfortunate men, who received me kindly in your name, welcomed me into their land, and took me as their patron; they have no human help against this great multitude from west Munster." The people of Ui Conaill trusted in the prayers of Ita . . . [and] returned highly victorious from the battle, and gave thanks to God and to Ita for the victory which they had received. . . . Then Ita said to one of her attendants: "Go to where the battle was fought and look for the one who promised me to do penance, and you will find him lying and wounded amid the destruction of the battle." Ita's messenger found him as she had indicated. He brought the brother back to Ita who received him kindly, and he was healed of his wounds. Later, he did a fitting penance, according to Ita's order, and died a happy death.[35]

Like Brigit, Samthann, and Moninna, Ita was truly one of the great spiritual leaders of the Irish, a teacher of forgiveness who was sought out because she was a mirror of God's mercy and love. She died in approximately 570; her feastday is January 15. Ita's monastery at Killeedy flourished for some time after her death, but then suffered severely, as many women's monasteries did, at the hands of the Vikings who raided it in 845, 847, and 916. It still continued to prosper as a place of learning and spirituality until the dissolution of the monasteries in the sixteenth century.

Personal Dimensions of Soul Friendship

Beyond the specific roles and pastoral skills associated with the *anamchara* in the rules, penitentials, and hagiographies, there are the more personal dimensions of soul friendship itself. These dimensions emerge when we take a closer look at the stories of the early Celtic saints who were *anamcharas* to one another. Reading between the lines, we can discern in those stories certain characteristics that typify such a close relationship.

Soul friendship is, first of all, synonymous with great affection, intimacy, and depth. As we learn from the eighth-century *Liber Angeli (Book of the Angel)*: "Between holy Patrick and Brigit, pillars of the Irish, there existed so great a friendship of charity that they were of one heart and one mind."[36] Although their relationship may not have been an historical reality, the passage speaks of an intimacy of great love that can exist between friends. In the Lives of the saints, this intimacy is manifest in very ordinary emotions and simple gestures. St. Brendan, for example, smiles warmly when he thinks of Ita, his foster-mother, and Ita, in turn, experiences the slow passage of time when Brendan is away. Finnian calls his student Ciaran "O little heart" and "dear one," and blesses him before Ciaran leaves the monastery of Clonard where he had studied under the older man.

Secondly, soul-friend relationships are characterized by great mutuality: a profound respect for each other's wisdom, despite any age or gender differences. They share an awareness, as did the desert Christians, that the other person is a source of many blessings. This quality of mutuality is expressed symbolically in the Celtic stories by an exchange of gifts. Brigit gives Finnian a ring, Columcille sends the holy virgin Maugina a little pine box that helps cure her, David of Wales gives Findbarr his horse, Gildas creates a fine bell with his own hands and presents it to Brigit. Even the great storyteller of the Celtic saints, the Venerable Bede (probably inspired by them), shared small gifts with his friends before he died.[37] Mutuality is also manifest in the tale of Brigit's and Brendan's confession to each other, as we've seen, and, perhaps most vividly, in a story from the *Life of St. Ciaran* as he prepares for death:

> When the time of his death at the age of thirty-three drew near to the holy Ciaran in his little church, he

said: "Let me be carried to a small height." When he
looked up at the sky and the vast open air above his
head, he said, "Terrible is the way of dying." . . . Then
angels went to meet his soul, filling as they did all the
space between heaven and earth. He was carried back
into the little church, and raising his hands, he blessed
his people. Then he told the brethren to shut him up in
the church until Kevin should come from Glendalough.
After three days Kevin arrived. . . . At once Ciaran's
spirit returned from heaven and re-entered his body so
that he could commune with Kevin and welcome him.
The two friends stayed together from the one watch to
another, engaged in mutual conversation, and
strengthened their friendship. Then Ciaran blessed
Kevin, and Kevin blessed water and administered the
eucharist to Ciaran. Ciaran gave his bell to Kevin as a
sign of their lasting unity which today is called
Coimgen's Boban [Kevin's Bell].[38]

From what the hagiographies imply, a third characteristic of
soul friends is that they share common values, a common vision
of reality, and, sometimes, an intuitive sense of the potential
leadership of younger protégés. Both vision and intuition are
referred to in the story of Ciaran and his spiritual mentor, Enda:

After that Ciaran went to the island of Aran to
commune with Enda. Both of them saw the same
vision of a great fruitful tree growing beside a stream in
the middle of Ireland. This tree protected the entire
island, and its fruit crossed the sea that surrounded
Ireland, and the birds of the world came to carry off
some of that fruit. Ciaran turned to Enda and told him
what he had seen, and Enda, in turn, said to him: "The
great tree which you saw is you, Ciaran, for you are
great in the eyes of God and of men. All of Ireland will
be sheltered by the grace that is in you, and many
people will be fed by your fasting and prayers. So, go in
the name of the God to the center of Ireland, and found
your church on the banks of a stream."[39]

Fourthly, soul friendships include, not only affirmation, but
the ability to challenge each other when it is necessary to do so.
This is sometimes the most difficult aspect of any intimate

relationship, but without that quality the friendship can soon become superficial, stunted, and eventually lost. The stories of Irish women who were courageous enough to be assertive have already been told, including those of Canair, and (through their appearance in others' dreams) of Samthann and the gospel-nun. Male leaders too show this same challenging and at times prophetic quality. A story of the handsome Mochuda, founder of Lismore monastery, shows that such challenge and prophecy can be done in a gentle manner, one that fosters reconciliation rather than further alienates people from one another:

> On a certain day about vesper time [evening prayer], because of the holiness of the hour, Mochuda said to his monks: "We shall not eat today till each one of you has made his confession," for he knew that some one of them had ill will in his heart against another. All the brethren thereupon confessed to him. One of them in the course of his confession stated: "I love not your miller and the cause of my lack of charity towards him is this, that when I come to the mill he will not lift the loads off the horses and he will neither help me to fill the meal sacks nor to load them on the horse when filled. And not this alone but he does everything that is disagreeable to me; moreover I cannot tell, but God knows, why he so acts. Often I have thought of striking him or even beating him to death." Mochuda replied, "Brother dear, the prophet says, *'Declina a malo et fac bonum.'* Avoid evil and do good. Following this precept let you act kindly towards the miller and that charity of yours will move him to charity towards you and you shall yet be steadfast friends." Things went on thus for three days—the monk doing all he could to placate the miller. Nevertheless the miller did not cease his persecution, nor the brother his hate of the miller. On the third day Mochuda directed the brother to confess to him again. The brother said,
>
> "This is my confession, Father; I do not yet love the miller." Mochuda observed, "He will change tonight, and tomorrow he will not break fast till you meet him and you shall sit on the same seat, at the same table, and you shall remain fast friends for the rest of your lives." All this came to pass, for that monk was,

———— ❧ ————

through the instruction of Mochuda, filled with the grace of the Divine Spirit. And he glorified and praised Mochuda, for he recognized him as a man favored by the Holy Spirit.[40]

A fifth characteristic of soul friendship is that it survives geographical separation, the passage of time, and death itself. In the early stories, even after Columcille moves to Iona in order to bring Christianity to the Scots, he continues to long for Derry and his friends in Ireland, and they for him; Brendan consistently returns to Ita for advice after his journeys to foreign lands; Lasrianus and Maedoc, in response to God, separate and go their own ways, but never forget what each has meant to the other. In the latter's life, in particular, we find reference to the lasting ties of friendship with Lasrianus, despite their geographical distance:

> Maedoc and Molaise of Devenish were comrades who loved each other very much. One day they sat praying at the foot of two trees. "Ah, Jesus!" they cried, "is it your will that we should part, or that we should remain together until we die?" Then one of the trees fell to the south, and the other to the north. "By the fall of the trees," they said, "it is clear that we must part." Then they told each other goodbye and kissed each other affectionately. Maedoc went to the south and built a noble monastery at Ferns in the center of Leinster, and Molaise went north to Lough Erne and built a fair monastery at Devenish.[41]

The same hagiography tells the story about Maedoc climbing a golden ladder to see his soul friend:

> Once Maedoc was teaching a student by a high cross at the monastery of Ferns. The student saw him mount a golden ladder reaching from earth to heaven. Maedoc climbed the ladder, and when he returned sometime later, the student could not look in his face because of the brilliance which transfused his countenance. . . . "Columcille has died," Maedoc told him, "and I went to meet him with the family of heaven. He was my own soul friend in this world, so I wanted to pay him my respects." The student told this story only after

Maedoc's death, when he had become an adult and a holy man himself.[42]

This story, along with numerous other accounts of the appearances of saints, after their death, to help those left behind attests to the firm belief that a relationship with a soul friend was not ended with death, but transformed. As St. Samson of Dol's hagiographer states, "Samson in the heavens, although absent from us in body, yet from some kind of excellence which he enjoys with God . . . is without any impediment ever at hand to us. . . ."[43]

A sixth aspect of *anamchara* relationships that can be learned from the hagiographies is that they are centered upon God, *the* soul friend in whom all other friendships are united. True soul friends do not depend upon each other alone, but root their relationship in God. All the stories of the saints refer to this spiritual dimension, but one story in the *Life of Findbarr* is the most explicit symbolically. In it we find intimations not only of this need for reliance upon God, but also of those qualities identified earlier, those of affirmation, mutuality, and deep love:

> After the death of Bishop MacCuirb, Findbarr was much concerned at being without a soul friend. So he went to visit Eolang, and God revealed to Eolang that Findbarr was coming to see him. Eolang immediately knelt before Findbarr, and said the following, "I offer to you my church, my body, and my soul." Findbarr wept openly, and said, "This was not my thought, but that it would be I who would offer my church to you." Eolang said, "Let it be as I have said, for this is the will of God. You are dear to God, and you are greater than myself. One thing only I ask, that our resurrection will be in the same place." Findbarr replied, "Your wish will be fulfilled, but I am still troubled about the soul friendship." Eolang told him, "You shall receive today a soul friend worthy of yourself." This was done as he said, for Eolang in the presence of the angels and archangels placed Findbarr's hand in the hand of the Lord. . . .[44]

Finally, according to hagiographies, *anamcharas* appreciate, as did the desert Christians, both friendship and solitude as resources ultimately for "soul-making." As the stories of Kevin and Ciaran, and Maedoc and Columcille have already intimated, soul friends help each other make the transition from this life, through death, to God. No hagiography expresses this better than Bede's *Life of St. Cuthbert*, about the seventh-century Anglo-Saxon saint from northern England whom some believed to have been born in Ireland, so immersed was he in Celtic spirituality. Cuthbert's life clearly reflects a spirituality that values both friendship and solitude, being active in ministry and having a cell. For years, he was involved in pastoral ministry and monastic leadership on the tiny island, Lindisfarne, yet consistently made time in his busy schedule to be away. Finally, to prepare for his own death, Cuthbert was given permission to build a solitary cell on Inner Farne Island nearby, where he "entered," Bede tells us, "with great joy . . . into the remoter solitude he had so long sought, thirsted after, and prayed for." Even then, great numbers of people continued to come to him, Bede says, "not just from Lindisfarne but even from the remote parts of Britain, attracted by his reputation for miracles. They confessed their sins, confided in him about their temptations, and laid open to him the common troubles of humanity they were laboring under—all in the hope of gaining consolation from so holy a man. They were not disappointed. No one left unconsoled; no one had to carry back the burdens he came with. Spirits that were chilled with sadness he could warm back to hope again with a pious word. Those beset with worry he brought back to thoughts of the joys of Heaven. He showed them that both good fortune and bad were transitory in this world. To men beset with temptation he would skillfully disclose all the wiles of the devil, explaining that a soul lacking in love for God or man is easily caught in the devil's nets, while one that is strong in faith can, with God's grace, brush them aside like so many spider's webs."[45] As is evident from the stories about him, Cuthbert's life was a constant struggle between serving others well and caring for his own solitary needs. Somehow, with God's grace and his own efforts, he was evidently able to maintain some balance—at least on his better days.

Despite his longing for solitude, this last story about Cuthbert shows us how he united in himself all the various roles identified in the writings, those of being a confessor, teacher, physician of souls, judge, discerning guide, and spiritual mediator. He also seems to have had the pastoral skills of listening, discernment, teaching, and challenging that might be expected of a soul friend. In many ways, Cuthbert represents the quintessential *anamchara:* someone who does not increase others' burdens, but helps alleviate their weight through the simple, yet crucial act of attentive listening. Through that form of discipline and art, others received gifts of hope, insight, and deepened faith. As the penitential of St. Gall reminds us by quoting the words of Jesus: "Woe unto you scribes, who oppress others and lay upon their shoulders heavy loads, but you yourselves do not touch these burdens with one of your fingers" (Lk 11:46).

Cuthbert, though a holy and gifted man, was not the only effective *anamchara* who helped others in their soul-making as he attended to his own. All of the early Celtic saints seem to have had wonderful abilities and qualities that drew people to them, both during their lifetimes and after their deaths, helping others experience healing and reconciliation, through their example, inspiration, and, at times, miraculous intercession.

Conclusion

When you place yourself under the guidance of someone else, you should seek out the fire. . . .

Maelruain

The early Celtic Church of Patrick, Brigit, Columcille, and the other spiritual leaders who founded it did not come to an end swiftly, but slowly, over centuries, as the church on the European continent with its strong Roman influence gradually assumed dominance. Numerous historical factors contributed to its demise, including the destructive incursions of the Vikings or Norsemen from the eighth through the eleventh centuries.[1] Other social, political, and religious events had their effect as well. In Britain, the Council of Whitby, called by the Anglo-Saxon King Oswy, met in 664 C.E. at Hild's double-monastery, high on the cliffs overlooking the ocean. There two sides fought each other verbally over what sort of church would survive in Northumbria. The Roman faction, represented by Wilfrid, and the other, represented by Colman of Lindisfarne, disagreed over such issues as the kind of tonsure each priest should wear, and how to calculate the date for the annual celebration of Easter.[2] What they were really arguing about was more fundamental: the type of church they wanted to exist, and what sort of spirituality

213

should survive. Although King Oswy ruled in favor of the Roman faction when he decided that he personally desired St. Peter, the "keeper of the keys" to heaven, on his side when he died, many of the same issues would reassert themselves nine hundred years later in the Protestant Reformation: diversity versus uniformity, local autonomy versus Roman authority, greater participation of laity in church worship and life versus clerical-dominated structures; simplicity versus extravagant wealth; and small communities versus larger, anonymous ones. Hurt by the rejection of his ecclesiology and spirituality, Colman resigned and went with his followers to a tiny island, Inishbofin, off the west coast of Ireland, where, before his death in 674, he built a monastery not far from the yellow sands of the ocean. Its medieval ruins and holy well can still be visited today, a fitting memorial to one man's love of his spiritual heritage and his persistence in preserving a different expression of Christianity.

In France, the entire Breton church maintained its independence of the Gallo-Frankish church until the ninth century. At that time, in order to promote greater ecclesial uniformity, Louis the Pious, the third son of Charlemagne, attempted to make all monasteries in Gaul follow the Rule of St. Benedict. He also asked them to abandon the traditional Irish tonsure which Breton priests wore.[3] The Celtic Church in Wales came to an end primarily with the arrival of the Normans who brought with them many of the Roman norms of continental Christianity. As in Ireland, the ancient Celtic foundations in Wales either gave way to the new continental orders or themselves conformed, frequently by adopting the Augustinian Rule and becoming canons.[4]

In Scotland, while the monks of Iona had accepted the Roman ways in the late eighth century, it was not until the eleventh century that the Celtic Church was merged with Roman structures. Margaret, Queen of Scotland (c. 1045-93), was instrumental in this final submersion, intent as she was on imposing Anglo-Norman manners and institutions that would displace the native Celtic ones.[5]

In Cornwall, Athelstan of England in the tenth century began to exert his political power and reorganize the church there, resulting in the creation of a diocese of Cornwall with a bishopric at St. Germans. From then on, Celtic monasticism was on the defensive as Canterbury increasingly urged Roman rules.

———— ❧ ————

In Ireland, the Roman assimiliation was exceptionally gradual, beginning with the Irish Synod of 697 at which churches in the north accepted the Roman discipline. Not until the twelfth century, however, did great changes begin to occur in the rest of the island. The old native monasteries collapsed as Cistercian, Franciscan, and Dominican communities took their place. St. Malachy with his friend, Bernard of Clairvaux, were leaders in this effort to promote what they saw as needed reforms. In 1142, the beautiful buildings of Mellifont Abbey were constructed when Malachy first introduced the Cistercian Order to Ireland. In 1111, at the Council of Rathbreasail the entire island was divided into dioceses with bishops appointed to head each of them, thus replacing the monastic system in which abbots and abbesses had dominant roles.[6] Both processes, the collapse of the monastic system and the emergence of the diocesan, were accelerated by the Anglo-Norman conquest of most of the country which began in 1169 with the arrival of a handful of Anglo-Norman knights and their supporters at Wexford. By 1250, three quarters of the country had been overrun by invaders and a centralized government in Dublin controlled the country. Some of the ancient monasteries have survived as cities and towns to the present day, such as Derry, Armagh, Kildare, and Kells, while others with their rich and creative history of spiritual accomplishments were gradually deserted, the fate of Durrow, Monasterboice, and Clonmacnoise.

Thus, on one level, the Celtic Church came to an end in the twelfth century after some seven hundred years of great creativity and learning. On another level, however, it still exists, its spirituality alive in Celtic landscape and ancestral memories, in the prayers that have been passed down from one generation to another, in the popularity of the holy wells, and in the enduring observances and rituals connected with the feast days of the saints. Of all the prayers and practices which still live, soul friendship itself is being increasingly valued in and outside of any formal confessional encounter with a priest.

A Spiritual Heritage

This book has been about that Celtic soul friend, its historical origins, landscape, and spirituality. To know and identify with the history of the *anamchara* makes us capable of

———— ❧ ————

incorporating that spiritual heritage into our self-understanding, relationships, work, ministries, and daily life. Looking back on that history as described in the ancient stories as well as the practice of it through the ages, certain awarenesses emerge that offer ongoing guidance.

First of all, as the popular saying of St. Brigit reminds us, everyone needs a soul friend, since "anybody without a soul friend is like a body without a head." Soul friends, we've come to see, share what the Greeks and Romans and the early church fathers and mothers equate with true friendship: one soul in two bodies, two hearts united as one. This bonding and exchange of soul and heart in a relationship of trust, respect, and mutuality is the greatest gift we can receive from others or give to them. In a world of increasing complexity, in a culture where fear, violence, and cynicism flourish and where Internet, e-mail, and voice-mail increasingly keep us from speaking face to face, it is no wonder that people today long for relationships of genuine intimacy, continuity, and depth. Being accepted and loved by another person is to be cherished, and not taken for granted—as is the experience of being heard when one is not even sure what it is one is trying to say.

A second awareness about soul friendship is that it is grounded in a spirituality of conversion and reconciliation. To be a soul friend or to have a soul friend can bring about significant change in our lives, and can help make it possible for that transformation to become more deeply rooted. Soul friendship thrives in a particular kind of spirituality: a spirituality of ongoing conversion and reconciliation, starting with ourselves. Through our willingness to change, and our efforts to bring about unity and reunion with those with whom we may feel insecure, misunderstood, alienated, and even hostile, we set an example of Christian leadership today. Such leadership incorporates the values of the saints and the wisdom of their stories.[7] Such leadership is grounded in a spirituality that is global in its vision and creation-centered in its scope. It invites the full participation of laity, women, and marginal peoples in church life, its sacraments and decision-making. It cherishes the warmth of the hearth, family life, and a circle of friends. It acknowledges the significance of daily life and work, the so-called "ordinary" aspects of our lives, as sacred soil for soul-making. Such leadership is willing to work, as did the saints, for qualitative changes in our culture and our Christian churches—especially in our churches. If they do not model inclusivity, equality, diversity, and respect for others, the truth and hope of the gospels can quickly be lost to this generation and the next, our children's and grandchildren's.

A third awareness concerning soul friendship is that it is about being a cell, a sanctuary for others, strong enough, like the beehive huts that cling to the cliffs of Skellig Michael, to withstand the force of wind and waves, traumas and transitions. As we learned from our study of both desert and Celtic Christians, an *anamchara* was originally someone who, as a companion, shared another's cell and to whom one confessed, revealing confidential aspects of one's life. These friendships were strong precisely because they were built, not on human perfection nor on the concealment of human faults, but on the courage to be vulnerable, to speak as truthfully as one can from the heart where identity, meaning, and passion dwell. Soul friendship is a relationship that acts as a container, a cell in which we can face the truth of our lives without fear. Soul friendship is a sanctuary where the worst part of us can be acknowledged so that genuine change can begin to occur. The cell of soul friendship is where we can lay down our lives for awhile, and put down the arms we carry of anger, resentments, blame, and jealousies. It is a place of quiet and solitude which, as the desert Christians believed about their own dwelling places, can teach us everything, especially the self-knowledge that we sometimes seek so hard to avoid. Soul friendship then becomes a place where our joys and accomplishments can be celebrated wholeheartedly. Ultimately, to be a soul friend is to be a cell where two people can speak, as friends do, heart to heart, and experience, in their mutual disclosure, the acceptance and forgiveness of God. Considering the shape of the beehive cells on Skellig Michael, what is frequently expressed and given between soul friends is precisely what the honeybee represents: fertility, creativity, generativity, wisdom.

To be fertile, creative, and generative, to obtain wisdom, the cell of soul friendship often becomes a kiln in which we are purified of the false loves and desires that make us sick so that we can better appreciate the goodness of this life as we prepare for the next. Maelruain, one of the founders of the Celi De Movement, linked soul friendship with fire, saying, "When you place yourself under the guidance of someone else, you should seek out the fire which will most fiercely burn, that is, which will spare you the least."[8] This image of fire Carl Jung associates with transformation when he quotes Origen quoting Jesus, "Whoever is near to me is near to the fire. . . ."[9] Life in the cell, life with a soul friend, is sometimes like being in a furnace where our illusions and obsessions are burned away, revealing what often lies behind them: our desire to control, our dread of change, and, ultimately, our fear of dying. Only when the illusions and falsehoods are stripped away can we see ourselves as we really are, while at the same time freeing ourselves to see the world as it really is. Facing reality, and living creatively within it, is what soul friendships can help us do. The cell which soul friendship provides teaches us how to face our illusions and fears—not alone, but with the help of a community of friends.

A fourth awareness is that soul friendship, while it can embody many leadership roles and be identified in numerous ways, is always rooted in the heart. As we learned from the penitentials and lives of the saints, those roles might include being a confessor, a teacher, a mentor, a spiritual guide, but however such soul friendship is expressed, it is about offering others an inviting presence, an attentive ear, a place to tell their story and to be honest with themselves. Whether we are soul friends in our personal relationships or in our professional work, being an *anamchara* is about the graceful art of listening, of discerning, of being attentive to the workings of the heart.

The desert and the Celtic spiritual traditions very realistically speak of the heart not only as a center from which our thoughts and desires, yearnings and aspirations originate, but also as the battleground where the struggle for integrity and the truth of our lives is fought. Our scriptures understood this, and make repeated references to that conviction. In the Old Testament we find frequent references to "hardness of heart" (cf. Ex 8:19) as well as to the change that is equated with conversion: "I shall give you a new heart, and put a new spirit in you; I shall remove the heart of stone from your bodies and give you a heart of flesh instead" (Ez 36:26). Ecclesiastes tells us, "the wise man's heart leads him aright; the fool's leads him astray" (10:2). In our hearts, wisdom is or is not learned: "Let your heart treasure what I have to say, keep my principles and you shall live; acquire wisdom, acquire perception" (Prv 4:4).

And, of course, there is the prayer of the wise person who has listened: "Lord, teach me wisdom in the secret of my heart" (Ps 90:12).

Jesus was obviously aware of this tradition and appreciative of it. Immersed in this spiritual heritage, he reveals a great respect for the reality of the heart. "Happy are the pure of heart," he tells us, "they shall see God" (Mt 5:8). That saying from the Beatitudes was honored by the desert Christians and Celtic saints, with the knowledge that it had much more to do with where one's heart is centered and for what purpose one's life is lived than only applying it to sins related to eros or sexuality. Warning his friends that "where your treasure is, there will your heart also be" (Lk 12:34), Jesus also includes reference to the heart when asked what the greatest commandment is: "You must love the Lord, your God with all your heart, with all your soul, with all your mind and with all your strength" (Mk 12:30). Later, like a wise soul friend, he says, "Do not let your hearts be troubled. Trust in God still, and trust in me" (Jn 14:1). Those who followed Jesus throughout the centuries often have been reminded of his words concerning the heart's reality, and then reminded others. Julian of Norwich, a fourteenth-century English anchoress whose writings reflect so many of the non-dualistic attributes of Celtic spirituality, including a great respect for the feminine side of God, equates the heart with the soul, and speaks of where the soul is found: "Our Lord opened my spiritual eyes, and showed me my soul in the midst of my heart."[10] Soul friends are attentive to the stirrings of the heart in their own lives and encourage others to do the same.

Finally, soul friendships are concerned, along with holiness, with the acquisition of wisdom. From the stories of desert Christians to those of the Celtic saints, we can see a movement in Christian history from external cells to the cell of the heart, what Augustine called the "royal cell of wisdom."[11] Conscious of this, soul friends today are aware that their friendships and mentoring are concerned with the pursuit of wisdom, that type of knowledge that has eternal value. Bernard of Clairvaux associated wisdom with the breasts of Christ, and an ancient hagiography of St. Berach states that "it is from the fount of all true wisdom, that is, from Jesus Christ, that all the saints were filled with the grace of wisdom."[12] The person considered a true

hero among the Christian Celts was someone who had
surrendered one's life to God, and sought to model his or her life
after the saints, expressed in the belief that "he [or she] is
wisdom of the saints who does God's will."[13] Aelred of Rievaulx
linked wisdom directly with friendship: "I might almost say that
friendship is nothing else but wisdom."[14] Thomas Merton, like
Aelred, also equates wisdom with friendship. Quoting scripture,
he says, "But with her friendship, one becomes truly the friend
of God" (Wis 7:14); "She makes them friends of God and
prophets, for God loves those who dwell in wisdom" (Wis 7:27-
28). Merton goes on to equate wisdom with beauty as well:[15]

> For she is fairer than the sun
>   and surpasses every constellation of the stars.
> Compared to light, she takes precedence;
>   for that, indeed, night supplants,
> but wickedness prevails not over Wisdom.
>   Indeed, she reaches from end to end mightily
> and governs all things well.
>   Her I loved and sought after from my youth;
> I sought to take her for my bride
>   and was enamored of her beauty (Wis 7:26-8:2).

Beauty, as we know from our study of the ancient Celts, was
loved and especially appreciated by them. They were enamored
of the beauty of the body, while Christian Celts, though not
unappreciative of physical beauty, emphasized the inner beauty
of the soul, a beauty of lasting value that transcends the rigors of
growing old and the supposed finality of death. Considering
their respect for the soul, they equated soul friendship itself with
the beauty of forgiveness, or, as the Welsh poem, "The Loves of
Taliesin," expressed it, with the beauty of "doing penance for
sin."[16] Often, like birth itself, true beauty and wisdom is born in
anguish and tears: the anguish of recognition and repentance,
the tears of gratitude. A soul friend is someone who, in the
process of integrating the wisdom which his or her own life
experiences and wounds have taught, accompanies another in
their own soul-birthing or soul-making, so that "in every
generation wisdom lives in holy souls and makes them friends of
God" (Wis 7:27).

Appendix

BCE

900-300	Celtic race comes to Ireland
750-450	La Tene—Celtic culture is identified
400	Classical Greek civilization reaches peak
387	Celts sack Rome
300s	Celts dominate Europe
146	Greece falls to Roman power
64-52	Caesar invades Gaul and Britain, 55 B.C.E.

CE

4	Birth of Christ
60s	First written gospel narrative: gospel of Mark
c. 90	Definitive break between Synogogue and newly consolidated Christian community

100

100-300s	Gnostics

200

200-300s	Fathers and Mothers of the church
	Persecutions of Christians
251-356	Antony
292-346	Pachomius

300

300s	Great influx into the desert
313	Edict of Milan: Christianity formally recognized
316-397	St. Martin of Tours

330-379	Basil
331-420	Jerome
	Roman friends Marcella, Melania, Lea, Paula, Eustochium
c. 331-395	Gregory of Nyssa
	Macrina, sister of Basil and Gregory of Nyssa
334-397	Ambrose of Milan
346-399	Evagrius of Pontus
354-430	Augustine of Hippo
357	Athanasius writes the *Life of Antony*
c. 360-435	John Cassian
362-432	Ninian of Candida Casa, Scotland
c. 380-461	Patrick of Ireland
385	Jerome in Bethlehem

400

407-8	First devastation of Scetis; death of many desert Christians, exodus of some
410	Sack of Rome by Alaric
c. 412	Rufinus, *History of the Monks of Egypt* completed
419-20	Palladius' *Lausiac History* written
421-6	Cassian writes the *Institutes* and *Conferences*
432	Patrick in Ireland
434	Second devastation of Scetis
c. 452-524	Brigit of Kildare
455	Sack of Rome by the Vandals
480-547	Benedict
489-570/83	Brendan of Clonfert
Late 400s-early 500s	Monasteries, convents, and double-monasteries begun in very primitive forms

500 (Middle Ages 500-1500)

mid/late 400s-early 500s	Declan of Ardmore
500s	Heroic Age of Irish monasticism begins; age of powerful founders

510	Rule of St. Benedict
512-545	Ciaran of Clonmacnoise
520-589/601	David of Wales
d. 549	Finnian of Clonard
?-570	Ita of Killeedy
521-597	Columcille of Iona
500-700	Irish penitential books written, Finnian's (550-575) the earliest
540-604	Gregory the Great
c. 543-615	Columbanus
550	Byzantine Empire at height
c. 560-623	Findbarr of Cork
563	Columcille arrives on Iona
597	Augustine of Canterbury brings Christianity to Anglo-Saxons in England

600

600s	Artistic flowering of Ireland, and growing affiliation with Roman-style Christianity; beginning of Celtic hagiographies
c. 600-651	Aidan of Lindisfarne
614-680	Hild of Whitby
d. 616	Kevin of Glendalough
c. 620-680	Cogitosus, author of *Life of Brigit*
d. 626	Maedoc of Ferns
d. 630	Gall of St. Gallen, Switzerland
628-689	Benedict Biscop
632	Agreement in southern Ireland for unity with Rome
633-709	Wilfrid, i.e., Book of Durrow (c.650-700): earliest illuminated gospel
	Irish missionaries to Gaul, Rhineland, Switzerland, Italy, Scotland, and England
634-687	Cuthbert of Lindisfarne
635	Aidan arrives on Lindisfarne
c. 640	Jonas's *Life of Columbanus* written
653	Benedict Biscop goes to Rome for the first time
664	Council of Whitby (greater unity with Roman "ways," including northern Ireland—although Celtic

————— ✺ —————

	Christianity and spirituality continue in Ireland until 1200s)
669	Theodore the Greek, Archbishop of Canterbury
c. 672-735	Bede the Venerable
673	Wearmouth monastery established
675	Cuthbert retires from being abbot on Lindisfarne and moves to Inner Farne
c. 675	Tirechan writes *Memoir of St. Patrick*
679-704	Adomnan, ninth abbot of Iona and author of *Life of Columba*
c. 680s	Muirchu's *Life of Patrick*
682	Jarrow monastery founded
685	Cuthbert made bishop of Lindisfarne
687	Death of Cuthbert on Inner Farne
c. 695	Lindisfarne gospels
697	Irish synod at which churches in north accept Roman discipline

700

700s	Irish monastic cities; transition from "spiritual fervor to temporal cupidity" (dePaors)
716	Iona community celebrates Easter for the first time according to Roman practice
731	Completion of Bede's *Ecclesiastical History*
c. 735-804	Alcuin of York at court of Charlemagne
	Celi De reform movement: hermits and anchorites concerned with spiritual perfection, meditation, excellence in liturgies, and soul friendship
d. 739	Samthann of Clonbroney
d. 792	Maelruain, founder of Tallaght Monastery
d. 824	Oengus the Culdee
795	First Viking attack against Irish monasteries

800

800	Charlemagne crowned emperor
early 800s	Book of Kells

| 800-1000 | Irish high crosses earliest: at Ahenny; finest: Cross of Muiredoch, at Monasterboice; latest: Dysert O'Dea, Kilfenora |
| 830-870 | worst period, Vikings increasingly attack Ireland, Scotland, England, Wales ("drowning books," stealing, destroying, killing) |

900 — Round towers

1000 — Gregorian Reform on the Continent

1014	Battle of Clontarf—total defeat of Vikings in Ireland and death of Brian Boru
1054	Schism of East and West
1066	William the Conqueror and Battle of Hastings
1094-1148	St. Malachy of Ireland (friend of Bernard of Clairvaux)
1095	Pope Urban II launches First Crusade

1100

1111	National Synod near Cashel: from monastic churches to dioceses and parishes; church reform from Canterbury; Continental orders (Cistercians, and later Franciscans, Dominicans) introduced to Ireland
c. 1110-1167	Aelred of Rievaulx
c. 1146-1223	Gerald of Wales
1157	Mellifont Abbey founded by Cistercians in Ireland— "end of Irish monastic period"
1168	Anglo-Norman invasion of Ireland
1170	Murder of Thomas Becket at Canterbury

1200-1500 — Urbanization of Ireland begins in earnest; Norman assimilation; Tudor pressure begins in 1521, Reformation introduced and resisted

———— ❧ ————

Notes

Introduction

1. Norman Maclean, in his book *A River Runs Through It and Other Stories* (New York: Pocket Books, 1992), p. 113, refers to this haunting, a quality with which many people of Celtic origins can identify.

2. Frank McCourt, *Angela's Ashes* (New York: Scribner, 1996), p. 69.

3. Stephen Gwynn, "Ireland, O Ireland," handcoloured print #295 (Dublin: The Cuala Press Limited, 1983).

4. C. S. Lewis, *Surprised by Joy: The Shape of My Early Life* (New York: Harcourt, Brace & World, Inc., 1955), p.16.

5. See Thomas Merton, trans., *The Wisdom of the Desert* (New York: A New Directions Book, 1960), p. 30.

6. See Cassian's Conference 16, chapter III, in P. Schaff and H. Wace, eds., *A Select Library of Nicene and Post-Nicene Fathers of the Christian Church*, Vol. XI (Grand Rapids, MI: Wm. B. Eerdmans, n.d.), p. 451.

7. See Peter Berresford Ellis, *The Druids* (London: Constable and Company, 1994), p. 177 where he states that Virgil "was born at Andes, near Mantua, in Cisalpine Gaul, and was of a Celtic family. . . . Virgil grew up with knowledge of the Celtic culture which still existed all around him."

8. Biographers refer to the Lincolns as among the English, Scotch, and Irish who settled in Kentucky, and tell of the influence of Scottish and Irish stories which Nancy Hanks, Lincoln's mother, told him as a boy. Lincoln certainly manifested an Irish temperament with his belief in dreams and portents, his telling of numerous stories, and what biographer Carl Sandburg describes as his "shifting moods." Besides the numerous stories he told, on more than one occasion Lincoln is said to have recited the ballad of "How St. Patrick Came to Be Born on the Seventeenth of March." See Carl Sandburg, *Abraham Lincoln: The Prairie Years I* (New York: Charles Scribner's Sons, 1951), pp. 3, 66, 174, 177, and 296 ff.

9. A. M. Allchin, *God's Presence Makes the World: The Celtic Vision Through the Centuries in Wales* (London: Darton, Longman and Todd Ltd., 1997), p. 148.

10. John Macquarrie, *Paths in Spirituality* (London: SCM Press Ltd., 1972), p.122.

11. See Rex Warner, trans., *The Confessions of St. Augustine* (New York: New American Library, 1963), book ten, pp. 210-256, where Augustine describes memory as a "great harbor" and "a vast and boundless subterranean shrine."

12. Rollo May, *The Cry of Myth* (New York: W.W. Norton & Co., 1991), p. 70.

13. Thomas Merton, *Conjectures of a Guilty Bystander* (New York: Doubleday, 1966), p. 21.

Chapter 1

1. Whitley Stokes, ed., *The Martyrology of Oengus the Culdee* (London: Henry Bradshaw Society, 1905), p. 65.

2. For information on the Celtic soul-friend tradition and its influence on the evolution of the sacrament of penance in the West, see O. D. Watkins, *A History of Penance,* Vols. I and II (London: Longmans, Green and Co., 1920), especially Vol. II on the "Keltic System," pp. 756 ff., and James Dallen, *The Reconciling Community: The Rite of Penance* (New York: Pueblo Publishing Co., 1986), pp. 103-118. An ironic part of that history is that the church in Rome, preferring the public forms of penitence and reconciliation that had developed in early Christian history, initially opposed this form of spiritual guidance; that is, until 1215 at the Fourth Lateran Council when participation *with a priest* in these encounters was made obligatory. Then, later, at the Council of Trent in the 1500s, these encounters were legally defined as one of the seven great sacraments of the Roman Catholic church: the sacrament of reconciliation, popularly referred to as "confession" before Vatican II.

3. John T. McNeill and Helena Gamer, *Medieval Handbooks of Penance* (New York: Octagon Books, 1979), p. 25. Besides the reference to the *acharya,* McNeill speaks of "the continuity of pagan elements" in Celtic Christianity.

4. See Robert O'Driscoll, ed., *The Celtic Consciousness* (New York: George Braziller, 1981), pp. xii, 11, 333 ff. Myles Dillon, in his *Early Irish Literature* (Chicago: University of Chicago Press, 1948), p. 173 comments on the similiarities between the Indian *kavi* and the Irish *fili* or poet. Reference to the native costumes and almond eye is found in Amy Oakley, *Enchanted Brittany* (New York: The Century Co., 1930), p. 305.

5. See Peter Berresford Ellis, *The Celtic Empire* (Durham, NC: Carolina Academic Press, 1990), pp. 9-22.

6. O'Driscoll, *The Celtic Consciousness,* p. xvi.

7. Aedeen Cremin, *The Celts* (New York: Rizzoli, 1998), p. 6.

8. Quoted in Prudence Jones and Nigel Pennick, *A History of Pagan Europe,* p. 93.

9. See Michael Richter, *Medieval Ireland: The Enduring Tradition* (New York: St. Martin's Press, 1988), pp. 20-21.

10. See, for example, Cecile O'Rahilly, ed., *Tain Bo Cualnge* (Dublin: Dublin Institute for Advanced Studies, 1984), for one of the most important epics of Irish literature which confirms statements on the Celts by the classical writers regarding their war-like qualities, nakedness in battle, head-hunting, belief in spirits, and strong passions. One of the best compilations of early Welsh literature is found in Jeffrey Gantz, trans., *The Mabinogion* (New York: Penguin Press, 1976).

11. One reason for the Celts going naked into battle may be related to what the Native American shaman, Black Elk, says about his own people, the Oglaga Sioux. In John G. Neihardt, *Black Elk Speaks* (New York: Pocket

Books, 1973), pp. 12-13, Black Elk describes how as a young man he and his friends would play a game of war to prepare themselves for the real thing: "We were always naked when we played it, just as warriors are when they go into battle if it is not too cold, because they are swifter without clothes."

12. W. F. and J. N. G. Ritchie, *Celtic Warriors* (Shire Publications, 1985), pp. 25, 29.

13. Quoted in Nora Chadwick, *The Celts* (New York: Penguin Books, 1970), p. 50.

14. See C. H. Oldfather, trans., *Diodorus Siculus: The Library of History, Books IV.59-VIII, Vol. III* (Cambridge, MA: Loeb Classical Library, Harvard University Press, 1939), pp. 167-171.

15. Ibid., pp. 173-177.

16. Quoted in Christiane Eluere, *The Celts: Conquerors of Ancient Europe* (New York: Harry Abrams Inc., Publishers, n.d.), pp. 141-142.

17. Athenaeus is quoted in Simon James, *The World of the Celts* (London: Thames and Hudson, 1993), p. 53.

18. See Cecile O'Rahilly, ed., *Tain Bo Cualnge*, pp. 220-233.

19. For a discussion of the fluidity of sexuality among the ancients, see Eva Cantarella, *Bisexuality in the Ancient World* (New Haven: Yale University Press, 1992), and David Halperin, John Winkler, and Froma Zeitlin, eds., *Before Sexuality: The Construction of Erotic Experience in the Ancient Greek World* (Princeton, NJ: Princeton University Press, 1990). Concerning sexuality among Native Americans, see Walter Williams, *The Spirit and the Flesh: Sexual Diversity in American Indian Culture* (Boston: Beacon Press, 1986), and Will Roscoe, *Changing Ones: Third and Fourth Genders in Native North America*, (London: Macmillan Press Ltd., 1998).

20. It may also reflect something of the conflict within oneself between good and evil. George Simms, in *Exploring the Book of Kells* (Dublin: O'Brien Press, 1989), p. 25, describes a similar scene in the Book of Kells as that found on the high cross. In the Book of Kells two men, pulling each other's beards, form a capital N, and introduce the words, "No man can serve two masters. He will either hate the one and love the other or hold to the one and despise the other." Simms says, "The little picture of the two men struggling gives us the clue to the words of Jesus which need to be thought about."

21. See Sean Connolly, "*Vita Prima Sanctae Brigitae*: Background and Historical Value," *Journal of the Royal Society of Antiquaries of Ireland*, Vol. 119, 1989, pp. 43-44, 49.

22. See C. H. Oldfather, trans., *Diodorus Siculus: The Library of History, Books IV.59-VIII, Vol. III*, pp. 171-181.

23. See Nora Chadwick, *The Celts*, p. 146.

24. For discussion of this topic on the meaning of "druid," and for direct quotations from Pliny and Lucanus, see Peter Berresford Ellis, *The Druids* (London: Constable & Co., 1994), pp. 37-49, and Miranda Green,

Exploring the World of the Druids, pp. 9 and 18. Both speak of early Christian writers, such as Hippolytus, Clement of Alexandria, and Cyril of Alexandria, as writers who saw the druids in a very positive light: as powerful mystical leaders, teachers, and philosophers. Green, however, says that they had no direct contact with the Celts, but relied upon second-hand written accounts in their idealization of the druids as "noble savages."

25. Quoted in Nora Chadwick, *The Druids* (Cardiff: University of Wales Press, 1966), pp. 29-30.

26. See S. A. Handford, trans., *Caesar: The Conquest of Gaul* (Baltimore, MD: Penguin Classics, 1951), pp. 31-33.

27. Ibid., p. 31.

28. See John T. McNeill, *Celtic Penitentials and Their Influence on Continental Christianity*, pp. 90 ff. He shows that while the patristic writers, such as John Cassian, Pachomius, and Basil (with whose works the Christian Irish were familiar) refer to the practice and value of confession which they learned from the desert monks, there is no specific reference in those writings to penances being assigned the penitent. That seems to be uniquely an Irish contribution, derived from the druids.

29. See S. A. Handford, trans., *Caesar: The Conquest of Gaul*, pp. 31-32, and Miranda Green, *Exploring the World of the Druids* (London: Thames & Hudson, 1997), p. 48.

30. The so-called Tolland Man of Denmark and Lindow Man of Britain, for example, show that both naked young men partook of a kind of ritual meal before having their throats cut. See "bog burial" and "sacrifice, human" in Miranda Green, *Dictionary of Celtic Myth and Legend* (London: Thames and Hudson, 1992), pp. 46-47,182-183. Also R. C. Turner and R. G. Scaife, eds., *Bog Bodies: New Discoveries and New Perspectives* (London: British Museum Press, 1995), for a full discussion of recent archaeological findings.

31. See S. A. Handford, trans., *Caesar: The Conquest of Gaul*, p. 33.

32. References to druidesses and druidical families are found in Nora Chadwick, *The Druids*, pp. 81-83, 99. See Cecile O'Rahilly, ed., *Tain Bo Cualnge*, p. 196, where "three druids and three druidesses" are sent forth to attack the Irish hero, CuChulainn.

33. See James Kenney, *The Sources for the Early History of Ireland: Ecclesiastical* (Dublin: Irish University Press, 1920), p. 358, and W. D. Killen, *The Ecclesiastical History of Ireland*, Vol. I (London: Macmillan & Co., 1975), pp. 28-29. For a very interesting comparison of the vestal and Brigittine cults, see Paul Lonigan, *The Druids: Priests of the Ancient Celts* (London: Greenwood Press, 1996), pp. 70-75.

34. Oliver Davies, *Celtic Spirituality* (New York: Paulist, 1999), p. 214.

35. T. F. O'Rahilly, *Early Irish History and Mythology* (Dublin, 1946), p. 323.

36. See Elissa Henken, *Traditions of the Welsh Saints* (Cambridge: D.S. Brewer, 1987), p. 81.

37. These terms for God are found in the ninth-century Irish "Rule of Carthage" which was influenced by the Celi De. See Uinseann O Maidin, *The Celtic Monk: Rules and Writings of Early Irish Monks* (Kalamazoo, MI: Cistercian Publications, 1996), p. 69.

38. Brian Friel, ed., *The Last of the Name* (Nashville, TN: J.S. Sanders and Co., 1999), p. 111.

39. See Anne Ross, "The Horned God in Britain," in *Pagan Celtic Britain* (Chicago: Academy Chicago Publishers, 1996), pp. 172-220, and Miranda Green, *Dictionary of Celtic Myth and Legend*, p. 60. In Green's *Symbol and Image in Celtic Religious Art* (London: Routledge, 1989), p. 94, she speaks about "the regenerative and prosperity roles of Cernunnos" and his function "as a god of healing and renewal."

40. See Elizabeth Gray, ed., *Cath Maige Tuired: The Second Battle of Mag Tuired* (Naas, Ireland: Irish Texts Society, 1982), pp. 47, 25.

41. For an informative study on the cult, see Fred Gustafson, *The Black Madonna* (Boston: Sigo Press, 1990). His focus is upon the Black Madonna of Einsiedeln in Switzerland, and although he traces the cult back to roots "deeply embedded in Swiss history," p. x, he does not allude to any Celtic associations. I would, especially considering the important ancient influence the Celts had in Switzerland, as is evident at the excavations at La Tene.

42. Jim Fitzpatrick, "The Dream of Nuada," in *The Book of Conquests* (Limpsfield, England: Dragon's World Ltd., 1978). For the various names associated with the mother-goddess of the Celts, see Elizabeth Gray, ed., *Cath Maige Tuired, the Second Battles of Mag Tuired*, p. 122.

43. See Alexander MacBain, *Celtic Mythology and Religion* (Stirling: Eneas MacKay, 1917), p. 128, regarding Ana or Danu as moon goddess. Jean Markale, in *Women of the Celts* (Rochester, VT: Inner Traditions International, 1975), pp. 16-17, describes the equality and "harmony between the roles of men and women that was not dependent upon the superiority of one sex over the other," and refers to "the well-documented knowledge we have of Celtic law, where women enjoyed privileges that would have made the Roman women of the same period green with envy."

44. See O'Donovan, "A poem attributed to Colum Cille," in *Miscellany of the Irish Archaeological Society*, I (Dublin, 1846), pp. 12-13.

45. See Edward Sellner, *Wisdom of the Celtic Saints* (Notre Dame, IN: Ave Maria Press, 1993), p. 133.

46. See H. Zimmer, *The Irish Element in Medieval Culture* (New York: Patnam's Sons, 1890), p. 33.

47. J. M. Clark, *The Abbey of St. Gall as a Centre of Literature and Art* (London: Cambridge University Press, 1926), p. 27.

48. John Ryan, *Irish Monasticism* (Dublin: Irish Academic Press, 1986), p. 207.

49. See, for example, Stuart Piggott, *The Druids* (New York: Thames and Hudson, 1975), pp. 119-121.

50. Myles Dillon, *Early Irish Literature* (Chicago: University of Chicago Press, 1948), p. 157.

51. Jeffrey Gantz, *The Mabinogion* (New York: Penguin Books, 1976), p. 243.

Chapter 2

1. See Julia Smith, "Celtic Asceticism and Carolingian Authority in Early Medieval Brittany," in W. J. Shields, ed., *Monks, Hermits and the Ascetic Tradition* (Oxford: Blackwell, 1985), p. 59.

2. Sandra LaWall Lipshultz, *Selected Works* (Minneapolis, MN: The Minneapolis Institute of Arts, 1988), p. 36.

3. See "Art and Architecture," in Father Gregory Telepneff, *The Egyptian Desert in the Irish Bogs: The Byzantine Character of Early Celtic Monasticism* (Etna, CA: Center for Traditionalist Orthodox Studies, 1998), pp. 44-49.

4. See Lionel Casson, *Travel in the Ancient World* (Baltimore, MD: John Hopkins University Press, 1994) for an excellent discussion of the topic, especially pp. 300-329 on travel to the Holy Land.

5. See Denis Meehan, ed., *Adamnan's De Locis Sanctis* (Dublin: Dublin Institute for Advanced Studies, 1983), pp. 97, 51-53. Adamnan says that the bishop saw and touched, in one of the chapels in Jerusalem, "the chalice of the Lord, which he himself blessed with his own hand and gave to the apostles when reclining with them at supper the day before he suffered. The chalice is silver, has the measure of a Gaulist pint, and has two handles fashioned on either side. . . . All the people of the city flock to it with great veneration."

6. See "Irish Pilgrims in Jerusalem and Rome," in Peter Harbison, *Pilgrimage in Ireland* (Syracuse, NY: Sycracuse University Press, 1991), pp. 29-31, and Aziz Atiya, *History of Eastern Christianity* (Notre Dame, IN: University of Notre Dame Press, 1967), pp. 55 ff.

7. Quoted in J. M. Clark, *The Abbey of St. Gall as a Centre of Literature and Art* (Cambridge: Cambridge University Press, 1926), p. 28.

8. See Charles Plummer, "Seven Monks of Egypt in Disert Uilaig," *Irish Litanies* (Rochester, NY: Boydell & Brewer Inc., 1992), pp. 65, 118.

9. Jerome, after he had moved to the Holy Land from Rome, asks a friend in a letter, "How long will you remain in the shadow of roofs, in the smoky dungeon of the cities? Believe me, I see here more light." Quoted in Susan Power Bratton, *Christianity, Wilderness, and Wildlife* (Scranton: University of Scranton Press, 1993), pp. 171-172.

10. Hilary of Poitiers is quoted in Philip Rousseau, *Ascetics, Authority, and the Church* (Oxford: Oxford University Press, 1978), p. 86.

11. For Sulpicius Severus's quotation, see "First Dialogue," in Bernard Peebles, trans., "Sulpicius Severus: Writings," from B. Peebles, ed., *The Fathers of the Church*, Vol. 7 (Washington, DC: Catholic University of America Press, 1949), p. 189.

12. Quoted in Alison G. Elliott, *Roads to Paradise: Reading the Lives of the Early Saints* (London: Brown University Press, 1987), p. 84.

13. Benedicta Ward, trans., *The Sayings of the Desert Fathers* (London: Mowbray, 1975), p. 191.

14. Helen Waddell, trans., *The Desert Fathers* (Ann Arbor, MI: University of Michigan Press, 1972), pp. 53-54.

15. Norman Russell, trans., *The Lives of the Desert Fathers* (London: Mowbray, 1980), p. 118.

16. See Rex Warner, trans., *The Confessions of St. Augustine* (New York: New American Library, 1963), in book eight, chapter six, pp. 171-173.

17. See Shirley Toulson, *The Celtic Year* (Shaftsbury, Dorset: Element, 1993), p. 94, where she states: "It was a Celt, born in Scythia in 360, who first brought monasticism out of Egypt to Gaul."

18. Norman Russell, trans., *The Lives of the Desert Fathers*, p. 8.

19. See George Gingras, trans., *Egeria: Diary of a Pilgrimage* (New York: Newman Press, 1970), p. 49. Hers is a fascinating story of her experiences on Sinai, the countless monastic cells for men and women found at the shrine of St. Thecla, and the churches and Holy Week liturgies of Jerusalem.

20. Robert Gregg, trans., *Athanasius: The Life of Antony and the Letter to Marcellinus* (New York: Paulist Press, 1980), pp. 42-43.

21. See the story in the "Life of St. Mary of Egypt" in Benedicta Ward, *Harlots of the Desert* (London: Mowbray, 1987), p. 41, in which the monk Zossima encounters Mary in the desert, "naked, her body black as if scorched by the fierce heat of the sun, the hair on her head was white as wool and short, coming down only to the neck."

22. Robert Meyer, trans., *Palladius: The Lausiac History* (New York: Newman Press, 1964), pp. 101-102.

23. Ibid., pp. 31-33, 113, and 171.

24. Roy Deferrari, ed., *Early Christian Biographies* (Washington, DC: Catholic University of America Press, 1952), pp. 248-249.

25. Quoted in Carlin Barton, *The Sorrows of the Ancient Romans* (Princeton, NJ: Princeton University Press, 1993), p. 52.

26. See Helen Waddell, trans., *The Desert Fathers*, p. 41.

27. Quoted in Deno Geanakoplos, "St. Basil, 'Christian Humanist' of the 'Three Hierarchs' and Patron Saint of Greek Letters," p. 236, in Everett Ferguson, *Personalities of the Early Church* (New York: Garland Publishing, Inc., 1993).

28. Thomas Taylor, trans., *The Life of St. Samson of Dol* (London: SPCK, 1925), p. 20.

29. Robert Meyer, *Palladius: The Lausiac History*, pp. 17-19, 117-119.

30. Benedicta Ward, trans., *The Sayings of the Desert Fathers* (London: Mowbray, 1975), pp. 229-230.

31. Kenneth MacKenzie, trans., *Hell*, canto five, in *The Divine Comedy* (London: The Folio Society, 1979), p. 21.

32. For a discussion on purity of heart, see Columba Stewart, *Cassian the Monk* (New York: Oxford University Press, 1998), pp. 40-47.

33. Kevin Corrigan, trans., *The Life of Saint Macrina* (Toronto: Peregrina Publishing Co., 1995), p. 40.

34. For the moving account of Socrates' death, see "Phaedo" in Erich Segal, *The Dialogues of Plato* (New York: Bantam Books, 1986), pp. 65-133.

35. Benedicta Ward, *The Sayings of the Desert Fathers*, pp. 82-84.

36. R. M. French, trans., *The Way of a Pilgrim* (London: Triangle, SPCK, 1995).

37. Elizabeth Bryson Bongie, trans., *The Life and Regimen of the Blessed and Holy Syncletica* (Toronto: Pergrina Publishing Co., 1998), p. 18.

38. See Ben Witherington III, *Women and the Genesis of Christianity* (Cambridge: Cambridge University Press, 1990), pp. 15-17.

39. Elizabeth Bryson Bongie, trans., *The Life and Regimen of the Blessed and Holy Syncletica*, pp. 32-33.

40. Benedicta Ward, *The Sayings of the Desert Fathers*, pp. 231-233.

41. Edward Sellner, *Wisdom of the Celtic Saints* (Notre Dame, IN: Ave Maria Press, 1993), pp. 198-199.

42. Elizabeth Bryson Bongie, trans., *The Life and Regimen of the Blessed and Holy Syncletica*, p. 19.

43. Ibid., pp. 31-38, 50-51.

44. Norman Russell, trans., *The Lives of the Desert Fathers*, p. 78.

45. Thomas Merton, *The Wisdom of the Desert* (New York: A New Directions Book, 1960), p. 77.

46. Norman Russell, trans., *The Lives of the Desert Fathers*, p. 106.

47. Benedicta Ward, ed., *The Desert of the Heart* (London: Darton, Longman and Todd Ltd., 1988), p. 21.

48. Armand Veilleux, trans., *Pachomian Koinonia*, Vol. I (Kalamazoo, MI: Cistercian Publications, 1980), p. 66.

49. Benedicta Ward, ed., *The Desert of the Heart*, p. 2.

50. Norman Russell, trans., *Lives of the Desert Fathers*, p. 3.

51. Ibid., p. 23.

52. Benedicta Ward, "Introduction," p. 32, in Norman Russell, trans., *Lives of the Desert Fathers*.

53. Ibid., pp. 70-71.

54. Ibid., pp. 59-61.

55. See Philip Rousseau, *Ascetics, Authority, and the Church* (Oxford: Oxford University Press, 1978), p. 133.

56. See Helen Waddell, trans., *The Desert Fathers*, pp. 30-39, from which all quotations of the *Life of Paul* were taken.

57. Norman Russell, trans., *Lives of the Desert Fathers*, p. 78.

58. See Derwas Chitty, trans., *The Letters of Ammonas* (Oxford: SLG Press, 1979), pp. 3-5.

59. See John Cassian, "Institutes," Book II, ch. 3, in P. Schaff and H. Wace, eds., *A Select Library of Nicene and Post-Nicene Fathers of the Christian Church,* Vol. XI (Grand Rapids, MI: Eerdmans, 1986), p. 206.

60. Ibid., p. 283.

61. Colm Luibheid, trans., *John Cassian: Conferences* (New York: Paulist Press, 1985), p. 64.

62. John Cassian, "Institutes," Book II, ch. 3, in P. Schaff and H. Wace, eds., *A Select Library of Nicene and Post-Nicene Fathers of the Christian Church,* Vol. XI, p. 234.

63. Colm Luibheid, trans., *John Cassian: Conferences,* pp. 57-58.

64. Ibid., pp. 68-70.

65. Ibid., p. 74.

66. John Cassian, "Institutes," Book II, ch. 3, in P. Schaff and H. Wace, eds., *A Select Library of Nicene and Post-Nicene Fathers of the Christian Church,* Vol. XI, p. 279.

67. Boniface Ramsey, *John Cassian: The Conferences* (New York: Paulist Press, 1997), p. 267.

68. James Charles Roy, *Islands of Storm* (Chester Springs, PA: Dufour Editions Inc., 1991), p. 191.

69. Colm Luibheid, *Conferences,* p. 37.

70. A. Veilleux, *Pachomian Koinonia,* Vol. III (Kalamazoo, MI: Cistercian Publications, 1982), p. 107.

71. See Norman Russell, trans., *The Lives of the Desert Fathers,* p. 91.

72. Robert Meyer, trans., *Palladius: The Lausiac History,* p. 28.

73. See George Gingras, trans., *Egeria: Diary of a Pilgrimage,* pp. 87 and 57.

74. Robert Meyer, trans., *Palladius: The Lausiac History,* p. 61.

75. Thomas Merton, *The Wisdom of the Desert,* p. 30.

76. Benedicta Ward, trans., *Sayings of the Desert Fathers,* p. 3.

77. Robert Meyer, trans., *Palladius: The Lausiac History,* p. 92.

78. Helen Waddell, trans., *The Desert Fathers,* p. 142.

79. See "Life of Ruadan," in Charles Plummer, *Lives of Irish Saints,* (Oxford: Oxford University Press, 1922), Vol. II, p. 308.

80. See "The Life of Gildas," in Hugh Williams, trans., *Two Lives of Gildas* (Cymmrodorion Record Series, 1899), p. 40.

81. See Nora Chadwick, *The Age of the Saints in the Early Celtic Church* (London: Oxford University Press, 1961), pp. 103 ff. and 149.

82. See Cassian's Conference 16, chapter III, in P. Schaff and H. Wace, eds., *A Select Library of Nicene and Post-Nicene Fathers of the Christian Church,* Vol. XI, p. 451.

83. Thomas Merton, *The Wisdom of the Desert,* p. 50.

84. In Ireland alone, by the sixth century, hermits had become so numerous that they posed a problem to the organized church. According to a report of the great Irish missionary Columbanus, Finnian of Clonard, one of the early monastic founders, had asked the writer Gildas in Britain about the

———— ✂ ————

large number of monks that were leaving their monasteries to become hermits against the wishes of their abbots. Another early Irish church document, *Catalogue of Irish Saints*, which outlines the development of Christianity in Ireland, designates "the Third Order" of Irish saints (from 598-664) as the period of anchorites "who dwelt in desert places, and lived on herbs and water and by alms, for the idea of possessing anything of their own was repugnant." See John Ryan, *Irish Monasticism* (Dublin: Talbot, 1931), pp. 260 and 220.

85. Robert Gregg, trans., *Athanasius: The Life of Antony and the Letter to Marcellinus*, p. 43.

86. Norman Russell, trans., *The Lives of the Desert Fathers*, p. 92.

Chapter 3

1. Bertram Colgrave and R. A. B. Mynors, eds., *Bede's Ecclesiastical History of the English People* (Oxford: Oxford at the Clarendon Press, 1981), pp. 15-19.

2. See E. G. Bowen, "Britain and the British Seas," from Donald Moore, ed., *The Irish Sea Province in Archaeology and History* (Cardiff: Cambria Archaeological Assoc., 1970), p. 14.

3. Nora Chadwick, "Early Literary Contacts Between Wales and Ireland," in Donald Moore, ed., *Irish Sea Province in Archaeology and History*, p. 66.

4. See Michael Winterbottom, trans., *Gildas: The Ruin of Britain and Other Works* (London: Phillimore & Co., 1978), p. 18.

5. See Joseph Duffy, trans., *Patrick in His Own Words* (Dublin: Veritas Press, 1975), pp. 20-21.

6. See Letter 123 in W. H. Fremantle, trans., "The Principal Works of St. Jerome," in Philip Schaff and Henry Wace, eds., *A Select Library of Nicene and Post-Nicene Fathers of the Christian Church*, Second Series, Vol. VI (Grand Rapids, MI: Wm. B. Eerdmans Publishing Company, 1989), p. 237.

7. G. A. Williamson, trans., *Eusebius: The History of the Church from Christ to Constantine* (London: Penguin Books, 1989), p. 141.

8. Lewis Thorpe, trans., *Gregory of Tours: the History of the Franks* (London: Penguin Books, 1974), p. 128.

9. For an examination of Irenaeus's life and thought, see Simon Tugwell, "The Apostolic Fathers and Irenaeus," in Cheslyn Jones, Geoffrey Wainwright, and Edward Yarnold, eds., *The Study of Spirituality* (New York: Oxford University Press, 1986), pp. 107-109, and W. R. Schoedel, "Theological Method in Irenaeus," in Everett Ferguson, ed., *Personalities of the Early Church*, Vol. I (New York: Garland Publishing, Inc., 1993), pp. 127-145.

10. Regarding Hilary's Celtic ancestry and prominence in Christianity, see Peter Berresford Ellis, *The Druids* (London: Constable and Co., 1994), p. 128. Hilary's significant thought on the Trinity is found in Stephen McKenna, trans., *Saint Hilary of Poitiers: The Trinity* (Washington, DC: Catholic University of America Press, 1954).

11. See Christopher Donaldson, *Martin of Tours: The Shaping of Celtic Spirituality* (Norwich: Canterbury Press, 1997), p. 104, where he states, "It is not certain whether Martin himself was born a Celt, though everything about him suggests that he acted like one."

12. See, for example, Rahnall O'Floinn, "Insignia Columbae I," in Cormac Bourke, ed., *Studies in the Cult of St. Columba* (Dublin: Four Courts Press, 1997), p. 160 who states that Martin's hagiography by Sulpicius Severus had much influence on early Irish hagiography. See also Christopher Donaldson, *Martin of Tours: The Shaping of Celtic Spirituality*, pp. 133-154, where he argues that, among the evidence pointing to Martin's influence are the early churches in England dedicated to the saint from Tours mentioned in Bede's *History of the English People*.

13. See Ben Witherington III, "Women in Roman Settings," *Women and the Genesis of Christianity* (Cambridge: Cambridge University Press, 1990), pp. 19-26. Elizabeth Clark, in *Jerome, Chrysostom, and Friends* (New York: The Edwin Mellen Press, 1979), pp. 37-40, discusses Aristotle's theory of friendship, and how he suggests that in a few cases marriage partners *might* be capable of such a relationship!

14. For more information of the Breton saints, see Michel Renouard and Nathalie Merrien, *Saints Guerisseurs De Bretagne* (Rennes: Editions Ouest-France, 1994), Andre Legrand, *Bretagne des Monasteres* (Rennes: Editions Ouest-France, 1993), and Melanie Hamon, *Vies de Saints Bretons et Regles Monastiques* (Rennes: Collection Hagiographie Bretonne, 1998).

15. See Roisin Ni Mheara, *In Search of Irish Saints* (Dublin: Four Courts Press, 1994), pp. 24-39 for an excellent discussion of Celtic Christian sites in Brittany.

16. See L. Duchesne, "Lovacat et Catihern, prêtres bretons du temps de St. Melaine," *Revue de Bretagne et de Vendee* 57, 1885, pp. 7-8.

17. See Anne L. Barstow, "Clerical Marriage in the Western Church Before 1050," in *Married Priests and the Reforming Papacy* (New York: Edwin Mellen Press, 1982), pp. 19 ff.

18. See Robert Meyer, trans., *Palladius: The Lausiac History* (New York: Newman Press, 1964), pp.41-43, concerning Amoun and his unnamed, but long-suffering "blessed companion."

19. See Rosemary Rader, "Syneisaktism: Spiritual Marriage," in *Breaking Boundaries: Male/Female Friendship in Early Christian Communities* (New York: Paulist Press, 1983), pp. 62-71

20. For an excellent article, including the examples of male saints living with women, see Roger Reynolds, "*Virgines Subintroductae* in Celtic Christianity," *Harvard Theological Review*, 61, 1968, pp. 547-566. The story of St. Ailbe and his women companions is found in Liam de Paor, *St. Patrick's World* (Dublin: Four Courts Press, 1993), p. 240.

21. See Jerome's Letter 22:14, in Charles Mierow, trans., *The Letters of St. Jerome*, Vol. I (New York: Newman Press, 1963), p. 146, where he says, "I am ashamed to speak of so scandalous a thing" and refers to those women in such relationships as "this new kind of concubines" and "one-man

harlots." "They are sheltered by the same house, by a single bedroom, often by one bed—and they call us suspicious if we think anything about it."

22. See Erik Erikson, *Gandhi's Truth* (New York: W.W. Norton & Co., 1969), pp. 402-403. This link with Indian and Celtic practices shows again the possibility of the Celts having originated from the land near India.

23. See Whitley Stokes, trans., *The Martyrology of Oengus the Culdee* (London: Henry Bradshaw Soceity, 1905), p. 41.

24. See B. E. Dodd and T. C. Heritage, *The Early Christians in Britain* (London: Longmans, Green and Co., 1966), p. 11.

25. For the sources of these stories, see Lionel S. Lewis, *St. Joseph of Arimathea at Glastonbury* (London: James Clarke & Co., 1955), pp. 92-111; 151-154, and especially James Carley, *Glastonbury Abbey: The Holy House at the Head of the Moors Adventurous* (Woodbridge, England: The Boydell Press, 1988).

26. See Lionel S. Lewis, *Glastonbury: Her Saints* (Orpington: R.I.L.K.O. Books, 1925), p. xix.

27. See Bertram Colgrave and R.A.B. Mynors, eds., *Bede's Ecclesiastical History of the English People*, pp. 29 ff.

28. See Oliver Davies, *Celtic Christianity in Early Medieval Wales* (Cardiff: University of Wales Press, 1996), p. 8.

29. See W. H. Fremantle, trans., "The Principal Works of St. Jerome," in Philip Schaff and Henry Wace, eds., *A Select Library of Nicene and Post-Nicene Fathers of the Christian Church*, Second Series, Vol. VI, p. 499. Aside from Jerome's usual acerbic remarks about perceived enemies, it seems he had some good reasons for not liking Pelagius' followers, since some of them attacked and burned the monasteries of Bethlehem, and Jerome himself only escaped by taking refuge in a tower.

30. For a brief discussion of Augustine's and Pelagius's views, see Nora Chadwick, *Poetry and Letters in Early Christian Gaul*, pp. 174-176. A modified version of Pelagius' teachings, to be known as "semi-Pelagianism," was also strongly opposed by Augustine and his followers. John Cassian was one of those reputable thinkers who supported this semi-Pelagian view. See Liam de Paor, *Ireland and Early Europe* (Dublin: Four Courts Press, 1997), pp. 68.

31. See Michael Winterbottom, trans., *Gildas: The Ruin of Britain and Other Works*, pp. 23, 74-76.

32. See Bertram Colgrave and R. A. B. Mynors, eds., *Bede's Ecclesiastical History of the English People*, pp. 133-135.

33. Ibid., pp. 137-141.

34. Ibid., p. 223.

35. See D. D. C. Pochin Mould, *Scotland of the Saints* (London: B.T. Batsford Ltd., 1952), p. 56.

36. See Iain MacDonald, ed., *Saint Mungo*, by Jocelinus, a Monk of Furness (Edinburgh: Floris Books, 1993), pp. 21-22.

37. See Wendy Davies, *Wales in the Early Middle Ages* (Leicester: Leicester University Press, 1982), p. 148.

38. For her story, see Donald Allchin, *Journey to Pennant Melangell: A Welcome for Pilgrims* (1997), and Oliver Davies and Fiona Bowie, eds., *Celtic Christian Spirituality* (New York: Continuum, 1995), pp. 65-67.

39. Oliver Davies, *Celtic Christianity in Early Medieval Wales*, p. 9.

40. Louis Gougaud, *Christianity in Celtic Lands* (Dublin: Four Courts Press, 1992), p. 112.

41. See Edward Sellner, *Wisdom of the Celtic Saints* (Notre Dame, IN: Ave Maria Press, 1993), pp. 146-147, and G. H. Doble, *Saints of Cornwall*, vol. 1 (Chatham: Parrett & Neves Ltd., 1960), pp. 89-94.

42. See Kathleen Hughes, *The Church in Early Irish Society* (London: Methuen & Co., 1989), p. 31.

43. This, at least, is the approximate date of his birth and the "traditional" date of his death. For a succinct summation of scholarly views concerning when and where he was born and died, see John Walsh and Thomas Bradley, *A History of the Irish Church, 400-700 A.D.* (Dublin: Columba Press, 1991), pp. 13-21.

44. Joseph Duffy, *Patrick in His Own Words* (Dublin: Veritas Publications, 1975), pp. 12, 17, 22.

45. See, for example, Maire de Paor, *Patrick: The Pilgrim Apostle of Ireland* (Dublin: Veritas, 1998), pp. 90-91.

46. From "Notes on Fiacc's Hymn," Whitley Stokes, ed., *The Tripartite Life of St. Patrick*, Vol. II (1887), p. 425.

47. See Richard Sharpe, "Some Problems Concerning the Organization of the Church in Early Medieval Ireland," *Peritia*, vol. 3, 1984: 230-270.

48. See "Life of Bairre of Cork" in Charles Plummer, trans., *Lives of Irish Saints*, Vol. II (Oxford: Oxford at the Clarendon Press, 1922), p. 12.

49. Joseph Duffy, *Patrick in His Own Words*, pp. 30-31.

50. Charles Plummer, trans., *Lives of Irish Saints*, Vol. II, p. 178.

51. For a discussion of married clergy in the Irish church, see Kathleen Hughes, "Sanctity and Secularity in the Early Irish Church" in David Dumville, ed., *Church and Society in Ireland: A.D. 400-1200* (London: Variorum Reprints, 1987), p. 29, and *The Church in Early Irish Society*, pp. 160 ff. A sign of married clergy in the Celtic Church is also found in condemnations from the First Synod of St. Patrick (c. 457) in which both cleric and wife will "be held in contempt by the laity and be removed from the Church" if the "wife goes about with her head unveiled." Regarding women's monastic leadership and inheritance, Lisa Bitel, in "Women's monastic enclosures in early Ireland: a study of female spirituality and male monastic mentalities," *Journal of Medieval History*, vol. 12, 1986, p. 29, says: "No evidence exists to show that mothers passed their functions as abbesses to their daughters, as fathers passed abbacies to sons."

52. Liam de Paor, *Ireland and Early Europe* (Dublin: Four Courts Press, 1997), p. 150.

53. Ludwig Bieler, *Ireland: Harbinger of the Middle Ages* (London: Oxford University Press, 1966), p. 136. This was my first thought when I visited

-------- ⚜ --------

Ravenna with my wife in 1988. Later, I discovered that Bieler and others before me had had similar speculations; see also, for example, George L. Barrow, *The Round Towers of Ireland* (Dublin: The Academy Press, 1979), p. 19.

54. See "The Rule of the Grey Monks" in Uinseann O Maidin, trans., *The Celtic Monk: Rules and Writings of Early Irish Monks* (Kalamazoo, MI: Cistercian Publications, 1996), p. 52.

55. See Conleth Manning, *Early Irish Monasteries* (Dublin: Country House, 1995), p. 32.

56. See J. M. Clark, *The Abbey of St. Gall as a Centre of Literature and Art* (London: Cambridge University Press, 1926), p. 23.

57. Quoted in James Charles Roy, *Islands of Storm* (Chester Springs, PA: Durfour Editions Inc., 1991), p. 210.

58. John Hennig, "Studies in Early Western Devotion to the Choirs of Saints," *Studia Patristica* (Berlin, 1966), p. 247.

Chapter 4

1. Mary Low, *Celtic Christianity and Nature* (Edinburgh: Edinburgh University Press, 1996), p. 7.

2. See St. Columbanus, for example, in Cardinal Tomas O'Fiaich, *Columbanus in His Own Words* (Dublin: Veritas Publications, 1974), pp. 80-85 where he writes Pope Boniface IV in 613 that "I grieve, I confess, for the disgrace of St. Peter's chair," and warns him that "the ship is in peril."

3. See G. H. Doble, *Lives of the Welsh Saints* (Cardiff: Univerity of Wales Press, 1971), p. 45.

4. For an examination of various views, see Ian Bradley, *Celtic Christianity: Making Myths and Chasing Dreams* (Edinburgh: Edinburgh University Press, 1999), pp. 119-188.

5. See, for example, Peter Schineller, *A Handbook of Inculturation* (New York: Paulist Press, 1990), Anscar Chupungo, *Liturgies of the Future: The Process and Methods of Inculturation* (New York: Paulist Press, 1989), and Robert Schreiter, *Constructing Local Theologies* (Maryknoll, NY: Orbis Books, 1985).

6. Yves Congar, *Diversity and Communion* (Mystic, CT: Twenty-Third Publications, 1985), p. 40.

7. Avery Dulles, *Models of the Church* (Garden City, NY: Doubleday, 1974), especially chapter 3, "The Church as Mystical Communion," pp. 43-57.

8. Diarmuid O'Laoghaire, *Irish Spirituality* (Dublin: M.H. Gill & Son, 1956), p. 2. Glosses are comments or explanations of texts written between the lines or in the margins—as footnotes are used today. Regarding the glosses to which O'Laoghaire refers, they were written on the Epistles of St. Paul, and now preserved in Wurzburg.

9. See John J. O'Riordan, *The Music of What Happens: Celtic Spirituality—A View From the Inside* (Dublin: The Columba Press, 1996), pp. 64-65.

10. Nora Chadwick, *The Age of the Saints in the Early Celtic Church* (London: Oxford University Press, 1961), p. 2.

11. See Marjory Kennedy-Fraser, and Kenneth Macleod, eds., *Songs of the Hebrides and Other Celtic Songs From the Highlands of Scotland* (London: Boosey & Co., 1909), p. 164. Ian Finlay, in *Columba* (London: Victor Gollancz, 1979), p. 187, discusses Columcille's qualities as including tenderness and devotion, as well as ruthlessness and irascibility. "The Celtic temperament," he says, "runs to extremes."

12. Quoted in a book review by Graham Frear in *Eire-Ireland*, Winter 1989, p. 135.

13. The poem, attributed to the Irish poet, is quoted in full in Robin Flower, *The Irish Tradition* (Oxford: Oxford at the Clarendon Press, 1947), pp. 51-52.

14. See "Life of Columcille" in Whitley Stokes, trans., *Lives of Saints from the Book of Lismore* (Oxford: Oxford at the Clarendon Press, 1890), p. 175.

15. See Gretel Ehrlich's excellent *The Solace of Open Spaces* (New York: Penguin Books, 1985), p. 103, where she says: "We live in a culture that has lost its memory. Very little in the specific shapes and traditions of our grandparents' pasts instructs us how to live today, or tells us who we are or what demands will be made on us as members of society." Along with this lack of ancestral voices to guide us, Mircea Eliade warns us in *Myth and Reality* (New York: Harper & Row, 1963), p. 121, that "the dead are those who have lost their memories."

16. John M. Synge, *The Aran Islands* (Marlboro, VT: The Marlboro Press, 1907), p. 64.

17. Belden Lane, *Landscapes of the Sacred* (New York: Paulist Press, 1988), p. 16.

18. Quoted in Frederick Turner, *Spirit of Place* (San Francisco: Sierra Club Books, 1989), p. 11.

19. Noel Dermot O'Donoghue, *The Mountain Behind the Mountain: Aspects of the Celtic Tradition* (Edinburgh: T & T Clark, 1993), p. 21.

20. Quoted in Donald Allchin, *God's Presence Makes the World* (London: Darton, Longman and Todd Ltd., 1997), pp. 16 and 98.

21. Ludwig Bieler, *The Patrician Texts in the Book of Armagh* (Dublin: Dublin Institute for Advanced Studies, 1979), p. 143.

22. Translation of Cogitosus's *Life of St. Brigit* by George Rochefort and Edward Sellner.

23. Quoted in Myles Dillon, *Early Irish Literature* (Chicago: University of Chicago Press, 1948), pp. 163-164.

24. See Charles Plummer, *Lives of Irish Saints*, Vol. II (Oxford: Oxford at the Clarendon Press, 1922), pp. 283, 177, 132.

25. See Joseph Duffy, *Patrick in His Own Words* (Dublin: Veritas Publications, 1972), p. 18.

26. See Richard Sharpe, trans., *Adomnan of Iona: Life of St. Columba* (New York: Penguin Books, 1995), pp. 230-231.

———— ✣ ————

27. See Liam de Paor, *St. Patrick's World* (Dublin: Four Courts Press, 1993), p. 239.

28. See Maud Joynt, trans., *The Life of St. Gall* (Ceredigion, Wales: Llanerch Publishers, 1927), pp. 91 and 104.

29. See G. H. Doble, *Saints of Cornwall*, vol. 1, (Chatham: Parrett & Neves Ltd., 1960), pp. 3-9, and Shirley Toulson, *Celtic Year* (Rockport, MA: Element Books, 1993), p. 239.

30. See Uinseann O Maidin, *The Celtic Monk* (Kalamazoo, MI: Cistercian Publications, 1996), pp. 173-174.

31. See Kenneth Jackson, *Studies in Early Celtic Nature Poetry* (Cambridge: Cambridge University Press, 1935), pp. 5, 3, 11.

32. Quoted in Jacques Le Goff, "The Wilderness in the Medieval West," *The Medieval Imagination* (Chicago: University of Chicago Press, 1988), p. 54.

33. D. D. C. Pochin Mould, *The Mountains of Ireland* (London: B.T. Batsford Ltd., 1955), p. 20.

34. See A. B. E. Hood, trans., *St. Patrick: His Writings and Muirchu's Life* (London: Phillimore & Co., 1978), pp. 88-89.

35. See Thomas Taylor, trans., *The Life of St. Samson of Dol* (London: SPCK, 1925), p. 49. Specific reference to the phallus worship is found in his *The Celtic Christianity of Cornwall* (first published 1916, reprint by Llanerch Publishers, 1995), p. 170.

36. Celtic phallic worship may even have taken place in North America some three thousand years ago. See Barry Fell, *America B.C.: Ancient Settlers in the New World* (New York: Pocket Books, 1976), in which the Harvard professor describes ancient European temple inscriptions found in New England and the Midwest that date as far back as 800 B.C.E., as well as phallic and other sexual carving and images that he associates with the beliefs of ancient Celtic fertility cults that, he says, were destroyed in Europe in early Christian times.

37. Kenneth Jackson, *Studies in Early Celtic Nature Poetry*, p. 22.

38. Quoted in *Songs of the Hebrides*, p. 164.

39. Most Rev. John Healy, *Ireland's Ancient Schools and Scholars* (Dublin: M.H. Gill & Son, 1890), p. vi and 368.

40. See Henry Beston, *The Outermost House: A Year of Life on the Great Beach of Cape Cod* (New York: Henry Holt and Co., 1928), pp. 43, 37, xxxv.

41. Robin Flower, *The Western Island* (Oxford: Oxford University Press, 1944), p. 31.

42. Thomas Cahill, *How the Irish Saved Civilization* (New York: Doubleday, 1995), p. 149.

43. Kenneth Jackson, in his *Studies in Early Celtic Nature Poetry*, p. 91, suggests that, among the Celts, at least in their literature, not all have such a positive attitude toward the sea. He says that the Irish regard it "with a genuine delight mingled with terror" while the Welsh ("not a seafaring people") show little feeling for it; Anglo-Saxon poetry, however, "so full of the sea," felt it to be "a sufficiently grey and cheerless element, and yet took a grim pleasure in its moods."

44. Carl Jung, *Symbols of Transformation* (Princeton: Princeton University Press, 1956), p. 205.

45. *Song of the Hebrides*, p. 164.

46. Kenneth Jackson, *Studies in Early Celtic Nature Poetry*, pp. 50-61.

47. James Charles Roy, "Landscape and the Celtic Soul," *Eire-Ireland*, Fall-Winter 1996, p. 252.

48. Kenneth Jackson, *Studies in Early Celtic Nature Poetry*, p. 63.

49. Thomas Tyler, trans., *The Life of St. Samson of Dol*, pp. 52-53.

50. So many of the early Celtic sagas are filled with scenes of horrendous bloodshed and a warrior ideal of vengeance against one's enemies. This is clear especially in the Irish epic of Cuchulainn (Cecile O'Rahilly, ed., *Tain Bo Cualnge* [Dublin: Dublin Institute for Advanced Studies, 1984], but is also found in numerous other works. See, for example, Myles Dillon, *Early Irish Literature* [Chicago: University of Chicago Press, 1948], and Jeffrey Gantz, *Early Irish Myths and Sagas* [New York: Penguin Books, 1981]). Their heroes' cries of anguish, as well as their search for Tir NaNog, the land of eternal youth, speaks, I believe, of their deep desire for something else.

51. Liam de Paor, *Ireland and Early Europe* (Dublin: Four Courts Press, 1997), p. 17.

52. Father Gregory Telepneff, *The Egyptian Desert in the Irish Bogs* (Etna, CA: Center for Traditionalist Orthodox Studies, 1998), p. 49.

53. See "Eddius Stephanus: Life of Wilfrid" in D. H. Farmer, ed., *The Age of Bede* (New York: Penguin Books, 1965), p. 118.

54. Bertram Colgrave and R. A. B. Mynors, eds., *Bede's Ecclesiastical History of the English People* (Oxford: Oxford University Press, 1969), p. 259.

55. Ibid., p. 227.

56. G. S. M. Walker, ed., *Sancti Columbani Opera* (Dublin: Dublin Institute for Advanced Studies, 1970), pp. 123, 127.

57. See Fergal McGrath, *Education in Ancient and Medieval Ireland* (Dublin: Skellig Press Ltd., 1979), pp. 72-81 on the subjects that were studies, and Kathleen Hughes, *Early Christian Ireland* (Ithaca, NY: Cornell University Press, 1972), p. 195.

58. Most Rev. John Healy, *Ireland's Ancient Schools and Scholars*, pp. v and 91.

59. Kathleen Hughes, *The Church in Early Irish Society*, p. 154.

60. Lisa Bitel, "Women's monastic enclosures in early Ireland: a study of female spirituality and male monastic mentalities," *Journal of Medieval History*, 12 (1986), p. 25.

61. Bertram Colgrave and R. A. B. Mynors, eds., *Bede's Ecclesiastical History of the English People*, p. 313.

62. Helen Waddell, *The Wandering Scholars* (Ann Arbor, MI: University of Michigan Press, 1989), pp. 30-31.

63. James King and Werner Vogler, eds., *The Culture of the Abbey of St. Gall* (Zurich: Belser Verlag, 1991), contains an excellent discussion on the significant heritage of St. Gall.

———— ❦ ————

64. See A. W. Haddan and W. Stubbs, eds., *Councils and Ecclesiastical Documents Relating to Great Britain and Ireland* (Oxford: Clarendon Press, 1873), Vol. II, pt. 1, pp. 292-293.

65. See footnotes in Bertram Colgrave and R. A. B. Mynors, eds., *Bede's Ecclesiastical History of the English People*, pp. 237, 356, 420.

66. See Benedicta Ward, "Theodore of Tarsus: a Greek archbishop of Canterbury," XI, in *Signs and Wonders* (Hampshire: Ashgate Publishing, 1992), pp. 41-53.

67. See Edward Sellner, *Wisdom of the Celtic Saints* (Notre Dame, IN: Ave Maria Press, 1993), for these stories alluding to women's leadership. See also the article, "Brigit of Kildare: A Study in the Liminality of Women's Spiritual Power," *Cross Currents*, 39, 1989, pp. 402-419.

68. See Bertram Colgrave and R. A. B. Mynors, eds., *Bede's Ecclesiastical History of the English People*, pp. 404-414, where Bede provides a short hagiography of Hild. The story of Caedmon is found on pp. 414-420.

69. Quotation from Brigit's hagiography by Cogitosus, found in J. P. Migne, *Patrologia Latina*, LXXII, cols. 777-790, are from the English translation by George Rochefort, Ph.D., and myself.

70. See Ian Bradley, *The Celtic Way* (London: Darton, Longman, and Todd Ltd., 1993), especially pp. 30, 39.

71. Sean Connolly, "*Vita Prima Sanctae Brigitae*: Background and Historical Value," *Journal of the Royal Society of Antiquaries of Ireland*, Vol. 119, 1989, p. 19.

72. Ibid., p. 22. A similiar story is found in Whitley Stokes, "Life of Brigit," *Lives of Saints From the Book of Lismore*, p. 191, although there, for some reason, all the sick and poor are men, not women.

73. Quoted in D. D. C. Pochin Mould, *The Celtic Saints* (New York: Macmillan Co., 1956), p. 102.

74. See Maud Joynt, trans., *The Life of St. Gall*, p. 82.

75. Patrick Kavanagh, *Tarry Flynn* (Penguin Books, 1948), p. 46.

76. For references to the beautiful Christ and Mary, see O'Dwyer, *Towards a History of Irish Spirituality* (Blackrock: Columba Press, 1995), pp. 42, 179, and Myles Dillon, *Early Irish Literature*, p. 158, and Robin Flower, *The Irish Tradition* (Oxford: Oxford Press, 1948), p. 119. An example of the flowing locks on males—without tonsure—can be seen in the Book of Kells in the figures of Christ, St. Matthew, and St. John, in colors, though somewhat faded, that are red, blonde, and tan. Even the "baby" Jesus, seated on Mary's lap, in one of the earliest depictions of Mary and child in Christian iconography, has long, curly hair. The dramatic styling of the hair of both male and female saints on the reliquary known as the Breac Maedhog, created about 1100, now on view at the National Museum in Dublin, is extraodinarily beautiful, showing a wealth of thick, intertwining hair on both genders' heads, long, decorative robes, and a variety of beards. In *The Irish Face*, published by the National Library of Ireland (Dublin: Mount Salus Press, 1986), the Celts' care for their hair is mentioned, evidenced by the numbers of combs and razors found in archaeological sites.

77. See Oliver Davies, trans., *Celtic Spirituality* (New York: Paulist, 1999), pp. 446-447.

78. These phrases are taken from prayers transcribed by Alexander Carmichael in the late nineteenth century. See his book, *Carmina Gadelica: Hymns and Incantations* (Hudson, NY: Lindisfarne Press, 1992), pp. 37-38, 74.

79. The quotation on Ita is from the *Life of Ita*, found in Charles Plummer's *Vitae Sanctorum Hiberniae*, vol. II (Dublin: Four Courts Press, 1997), pp. 116-130, and translated into English by the Irish scholar Fr. Diarmuid O' Laoghaire, S.J. Mochuda's is from Charles Plummer, *Lives of Irish Saints*, Vol. II (Oxford: Oxford University Press, 1922), p. 286.

80. See Rev. P. Power, ed., *Life of St. Declan of Ardmore and Life of St. Mochuda of Lismore* (London: Irish Texts Society, 1914), p. 81.

81. Oliver Davies and Fiona Bowie, eds., *Celtic Christian Spirituality* (New York: Continuum Publishing Co., 1995), pp. 54-56.

82. Patrick Kavanagh, *The Complete Poems* (Newbridge, Ireland: The Goldsmith Press, 1972), pp. 291-292.

83. See Charles Plummer, ed., *Irish Litanies* (Rochester, NY: Boydell & Brewer Inc., 1992), pp. 5-7.

84. Ibid., p. 13. The Latin text quotes Psalm 51, "Against you only have I sinned."

85. See Oliver Davies and Fiona Bowie, eds., *Celtic Christian Spirituality*, pp. 33-34.

Chapter 5

1. Unfortunately, only about one hundred Latin Lives and fifty written in Irish survive. For an excellent introduction to the subject and history of Celtic hagiographies, see Kathleen Hughes, *Early Christian Ireland* (Ithaca, NY: Cornell University Press, 1972), pp. 219-247, and Richard Sharpe, *Medieval Irish Saints' Lives* (Oxford: Clarendon Press, 1991). Besides my own collection, found in *Wisdom of the Celtic Saints* (Notre Dame, IN: Ave Maria Press, 1993) which contains selections from primary sources and original translations of two female saints, Ita and Samthann, other collections of Celtic hagiographies can be found in such sources as Ludwig Bieler, *The Patrician Texts in the Book of Armagh* (Dublin: Dublin Institute for Advanced Studies, 1979); Gilbert H. Doble, *The Saints of Cornwall* (Oxford: Holywell Press, 1970); Charles Plummer, ed., *Lives of Irish Saints*, Vols. I & II (London: Oxford University Press, 1922); and Whitley Stokes, trans., *Lives of Saints From the Book of Lismore*, (Oxford: Oxford at the Clarendon Press, 1890).

2. See Thomas Taylor, trans., *The Life of St. Samson of Dol* (London: SPCK, 1925).

3. See Dana Carleton Munro, ed., *Life of St. Columban by the Monk Jonas* (Felinfach: Llanerch Publishers, 1993).

4. See Robin Flower, *The Irish Tradition* (Oxford: Oxford University Press, 1947), p. 41.

5. Whitley Stokes, *The Martyrology of Oengus the Culdee* (London, 1905), p. 26.

6. George O. Simms, *Exploring the Book of Kells* (Dublin: The O'Brien Press, 1989), p. 26.

7. *The Book of the Angel*, in Ludwig Bieler, ed., *The Patrician Texts in the Book of Armagh* (Dublin: Dublin Institute for Advanced Studies, 1979), p. 191.

8. John Ryan, *Irish Monasticism* (Dublin: Talbot Press Limited, 1931), p. 197.

9. See Lisa Bitel, "Women's monastic enclosures in early Ireland: a study of female spirituality and male monastic mentalities," *Journal of Medieval History*, 12 (1986), p. 25, where she says: "We do not know whether any of the hagiographers, poets, and scholars who recorded the corpus of Irish literature and learning were women, since no woman ever left her name on a document. But on the Continent many manuscripts attributed to men have been shown to be the products of women's hands; perhaps this will be the case in Ireland as well." For reference to Kildare's scriptorium, see Kathleen Hughes, *Early Christian Ireland*, p. 227.

10. The litanies of the saints which have survived also refer to the many holy women. In a "Litany of the Virgins," twenty-eight are mentioned by name, including "Brigit, bright and glowing." See Charles Plummer, *Irish Litanies* (The Henry Bradshaw Society, 1925), p. 93.

11. William Reeves, "Adamnan's Life of Saint Columba," *Historians of Scotland* (Edmonston and Douglas, 1874), p. 34.

12. Aelred of Rievaulx, "The Life of S. Ninian," in *Two Celtic Saints* (Dyfed: Llanerch Enterprises, 1989), p. 3.

13. Robert Meyer, trans., *Bernard of Clairvaux's Life and Death of Saint Malachy the Irishman* (Kalamazoo, MI: Cistercian Publications, 1978), p. 11.

14. Jocelinus, "The Life of S. Kentigern," in *Two Celtic Saints*, p. 119.

15. J. W. James, trans., *Rhigyfarch's Life of St. David* (Cardiff, Wales: University of Wales, 1967), p. 48.

16. See Colgrave and Mynors, *Bede's Ecclesiastical History of the English People* (Oxford: Oxford at the Clarendon Press, 1969), p. 414.

17. See C. Jung, *Psychology and Religion: West and East* (Princeton, NJ: Princeton University Press, 1958), and *The Structure and Dynamics of the Psyche* (Princeton: Princeton University Press, 1960).

18. See, for example, Reeves, "Adamnan's Life of Saint Columba," p. 35.

19. See Alan Orr Anderson and Marjorie O. Anderson, eds., trans., *Adomnan's Life of Columba* (Oxford: Clarendon Press, 1991), p. lvii, who state that the idea for two prefaces by Adomnan "was borrowed from the *Life of Martin* written by Sulpicius Severus," thus revealing that Adomnan himself was familiar with Severus's writings.

20. See, for example, George Otto Simms, *St. Patrick: The Real Story of Patrick* (Dublin: The O'Brien Press, 1993), p. 68.

21. See Plummer, *Lives of Irish Saints*, Vol. II, p. 44.

22. Ancient peoples, including the Celts, Greeks, and Romans, believed strongly in the power of the curse, and relied upon the practice of getting even with their enemies by writing out curses against them, and throwing them into sacred springs or wells. Many of these curses have been found and can be seen in such places as the Roman baths in Bath, England. For a popular description of the practice, see Patrick Power, *The Book of Irish Curses* (Springfield, IL: Templegate Publishers, 1974).

23. See Kathleen Hughes, *Early Christian Ireland*, pp. 220 and 246. She also points out how hagiographers "are often influenced by the conventions of the secular storytellers."

24. See Felim O. Briain, "Miracles in the Lives of the Irish Saints," *Irish Ecclesiastical Record*, No. 66, 1945: 331-42, and "Saga Themes in Irish Hagiography," in *Feilsgribhinn Torna*, ed. Seamus Pender (Cork: 1947): 25-40.

25. See Kathleen Hughes, *Early Christian Ireland* (Ithaca, NY: Cornell University Press, 1972), pp. 190-192.

26. See Peter O'Dwyer, *Celi De: Spiritual Reform in Ireland, 750-900* (Dublin: Editions Tailliura, 1981), pp. 16 ff, William Reeves, *The Culdees of the British Islands* (Dublin: M.H. Gill, 1864), pp. 4-5, 66, and Padraig O'Fiannachta, "The Spirituality of the Ceili De," in Michael Maher, ed., *Irish Spirituality* (Dublin: Veritas, 1981), pp. 22-25. O'Fiannachta states that the earliest occurrence of the phrase *Ceili De* is found in the Milan glosses, dated about 800. He also says that a title associated with them, "sons of life," is "reminiscent of Qumran," the site of a strict Jewish sect which lived outside of Jerusalem, and predated Christianity. Reeves believes that there is evidence of the term originating in India, "applied to a Brahmin chief, who lived in the year 326 before Christ . . ." (pp. ix-x). There may, of course, have been sources closer to home: Jesus calls all of his followers "friends" of God (John 15), and John Cassian uses the phrase "servants of God" throughout his *Institutes* (i.e., Book I:2, and Book II: 2, etc.), and *Conferences* (i.e., 18:16, etc.).

27. There are numerous references to the Celi De clergy as married; see Reeves, *The Culdees of the British Isles*, p. 42, who quotes a fifteenth-century historian who states that "religious men, commonly called Kelledei . . . after the usage of the Eastern church, had wives. . . ."

28. See Bernard Peebles, trans., "Writings of Sulpicius Severus," in B. Peebles, ed., *The Fathers of the Church*, Vol. 7 (Washington, DC: Catholic University of America Press, 1949), p. 208.

29. See Robin Flower, *The Irish Tradition*, pp. 41 ff; Ludwig Bieler, *Irish Penitentials*, (Dublin, 1963), p. 47; O'Fiannachta, "The Spirituality of the Ceili De," p. 24; and O'Dwyer, *Celi De: Spiritual Reform in Ireland 750-900*, pp. 167 ff.

30. Robin Flower, in *The Irish Tradition*, p. 42, says about the Celi De: "It was not only that these scribes and anchorites lived by the destiny of their dedication in an environment of wood and sea, it was because they brought into that environment an eye washed miraculously clear by a

continual spiritual exercise, that they, first in Europe, had that strange vision of natural things in an almost unnatural purity."

31. See Kathleen Hughes, *Early Christian Ireland*, p. 232.

32. Passages from Samthann's hagiography were translated by Peter O'Dwyer for my book, *Wisdom of the Celtic Saints*, which can be found on pp. 194-199. The full hagiography, however, remains unpublished. It appears in Charles Plummer, *Vitae Sanctorum Hiberniae*, Vol. II (Oxford: Clarendon Press, 1997), pp. 253-261.

33. Stokes, *The Martyrology of Oengus the Culdee*, pp. 9-11.

34. Ibid., p. 65.

35. Ibid., see pp. 161, 26, 267.

36. Ibid., p. 23.

37. Specific references to "sons" and "children of life" are found in the lives of Ciaran and Findbarr in Sellner, *Wisdom of the Celtic Saints*, pp. 80, 130, 133; "servant of Almighty God" in the Life of Samthann, *Wisdom of the Celtic Saints*, p. 194. A life of St. Brigit, found in the *Book of Lismore*, includes a specific reference to the Culdees. See Iain MacDonald, *Saint Bride* (Edinburgh: Floris Books, 1992), p. 44. Kathleen Hughes, in *Early Christian Ireland*, pp. 232-234, discusses the influence and common themes of the Celi De upon the lives of Sts. Samthann and Ita.

38. See E. J. Gwynn and W. J. Purton, "The Monastery of Tallaght," *Proceedings of the Royal Irish Academy*, Vol. XXIX, Section C (Dublin, 1911), pp. 122, 133.

39. Ibid., pp. 136-137.

40. See William Reeves, *The Culdees of the British Islands*, for a comprehensive discussion of the movement's history and the places where the Celi De were located. He states that at Bardsey "the ancient monastic discipline of the country [Wales], akin to that of Ireland and Scotland, lingered to a later date than on the mainland" (p. 61). Gerald of Wales, in the twelfth century, specifically asssociates Bardsey Island with the Celi De whom he describes as "extremely devout monks." See his *The Journey Through Wales/The Description of Wales*, Lewis Thorpe, trans. (New York: Penguin Books, 1978), pp. 183-184. Donald Allchin has written a wonderful booklet, *Bardsey: A place of pilgrimage*, 1991, available at The Vicarage, Cropthorne, Worcester WR10 3LU.

41. Quoted in Peter O'Dwyer, *Celi De*, p. 28.

42. See, for example, the "Metrical and Prose Rules of the Celi De" in Reeves, *The Culdees of the British Isles*, pp. 82-97.

43. David of Wales (520-589/601) was nicknamed "Waterman," possibly because of his abstinence from alcohol. See his monastic "Rule" in J.W. James, trans., *Rhigyfarch's Life of St. David* (Cardiff, Wales: University of Wales, 1967), pp. 35 ff.

44. Gwynn and Purton, "The Monastery of Tallaght," pp. 129-130.

45. Ibid., p. 131. For the Brendan story, see "Brendan and a Young Harpist," in Sellner, *Wisdom of the Celtic Saints*, pp. 65-66.

———— ❧ ————

46. See Gwynn and Purton, "The Monastery of Tallaght," p. 145.

47. Ibid., p. 161.

48. See Bernard Peebles, trans., "Life of Saint Martin, Bishop and Confessor," in B. Peebles, ed., *The Fathers of the Church*, Vol. 7, p. 136.

49. See Reeves, *The Culdees of the British Isles*, pp. 39, 77-78.

50. Gwynn and Purton, "The Monastery of Tallaght," pp. 157-158.

51. Ibid., pp. 133-134.

52. Gwynn and Purton, "The Monastery of Tallaght," p. 119.

53. See, for example, the stories about soul friendship in the lives of Ciaran, Findbarr, and Maedoc in Sellner, *Wisdom of the Celtic Saints,* pp. 80, 128, 131, 168, 173.

54. Gwynn and Purton, "The Monastery of Tallaght," p. 144.

55. See Uinseann O Maidin, *The Celtic Monk: Rules and Writings of Early Irish Monks* (Kalamazoo, MI: Cistercian Publications, 1996), p. 106, note 29, where he says that this Helair "was held in very high esteem as a spiritual guide and confessor," as well as being "the patron, if not actually the founder, of the monastery of Loch Cre, near Roscre. He died in 807 and his feast is celebrated on 7 September."

56. Gwynn and Purton, "The Monastery of Tallaght," p. 135.

57. Ibid., pp. 135-136.

58. Ibid., pp. 163-164.

59. See Jacques Le Goff, *The Birth of Purgatory* (Chicago: Chicago University Press, 1984), pp. 1-17.

60. Gwynn and Purton, "The Monastery of Tallaght," p. 132.

61. Ibid., pp. 149-151.

62. See Kathleen Hughes, *The Church in Early Irish Society* (London: Methuen, 1966), p. 177, where she says, "In their attitude to the body the reformers [Celi De] reacted violently against the practices of the established church" [of their time], and "the story [of Samthann] expresses the views of Mael-ruain rather than the views of Samthann."

63. Reeves, "Prose Rule of the Celi De," *The Culdees of the British Islands*, p. 96.

64. Many desert Christians seemed to have overwhelmingly negative attitudes toward the body, women, homoerotic behavior, and the spiritual dimension of eros itself. Sexual desires were interpreted in the worst possible light, leaving no room for honest, loving expressions between men and women, and increasingly little or no room for affectionate bonds between those of the same gender. In their attempts to control all desires, they demonized sex, associating it only with lust and fornication, and often giving the impression that it was the worst possible sin. In their quite legitimate goal of choosing to live celibate lives, they frequently gave the impression that marriage itself was an inferior vocation, if not worse, compared to theirs. Jerome, for one, compared the married state to "vomit," recommending that widows certainly not consider marrying a second time. See F. A. Wright, trans., *Select Letters of St. Jerome*

(Cambridge, MA: Harvard University Press, 1933), p. 233. Although there are some exceptions, such as found in Palladius's writings, the *Life of Macrina*, and the sayings of Syncletica, for the most part women are portrayed as overwhelmingly dangerous, to be avoided at all costs. It is telling that one of the most influential hagiographies, the *Life of Antony*, portrays the saint's first tempters as a woman and a black youth. While the first figure, the woman as temptress, is unfortunately a familiar one in later hagiographies of male saints, the second symbolizes, according to scholars, a homosexual. See Robert Gregg, trans., *Athanasius: The Life of Antony and the Letter to Marcellinus* (New York: Paulist Press, 1980), pp. 35 and 135.

65. O'Dwyer, *Celi De*, p. xii.

66. They maintained their independence for centuries, but some seem to have been eventually merged with canons regular of St. Augustine. Records, however, show them to still be in Scotland by the late thirteenth and early fourteenth centuries; see Reeves, *The Culdees of the British Islands*, pp. 37-40.

Chapter 6

1. See Diarmuid O'Laoghaire, "Irish Spirituality" pamphlet (reprinted from *The Furrow*, January, 1956), p. 8. He quotes the *Life of Colman mac Luachain* in which four sons were born to Luachan who "at the end of seven years were taken to spiritual directors."

2. See Joseph Colleran, trans., *St. Augustine: The Greatness of the Soul* (New York: Newman Press, 1978), in which Augustine describes the "seven levels" of the soul and states that the soul's "proper abode" and "homeland" is God.

3. See Marjory Kennedy-Fraser, and Kenneth Macleod, eds., *Songs of the Hebrides and Other Celtic Songs From the Highlands of Scotland* (London: Boosey & Co., 1909), p. 104. The ancient Greeks also took dying very seriously. Plato says, in fact, that "those who are really philosophers practice dying, and death has less terror for them than for anyone else." See Plato's "Phaedo" in Erich Segal, trans., *The Dialogues of Plato* (New York: Bantam Books, 1986), p. 76.

4. See Bernhard Poschmann, *Penance and the Anointing of the Sick* (New York: Herder and Herder, 1964), especially pp. 87-99.

5. See O. D. Watkins, *A History of Penance,* Vol. II (London: Longmans, Green and Co., 1920), p. 609.

6. A third source, the rules of various monastic communities, primarily associated with the Celi De, provide some understanding of the *anamchara*. The earliest Celtic rules, however, do not use the term at all. See, for example, G. S. M. Walker, *Sancti Columbani Opera* (Dublin: Dublin Institute for Advanced Studies, 1970), and Uinseann O Maidin, *The Celtic Monk: Rules and Writings of Early Irish Monks* (Kalamazoo, MI: Cistercian Publications, 1996). In the *Rule of Comgall* of Bangor,

composed in the late eighth century, although there is no specific reference to a soul friend, a monk is recommended to place himself "in the hands of a holy mentor that he may direct one's path through life"; it also suggests that "the advice of a devout sage is a great asset." "No matter how much you esteem your strength of will," it says, "place yourself under the direction of another." See "The Rule of Comghall," in O'Maidin, *The Celtic Monk*, pp. 31-36. The Celi De documents examined in the previous chapter are more specific. The *Rule of Carthage* (or of Mochuda, as he's also known) possibly written at Lismore in the ninth century, is certainly the product of the Celi De movement. In it, specific duties of an *anamchara* are given, in addition to guidelines for certain monastic activities: "If you are a spiritual director to a man, do not barter his soul; be not as the blind leading the blind; do not leave him in neglect. Let penitents confess to you with candor and integrity, and do not accept their alms if they refuse to be led by you." Describing responsibilities of a soul friend, this rule also advocates a certain amount of professional distance: "Even though you accept offering from your penitents, do not allow these people a great part in your affections; rather let them be as fire on your body, a danger to your strength." See "The Rule of Carthage," in O'Maidin, *The Celtic Monk*, p. 59, 65-67. The longest of Celi De rules, the *Rule of Tallaght*, with its references to "sons of life," suggests that the "office" of a spiritual director (*anamchara*) is "perilous," and that a person should terminate one confessor relationship before beginning another. This rule, quoting Maelruain, also implies that the first year of being with an *anamchara* constitutes some sort of initiation: "We regard the first year spent under our spiritual direction as a year of purification, and so you will have to spend three periods of forty days on bread and water, except for a mouthful of milk on Sundays, and during the summer Lent a mixture of whey and water." Maelruain obviously believed that for true healing to occur or for genuine self-knowledge to be attained, discipline and commitment are needed. See "The Rule of Tallaght or the Teaching of Maelruain," O'Maidin, *The Celtic Monk*, pp. 97-130.

7. Hugh Connolly, *The Irish Penitentials* (Dublin: Four Courts Press, 1995), p. 11.
8. See John T. McNeill and Helena Gamer, *Medieval Handbooks of Penance* (New York: Octagon Books, 1979), p. 29.
9. Ibid., p. 28.
10. See John T. McNeill, *Celtic Penitentials and Their Influence on Continental Christianity*, pp. 90 ff.
11. Quoted in Diarmuid O'Laoghaire, "Old Ireland and Her Spirituality," in Robert McNally, ed., *Old Ireland* (New York: Fordham University Press, 1965), p. 30.
12. Ludwig Bieler, ed., *The Irish Penitentials* (Dublin: Dublin Institute for Advanced Studies, 1975), p. 3.
13. See John Walsh and Thomas Bradley, *A History of the Irish Church, 400-700 A.D.* (Dublin: Columba Press, 1991), p. 123, who say that "the basic principles of Irish penitential thinking originated with Cassian."

14. Pierre Payer, *Sex and the Penitentials* (Toronto: University of Toronto Press, 1984), p. 3. Allen Frantzen, in *The Literature of Penance in Anglo-Saxon England* (New Brunswick, NJ: Rutgers University Press, 1983), p. 201, notes that "sexuality has always been the main focus of confession—no sins outnumber sexual offenses in the early penitentials—even in non-Christian cultures."

15. See "Here Begins the Preface of Gildas on Penance," in Bieler, *The Irish Penitentials*, pp. 61-65.

16. See John Cassian, "Institutes," Book II, ch. 3, in P. Schaff and H. Wace, eds., *A Select Library of Nicene and Post-Nicene Fathers of the Christian Church*, Vol. XI (Grand Rapids, MI: Eerdmans, 1986), p. 232. This principle of "contraries," enunciated by Cassian, was not unique to him. Originally a medical concept advocated by Greek and Roman physicians, it can also be found in a number of other works. See Sr. Monica Wagner, trans., *Saint Basil: Ascetical Works* (New York: Fathers of the Church, Inc., 1950), pp. 328-329, where Basil states in his "Long Rules" #51, that "the cure of those afflicted by evil passions should be effected according to the method used by physicians;" that is, a religious superior should "wage war upon their malady by setting up a counter-irritant to the vice, curing the infirmity of soul by drastic measures, if need be."

17. Above quotations from "Penitential of Finnian," in Bieler, *The Irish Penitentials*, pp. 75-95.

18. See, for example, his Letter 4: 5-7 in G. S. M. Walker, *Sancti Columbani Opera*, p. 35, where he says: "If you remove the foe, you remove the battle also; if you remove the battle, you remove the crown as well. . . ."

19. See "Penitential of St. Columbanus" in Bieler, *The Irish Penitentials*, pp. 96-107.

20. James Kenney, *The Sources for the Early History of Ireland: Ecclesiastical*, p. 188.

21. See "Penitential of Cummean" in Bieler, *The Irish Penitentials*, pp. 109-135.

22. See Carl Jung's writings, especially *Modern Man in Search of a Soul* (New York: A Harvest Book, 1933).

23. See "Selections from the Tripartite St. Gall Penitential," in John T. McNeill and Helena Gamer, *Medieval Handbooks of Penance*, pp. 282-285. I have slightly modernized the translation, removing Thees and Thous and other archaic language in order to make it more meaningful.

24. See Kathleen Hughes, *Early Christian Ireland* (Ithaca, NY: Cornell University Press, 1972), p. 89, where she refers to Brittany and penitential manuscripts found there.

25. The evolution of sacraments in the church has a long history with various councils and theologians differing on the numbers and meaning of the term. Not until the Council of Florence (1439) and, after the Protestant Reformation, the Council of Trent (1545-63) was the number seven agreed upon. When it comes to discussing the sacrament of penance or, as it is more commonly called today, reconciliation, one cannot expect to

discern clear distinctions between "confessions" that were sacramental and those that were "devotional" in the early Celtic Church. Thus, Allen J. Frantzen, in his *The Literature of Penance in Anglo-Saxon England*, pp. 52-53, is not particularly helpful when he says, "Although penance is often mentioned in Irish saints' Lives, it rarely takes sacramental form, either public or private." The true distinctions are those encounters that are confessional with an *anamchara* and those that were done in a monastic "chapter of faults" with the abbot or abbess traditionally hearing those sins and communal infractions.

26. See Lisa Bitel, *Isle of the Saints: Monastic Settlement and Christian Community in Early Ireland* (Ithaca: Cornell University Press, 1990), p. 9.

27. See Whitley Stokes, trans., "Life of Brigit," *Lives of Saints From the Book of Lismore* (Oxford: Oxford at the Clarendon Press, 1890), p. 194.

28. *Idem*, "Life of Senan," *Lives of Saints From the Book of Lismore*, pp. 219-220.

29. Quoted in Diarmuid O'Laoghaire, S.J., "Old Ireland and Her Spirituality," published in Robert McNally, S.J., ed., *Old Ireland* (New York: Fordham University Press, 1965), p. 52.

30. See Whitley Stokes, trans., "Life of Brigit," *Lives of Saints From the Book of Lismore*, p. 196.

31. Ibid., pp. 199 and 333-334.

32. The story is from "Vita Sancte Samthanne," in Charles Plummer, trans., *Vitae Sanctorum Hiberniae*, Vol. II (Oxford: Clarendon Press, 1997), pp. 253-261, translated here by Peter O'Dwyer.

33. Moninna's stories are found in her Life, translated by Liam De Paor in his *Saint Patrick's World* (Black Rock, Ireland: Four Courts Press Ltd., 1993), pp. 281-294.

34. Whitley Stokes, trans., *The Martyrology of Oengus the Culdee* (London, 1905), p. 43.

35. Stories of St. Ita are taken from "Vita Sancte Ite Virginis," found in Charles Plummer, trans., *Vitae Sanctorum Hiberniae*, Vol. II, pp. 116-130.

36. See Ludwig Bieler, *The Patrician Texts in the Book of Armagh* (Dublin: Dublin Institute for Advanced Studies, 1979), p. 191.

37. Bertram Colgrave and R. A. B. Mynors, eds., *Bede's Ecclesiastical History of the English People* (Oxford: Oxford at the Clarendon Press, 1969), p. 585.

38. See Whitley Stokes, trans., "Life of Ciaran of Clonmacnois," *Lives of Saints From the Book of Lismore*, pp. 278-279. Translation is from Edward Sellner, *Wisdom of the Celtic Saints* (Notre Dame, IN: Ave Maria Press, 1993), pp. 86-87.

39. Ibid., p. 273, with translation in Sellner's *Wisdom of the Celtic Saints*, pp. 84-85.

40. See Rev. P. Power, trans., *Life of St. Mochuda of Lismore* (London: Irish Texts Society, 1914), pp. 113-115.

41. Edward Sellner, *Wisdom of the Celtic Saints*, p. 169.

———— ✺ ————

42. See Charles Plummer, *Lives of Irish Saints*, Vol. II (Oxford: Oxford University Press, 1922), pp. 232-233.

43. Thomas Taylor, trans., *The Life of St. Samson of Dol* (London: SPCK, 1925), p. 73.

44. Charles Plummer, *Lives of Irish Saints*, Vol. II, pp. 17-18.

45. See "Bede: Life of Cuthbert" in D. H. Farmer, ed., *The Age of Bede* (New York: Penguin Books, 1965), p. 71.

Conclusion

1. For an examination of the Vikings' destruction and contribution to Celtic lands, see John Marsden, *The Fury of the Northmen* (New York: St. Martin's, 1993).

2. The Council or Synod of Whitby is described by Bede in Bertram Colgrave and R. A. B. Mynors, eds., *Bede's Ecclesiastical History of the English People* (Oxford: Oxford University Press, 1969), pp. 296-309.

3. See Julia Smith, "Celtic Asceticism and Carolingian Authority in Early Medieval Brittany," in W. J. Sheils, ed., *Monks, Hermits and the Ascetic Tradition* (Oxford: Basil Blackwell, 1985), p. 60.

4. Oliver Davies, trans., *Celtic Spirituality* (New York: Paulist, 1999), p. 22.

5. Peter Berresford Ellis, *Celtic Inheritance* (London: Muller, Blond & White Ltd., 1985), pp. 114-116.

6. See John Watt, *The Church in Medieval Ireland* (Dublin: Gill and Macmillan, 1972), pp. 12-20.

7. For an excellent exposition on the contemporary relevance of the saints, see Elizabeth Johnson, *Friends of God and Prophets* (New York: Continuum, 1999).

8. See Uinseann O'Maidin, *The Celtic Monk: Rules and Writings of Early Irish Monks* (Kalamazoo, MI: Cistercian Publications, 1996), p. 122.

9. See C. G. Jung, *Psychology and Religion: West and East* (Princeton: Princeton University Press, 1969), pp. 36-37.

10. Edmund Colledge and James Walsh, trans., *Julian of Norwich: Showings* (New York: Paulist Press, 1978), p. 163.

11. Quoted in Philip Rousseau, *Ascetics, Authority, and the Church in the Age of Jerome and Cassian* (Oxford: Oxford University Press, 1978), p. 46.

12. Charles Plummer, trans., *Lives of Irish Saints*, Vol. II (Oxford: Oxford at the Clarndon Press, 1922), p. 22.

13. Caitlin Matthews, *The Elements of the Celtic Tradition* (Longmead, Shaftesbury, Dorset: Element Books, 1989), p. 105.

14. Aelred of Rievaulx, *Spiritual Friendship*, p. 65.

15. Thomas Merton, *Contemplation in the World of Action* (New York: Image Books, 1973), p. 259.

16. Oliver Davies and Fiona Bowie, eds., *Celtic Christian Spirituality* (New York: Continuum Publishing Co., 1995), pp. 54-56.